TRAVEL and TOURISM MARKETING

Dotty Boen Oelkers

THOMSON
─────✦─────™
SOUTH-WESTERN

Australia · Brazil · Canada · Mexico · Singapore · Spain · United Kingdom · United States

Travel and Tourism Marketing
Dotty Oelkers

VP/Editorial Director:
Jack W. Calhoun

VP/Editor-in-Chief:
Karen Schmohe

Acquisitions Editor:
Eve Lewis

Project Manager:
Penny Shank

Sr. Marketing Manager:
Nancy Long

Production Project Manager:
Darrell E. Frye

Manager of Technology, Editorial:
Liz Prigge

Technology Project Editor:
Scot Hamilton

Web Coordinator:
Ed Stubenrauch

Manufacturing Coordinator:
Kevin Kluck

Production House:
Pre-Press Company, Inc.

Printer:
Courier
Kendallville, IN

Art Director:
Tippy McIntosh

Internal and Cover Designer:
Ann Small, a small design studio

Cover Images:
© Getty Images/PhotoDisc; Eyewire, Brand X; Media Images; Corbis

Photo Researcher:
Darren Wright

For more information about our products, contact us at:

Thomson Higher Education
5191 Natorp Boulevard
Mason, Ohio 45040
USA

REVIEWERS

Teresa Chavis
Waldorf, MD

Sam R. Clark, Jr.
Malvern, AR

Jamie L. Currier-Dix
Hannibal, NY

Diane Ross Gary, Ed.D.
Hartford, CT

Jane Jordan Jaeger, NBCT
Cincinnati, OH

Jennifer Klock
Hannibal, NY

Polly A. Lazzeri
Oviedo, FL

Kathy L. M. Miles
Lakeview, OR

Kathryn L. Myers
Jamestown, NY

Joanne Savini
Uniontown, PA

ABOUT THE AUTHOR

Dotty Boen Oelkers is an author, educator, and traveler. She is the owner of an educational consulting business, Developing Educational Solutions (DES), in Conroe, Texas. DES helps school districts find dynamic ways to improve career and technology education programs. Dotty was previously a marketing education teacher and director of career and technology education in Texas.

Travel and Tourism Marketing
Contents

Destination: Marketing Success

Travel and Tourism Marketing is a brand new package that brings excitement and relevance to your marketing course. By presenting key marketing concepts using real examples from the travel and tourism industry, learning becomes easier and more permanent. DECA Prep activities in every chapter allow users to participate in competitive events in a non-threatening environment, while building presentation skills, marketing competencies, and confidence. Icons in the text visually identify the marketing concepts covered, linking theory to practice.

Instructors save time and improve planning using the wealth of resources in the Multimedia Module. The variety of review and assessment activities integrated throughout the text and supplements streamlines assessment and provides lots of opportunities for reinforcement. Minimize prep time and maximize learning by using these multimedia instructional materials: Annotated Instructor's Edition, Video, ExamView electronic testing CD, and Instructor's Resource CD.

Manage the Course with Multimedia

- **Multimedia Module** Keep interest levels high and instruction relevant with the wealth of resources included in the Multimedia Module: Video, Instructor's Resource CD, Annotated Instructor's Edition, and ExamView CD

- **Annotated Instructor's Edition*** Teaching suggestions, lesson plans, answers to text activities, and additional resources at point of use make planning, teaching, and assessment easier

- **Instructor's Resource CD*** Lesson plans, PowerPoint presentations, and video discussion guide questions are portable and easily accessible

- **ExamView CD*** Test creation, delivery, and grading are quick and easy with this complete test bank and electronic assessment tool

- **Video*** Video clips and related discussion questions present real-world examples of chapter content and generate discussion about travel and tourism marketing

* Included in the Multimedia Module

National Marketing Standards— We've Got You Covered

Your planning and teaching just got a little easier. You can cover national marketing standards using an industry that brings relevance to learners. *Travel and Tourism Marketing* follows the **Marketing Education Resource Center**® core standards for the marketing curriculum, described as follows:

Distribution Understands the concepts and processes needed to move, store, locate, and/or transfer ownership of goods and services

Marketing-Information Management Understands the concepts, systems, and tools needed to gather, access, synthesize, evaluate, and disseminate information for use in making business decisions

Pricing Understands concepts and strategies utilized in determining and adjusting prices to maximize return and meet customers' perceptions of value

Product/Service Management Understands the concepts and processes needed to obtain, develop, maintain, and improve a product or service mix in response to market opportunities

Promotion Understands the concepts and strategies needed to communicate information about products, services, images, and/or ideas to achieve a desired outcome

Selling Understands the concepts and actions needed to determine client needs and wants and respond through planned, personalized communication that influences purchase decisions and enhances future business opportunities

Welcome to *Travel and Tourism Marketing*!

The field of travel and tourism marketing is rapidly growing. Many universities, colleges, and high schools now offer specializations in travel and tourism marketing. The general principles of marketing that are presented throughout this book are intended to be a guide in taking your first career step into the exciting world of travel and tourism. Begin your journey by learning how to plan and market travel and tourism products and services.

The **core standards of marketing** are visually identified by icons throughout the text.

MARKETING CORE STANDARDS

DISTRIBUTION

MARKETING–INFORMATION MANAGEMENT

PRICING

PRODUCT/SERVICE MANAGEMENT

PROMOTION

SELLING

FINANCING

In addition to the six core standards, the text also covers the important topic of **financing**.

Winning Strategies presents successful, real-world strategies used in travel and tourism marketing.

Winning Strategies

E-Ticket investigates the impact of technology and the Internet on travel and tourism.

E-Ticket

All Aboard begins each lesson and encourages you to explore the material in the upcoming lesson. All Aboard also gives you opportunities to work with other students in your class.

All Aboard

Missing the Boat examines ethical issues in travel and tourism businesses.

Missing the Boat

Marketing Myths explores questionable travel and tourism marketing strategies or other marketing-related assumptions.

Marketing Myths

Stopover provides you with an opportunity to assess your comprehension at key points in each lesson. Ongoing review and assessment helps you understand the material.

Time Out introduces you to interesting facts and statistics about travel and tourism marketing.

Time Out

travel.swlearning.com includes Internet activities and crossword puzzles for every chapter.

▶ ▶ ▶ ▶ travel.swlearning.com

Extended Stay provides you with projects to improve your skills in planning and marketing travel and tourism products and services.

Five-Star Traveler acquaints you with people who have succeeded in travel and tourism marketing.

Five-Star Traveler

DECA Prep prepares you for competitive events with a Case Study and Event Prep in every chapter.

Travel and Tourism Industry

CHAPTER 1 · CHAPTER 1 · CHAPTER 1 · CHAPTER 1

1

Photodisc

Point Your Browser

travel.swlearning.com

▶ ▶ ▶ ▶

The Peninsula Hotels

When the wealthy think about upscale hotels for business or leisure travel, a Peninsula property is sure to make the list of top choices. There are seven Peninsula hotels in key locations— Hong Kong, Bangkok, Beijing, Manila, New York, Chicago, and Beverly Hills. An eighth hotel is under construction in Tokyo. The Peninsula Hotels is a division of The Hongkong and Shanghai Hotels, Limited (HSH).

The Peninsula hotels consistently rate as world-class hotels for their quality of service and attention to detail. The Peninsula hotels set a standard for other hotels to achieve. Peninsula hotels are consistently chosen as "Best U.S. Hotel" by industry reviewers such as *Travel + Leisure* magazine and *Andrew Harper's Hideaway Report*.

Peninsula hotels offer unique guest services and amenities, such as a nine-hole putting green on a terrace at the Chicago Peninsula. The Bangkok hotel provides transportation to and from the airport in chauffeur-driven Mercedes S-Class cars. Chinese cooking classes are offered at the Hong Kong Peninsula. While many upscale hotels offer frequent guests a bonus service, such as cookies or bottled water in their rooms upon arrival, Peninsula hotels provide flowers, fruit baskets, newspapers, and a full breakfast.

HSH has focused its business on developing the Peninsula hotels as premier destinations within major international cities. Using its expertise in the hospitality industry, HSH works with local partners to assure that each hotel is tailored to the location's customers.

THINK CRITICALLY

1. List at least three elements that help HSH successfully market Peninsula hotels.

2. Who is the target customer for Peninsula hotels?

Lesson 1.1

Marketing Basics

Goals

Describe the foundations of travel and tourism marketing

Explain the six core standards of marketing.

All Aboard

Sixty or seventy years ago, a vacation or business trip across the United States frequently included taking a train. The railroad was the fastest, most economical mode of transportation available. Thirty years later, the railroads were begging for government assistance in order to survive. The railroads had made some near-fatal marketing mistakes.

According to Theodore Levitt in an article titled "Marketing Myopia" in the July–August 2004 *Harvard Business Review*, the railroads failed to "discover, create, arouse, and satisfy customer needs." The rail companies saw their business as building railroads rather than serving customers. The railroads had failed to understand and apply the core standards of marketing. Today, the United States is in need of the safe, efficient, and fast nationwide passenger transportation system that rail provides other countries.

Work with a partner. Brainstorm ways a railroad could "discover, create, arouse, and satisfy customer needs."

MARKETING FOUNDATIONS

A series of activities that creates an exchange that satisfies the individual customer as well as the travel and tourism business is known as **travel and tourism marketing**. The activities begin with identifying a customer need and planning to meet that need. Next, the goods or services must be made available at a price the customer is willing to pay.

Photodisc

Owners and managers of resort rental properties in Hilton Head, South Carolina, use marketing knowledge and skills to assure that their vacation homes are rented for the entire season. Prime rentals in Hilton Head may go for $8,000 to $10,000 per week. Renters expect them to be professionally managed by customer-focused staff. Some rental property companies offer incentives to repeat customers who book the ocean-side homes early. For example, customers willing to book reservations with a 50 percent deposit a year in advance receive price discounts. The customers are pleased to lock in the rental of a house in a high-demand location because they are satisfied with the exchange of their money for the vacation rental property. In return, the business owners are assured of fully booked properties.

Entrepreneurship

When an individual enters the travel and tourism industry as an employee or business owner, the intent is to discover what customers want and create a customer base for the intended product. A travel and tourism product may be a service, goods, or a combination of both.

Effective businesses analyze the potential opportunities and weigh the associated risks. Then, they create a business plan that will result in sustaining the business and providing an ongoing livelihood for the employees and owner.

When a travel and tourism business is first being developed, there may be only a few customers who want to purchase its product. Even though little or no income is being produced, costs of operating the business will begin to grow. Employees need to be paid. Payments must be made for rent and utilities. Adequate economic resources must be available to sustain the business until the right balance is found between the cost of supplying the product and the amount customers are willing to pay. Eventually, the business needs a large enough customer base to generate a profit for those who have invested funds in the business. A **profit** is the amount of money, from sales and services, remaining after

Missing the Boat

In June 2004, the founder of AeroContinente, the main Peruvian airline, was placed on a list of drug kingpins by the U.S. Treasury Department. Fernando Melciades Zevallos Gonzales was identified as a major drug trafficker. Under the Kingpin Act, people under U.S. jurisdiction cannot conduct business transactions with persons on the kingpin list or with any of their businesses.

As a result, insurance companies canceled all policies for AeroContinente, and its flights into the United States were canceled. About a month later, the airline reemerged as Nuevo Continente and offered low-priced airfares. Some travel agents illegally booked Americans on flights of the new airline. Both the agents and their customers could be subject to fines and jail time for violating the law.

THINK CRITICALLY

1. Do you think the U.S. government should enforce the Kingpin Act when doing so causes inconvenience and extra expense for U.S. consumers? Why or why not?

2. Should an airline be closed down due to the acts of an owner? Discuss your opinion with others.

Time Out

The 100 largest metropolitan areas in the United States account for almost half of the tourism-related employment in the country.

all costs have been paid. Costs include salaries, advertising, utilities, and other expenses. People start businesses with the intent of making a profit.

Personal and Professional Development

Owners and managers of travel and tourism businesses must be able to communicate clearly with business partners and suppliers. All personnel must be able to communicate effectively with customers. Successful businesses involve teams of people working to meet customer needs.

Travel and tourism communication requires mastering both verbal and written communications skills. Verbal communications include making group presentations as well as talking with individuals. Written communications include writing effective business letters, brochures, and news articles that let consumers know why the product or service is the best choice for them. Technology, such as word-processing and presentation software or the Internet, is a critical tool for facilitating marketing communications.

The ability to work successfully with people from around the world is a vital skill for businesses. A diverse customer base can present unique challenges. In today's global marketplace, cultural sensitivity can make the difference between success and failure.

A variety of careers related to travel and tourism marketing require a range of educational levels, from a high school diploma to a bachelor's degree and beyond. Travel and tourism is a constantly changing industry. Those engaged in it need continual educational and professional development to remain current.

Stopover Describe travel and tourism marketing.

_____

_____

MARKETING CORE STANDARDS

The core standards of marketing identified in the National Standards for Marketing Management, Entrepreneurship, and Business Administration include distribution, marketing-information management, pricing, product/service management, promotion, and selling. All travel and tourism businesses use the six core marketing standards.

Distribution involves moving the products and services from producer to consumer by the best means possible. In travel and tourism marketing, the methods used to make products and services available to consumers are critical for customer satisfaction.

Marketing-information management involves collecting and using data to make decisions for the business. The information must include data about what potential customers want and how much they are willing to pay to obtain the products and services.

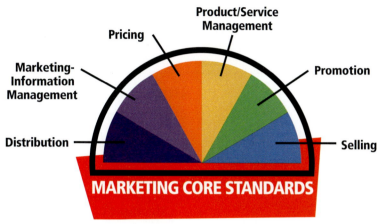

©2005, Marketing Education Resource Center®

Pricing means establishing the price of the products and services. Customers want to know that they are getting a fair value for the money they are spending. A business must price its products and services low enough that customers are willing to buy, but high enough that the business can make a profit.

Product/service management combines the right mix of products and services to match customer wants and needs. Once information is known about what customers want and need, products and services can be created to fill those requirements.

Promotion is communicating to potential customers about the travel and tourism products and services. Promotion can occur through various avenues, including advertising, publicity, public relations, sales promotions, and personal selling.

Selling involves communicating directly with customers to determine, and then satisfy, their wants and needs with appropriate products and services. Selling requires strong verbal and nonverbal communications skills as well as the ability to listen.

In addition to these six core standards, this text will also cover the important topic of financing. **Financing** requires budgeting, finding investors, record keeping, funding the business operations, and helping customers find ways to afford the products and services. With a new business, personnel must be paid a salary often before the first customer has even made a purchase. All six core standards of marketing, as well as financing, are involved in every transfer of travel goods and services to the consumer. Satisfying the customer and making a profit require knowledge and a practical application of each standard.

Name the six core standards of marketing.

_____

_____

At the Gate

Understand Marketing Concepts

Circle the best answer for each of the following questions.

1. Marketing is
   a. getting people to buy things.
   b. understanding business motives.
   c. creating satisfying exchange relationships.
   d. none of the above.

2. Four of the six core standards of marketing are
   a. selling, distribution, promotion, and pricing.
   b. exchanges, distribution, pricing, and promotion.
   c. purchasing, planning, advertising, and distribution.
   d. planning, distribution, pricing, and advertising.

Think Critically

Answer the following questions as completely as possible. If necessary, use a separate sheet of paper.

3. Briefly describe a positive travel and tourism marketing experience that you or someone you know has had. Why was it a positive experience?

_____

_____

_____

_____

_____

_____

_____

4. **Communication** Your community has a beautiful park full of tulips that bloom in April. Write a persuasive letter to a tour company about why it should add the park to its spring tours.

_____

_____

_____

_____

_____

_____

_____

The Nature of Travel and Tourism Marketing

Goals

● Understand the early development of the travel and tourism industry.

● Describe the importance of history and geography to travel and tourism.

All Aboard

One of architect Frank Lloyd Wright's most magnificent and best-known works is the residence called the Louis Penfield House in Willoughby Hills, Ohio. There are about 400 remaining structures that Wright designed during his lifetime, and Penfield House is one of only three that are open to overnight guests. Spending the night at Penfield House provides the visitor a glimpse of history and a sense of being outdoors while inside.

A walking tour through the house does not offer the serene sensation that an overnight stay provides.

Work with a partner. Find information about a historical site in your area that has been preserved and is open to tourists. List five ideas to attract tourists to the site.

ORIGINS OF TRAVEL AND TOURISM

Traveling for pleasure, or **tourism**, has evolved from limited beginnings into a major worldwide industry. People have always moved from their home base for many reasons, including to gather food, for social or religious purposes, or due to conflicts and wars.

Tourism began its historical expansion in the eighteenth century, due in part to improvements brought about by the Industrial Revolution. Great improvements in three areas—transportation, communication, and leisure time—influenced the vast expansion of tourism into the major industry of today.

Tourism generally includes travel, but much travel is done for reasons besides pleasure, including business and personal reasons. **Traveling** can be defined as leaving overnight the region in which one lives. Traveling for pleasure has grown from an infrequent activity for the wealthy to an expectation of the middle class.

Brand X Pictures

Transportation

DISTRIBUTION

The invention and refinement of the steam engine made rail and ship transportation a reliable and convenient method of travel. Prior to the steam engine, oceans were crossed in sailing ships. The passengers and crew were left to the mercy of the unpredictable weather. The trips were dangerous and uncomfortable. Only very hardy passengers could survive such a trip. The steam engine provided reliable power for both ships and rail transportation, making it possible for people to choose to travel for pleasure.

Later, the inventions of the airplane and automobile would make it easier and even more convenient to travel.

Brand X Pictures

Communication

PROMOTION

As people were able to travel in more affordable and convenient ways, they wrote about their travels. Accounts of their adventures were included in newspapers and sent via postal mail and telegraph, increasing the number of people who wanted to travel. In 1805, letters received from explorers Lewis and Clark were front-page news. By 1807, books describing the journey and copies of the maps created on the trip were for sale. News of the successful adventure opened the North American continent to travel.

During the Industrial Revolution, improvements in mass communication made people aware of distant places and potential ways to get to the destinations. From the postal service to the Internet, mass communication has played a major role in creating a desire to travel for pleasure.

Leisure Time

Once transportation was available and the desire to see the world had been sparked by mass communication, people only lacked the time and money. The Industrial Revolution made it possible for people to work all year in one location. The growth of organized labor helped limit the number of hours per week that people worked. The standard workweek was reduced to 40 hours over five days, leaving a large number of people with a two-day weekend.

Following the end of World War II, in 1945, a middle-class level of prosperity made extra income available for pleasure trips. Additionally, a full week of paid vacation time became a benefit of most full-time jobs. Today, many people in the United States have two or more weeks of paid vacation. People in France and other countries may work 35 hours per week and have as many as six weeks of vacation per year.

Changes over the years provided people with convenient and comfortable transportation, interesting information about new places, and the time and the money to travel for pleasure. The tourism industry has grown to help travelers use their leisure time and fulfill their desires to see the world.

Why has tourism grown in popularity?

Stopover

_____

_____

WHERE ARE WE GOING?

Think about a career in travel and tourism! You will open doors to all of the geographical regions of the world and possibly beyond. To help people travel for business or pleasure requires a vast understanding of the options beyond their current surroundings. Knowing how to find information about locations around the world, including their history, culture, and economic and political conditions, is a major requirement for success in travel and tourism.

Geography

Maps of the world are constantly changing. Countries change names and boundaries, and people in the travel and tourism business must stay on top of the changes. Businesspeople may be traveling to help start a new industry in a recently formed country. Adventure travelers may want to go where few have gone before. The Internet has made information about the world much more accessible, but it should not be the only source used. Business contacts made through public agencies and professional organizations can provide valuable informa-tion and should be used frequently.

Assume you are a travel agent who puts together trips for customers. You must stay current with economic and political changes in all geographic areas of the world. Your clients must be able to trust you to provide current, useful information about their destinations. You can help them be smart travelers in dangerous places. For example, if a customer is picked up by a bogus taxi in Rome and dropped miles from his or her destination after being charged a large fee, the customer's trip will be spoiled. A little ground transportation knowledge can make travel less stressful.

E-Ticket

To encourage students to understand the importance of geography and history, the American Automobile Association (AAA) sponsors a competition for high school students. Travel Challenge begins with an online, 40-question exam open to students in grades 9–12. The top five scorers in each state take a written exam. The top winner from each state wins an expense-paid trip to compete for a $25,000 scholarship.

THINK CRITICALLY

Visit AAA's web site and read about the Travel Challenge competition. Take the practice quiz and consider entering the contest.

Travel and tourism professionals who provide services to inbound customers from outside the country need to be versed in local geography and history. They also must have knowledge of the visitors' culture, important services they might want, and their level of service expectation. Learning about other countries provides knowledge to help please the consumer.

Japan is geographically a small country with a big travel appetite. Learning about the country and its history, customs, and culture can go a long way in earning repeat business from Japanese visitors. For example, Japanese businesspeople bow as a form of greeting, although most will shake hands with westerners. Learning to bow will indicate an interest in pleasing Japanese customers.

Doing as the Romans Do

A sense of history is an asset for success in the travel and tourism industry. Travel tours that explore both natural and cultural history are growing in popularity. Learning about U.S. history can be fun when it is brought to life in places like Williamsburg, Virginia. Parts of Colonial Williamsburg have been preserved and replicated to offer a walking history lesson. Trips that are based on providing historical information about a location and its most prominent historical sites are often called **heritage tours.**

People frequently want to visit regions where their ancestors may have originated many generations ago. These *genealogical trips* may include visits to find legal documents, such as birth and death records, or to discover long-lost relatives. Genealogy trips can be enhanced with area history from a local perspective.

Photodisc

If travel for business or pleasure involves a country like Egypt, the traveler will likely want to visit the country's landmarks, such as the Great Pyramids. Additionally, the traveler may discover the history of civilization through a Nile River cruise. A travel professional isn't required to visit every location or know every detail about its history, but knowing where to find the information is important. As with most aspects of travel and tourism, the Internet offers a great deal of information that can be found through search engines such as Yahoo! and Google.

Stopover

Why should travel and tourism professionals have a strong background in geography?

_____

_____

Understand Marketing Concepts

Circle the best answer for each of the following questions.

1. Improvements in three areas that have dramatically increased the expansion of travel are
   a. buses, trains, and automobiles.
   b. hotels, restaurants, and movie theaters.
   c. transportation, communication, and leisure time.
   d. none of the above.

2. Tourism is travel
   a. out of necessity.
   b. for business.
   c. for pleasure.
   d. for all of the above.

Think Critically

Answer the following questions as completely as possible. If necessary, use a separate sheet of paper.

3. **History** How have improvements in mass communications affected the travel industry?

_____

_____

_____

_____

_____

_____

4. Write a paragraph about the application to the tourist industry of the phrase, "When in Rome, do as the Romans do."

_____

_____

_____

_____

_____

_____

_____

_____

Travel and Tourism Business Operations

Goals
- List and describe the major components of the travel and tourism industry.
- Describe factors of service and quality.

All Aboard

First-class seats on airplanes are generally larger and more comfortable than coach seats. Passengers in first class typically receive a higher level of service than coach passengers. First-class passengers also pay more for their seats with the expectation of receiving a higher level of service. When Delta Air Lines rolled out a new ticket price structure, the cost of a first-class ticket was only $100 more than the cost of an economy ticket. Delta was sending a message that the service level it would provide was only worth $100 more. First class was losing its distinction as a special, limited service.

In a group, discuss how airlines might add distinction between levels of service. What could they offer that would not increase costs?

PUTTING IT TOGETHER

The travel and tourism industry is made up of a diverse group of businesses, service providers, and public-sector agencies. The travel and tourism segments of the industry can be discussed separately, but they also overlap in many areas. Tourism involves travel, unless the tourist is visiting destinations within his or her own region. Travel has many purposes beyond tourism, including business. The major interacting components of travel and tourism are

Photodisc

- transportation
- lodging, hospitality, and distributors
- regulatory agencies
- public-sector organizations
- conference, event, and destination planners
- professional organizations
- other related businesses

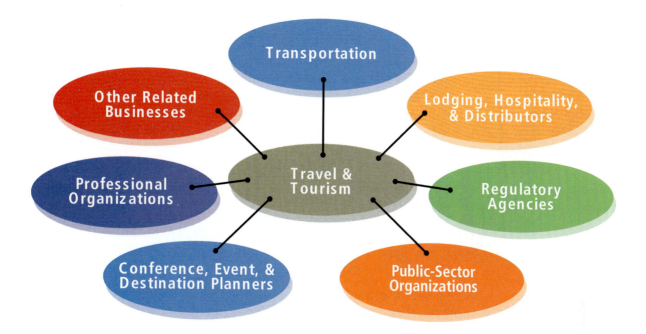

All of these components work together to shape one of the largest industries in the world. Each is needed to assure that the customer is satisfied.

Transportation includes cars, trains, airplanes, buses, ships, and any other mode of moving people. Whether for business or for pleasure, when people travel they must move from one location to another. Sometimes several forms of transportation are used in one trip. The traveling public counts on transportation businesses to get it to its destinations safely, comfortably, and on time.

Transportation businesses are heavily regulated. Some are operated by a public agency. Amtrak is a national public-railroad passenger service that operates primarily on rail tracks owned by private freight railroads. Most other transportation businesses are privately owned corporations, but operate within governmental rules set up to protect the public interest and safety.

DISTRIBUTION

Lodging, hospitality, and distributors are the most visible of the travel and tourism segments. They are the face of the industry to the consumer.

A place to stay and meals to eat are critical parts of any travel adventure, whether for business or pleasure.

The range of places to stay is wide, starting with youth hostels that offer shelter and a bed for a few dollars per day. At the other extreme is the luxurious Ritz-Carlton in Paris, where a suite can cost thousands of dollars per night.

The lodging and hospitality segments include businesses that are one-of-a-kind, privately owned facilities, as well as huge hotel chains that are the result of many mergers of major hotel companies. A **merger** is when two companies are integrated into one company.

Distributors of travel and tourism are the businesses that sell products and services directly to the consumer. They include travel agencies, call centers, and online services. The Internet has dramatically affected the way

Time Out

Black Hills State University in Spearfish, South Dakota, hosts the Center for Tourism Research. Over 125 travel and tourism organizations are listed with links at its web site.

travel agencies operate. The travel agencies that did not adjust to the changing technology have ceased to exist.

Regulatory agencies are governmental entities with the legal authority to issue rules and regulations that impact travel and tourism businesses. The U.S. Department of Transportation is the umbrella organization for all of the administrative agencies that oversee transportation in the United States, such as the Federal Aviation Administration and the Federal Highway Administration.

States, counties, and cities also have regulatory agencies that are dedicated to protecting the public. Florida's Division of Hotels and Restaurants issues operating licenses and inspects public lodging and food establishments to assure their compliance with health and safety standards. The potential for harm due to neglect of health and safety standards makes regulatory agencies an important aspect of building travelers' trust.

Public-sector organizations are agencies set up by governments to promote travel and tourism in their areas. Each of the 50 states and the District of Columbia has a state-level tourism organization. Some state legislators see travel and tourism as a major source of income for the people of the state. In those states, the state tourism organization receives tax-generated funding to market the area to potential visitors from other states and countries. The tourism organization's goal is to build an image of the state as a place people want to visit.

Part of the job of the tourism offices is to collect and analyze data about visitors. The data are used to gauge the perceived image of the region and to plan ways to improve that image so that additional travelers will choose to visit.

MARKETING – INFORMATION MANAGEMENT

At the international level, the World Tourism Organization is an agency of the United Nations. It has 144 member countries and 300 affiliate members. The affiliate members represent private businesses and professional travel and tourism organizations.

Conference, event, and destination planners market places, occasions, and happenings that will attract travelers and tourists. Business conferences are events that bring together people employed in the same industry to learn, share, and socialize. The conference attendees need transportation to the conference city, local transportation, hotel rooms, and meals. Additionally, they need meeting rooms, exhibition halls for vendor booths, leisure-time activities, and entertainment. They also spend money on clothing, gifts, and souvenirs.

In addition to business conferences, people travel to attend large-scale events such as a NASCAR race or the Super Bowl. A major event like the Super Bowl requires a city to have about 18,000 hotel rooms and 1,000 buses available to accommodate fans.

Major stops or attractions for travelers are called *destinations*. A destination can be a specific city, resort, or theme park, such as Disney's Magic Kingdom. Profitable destinations use all of the core standards of marketing to perfection.

Professional organizations are groups of people who meet for professional growth and to network with people employed in related businesses. In the travel and tourism industry, there are many such professional organizations at the international, national, state, and local levels. There are associations that address broad issues for the industry as a whole. The Travel Industry Association brings together thousands of U.S. and international travel buyers and journalists at its annual International Pow Wow. There are also professional organizations that serve specific segments of the industry. The Dude Ranch Association was formed in 1926 and has 120 members. It sets industry standards for its members. Membership assures visitors that they are booking a vacation at a real ranch, not just a hotel with horses.

Photodisc

Large and small professional organizations play a key role in the sharing of best practices, keeping the industry current, and finding new ways to market to customers. Many attendees at meetings of professional organizations say they learn the most from talking informally with others in between the scheduled, formal meetings.

Other related businesses include insurance companies, financial institutions, law firms, and publishing groups that interact with travel and tourism businesses. Travel insurance companies provide

- coverage for medical needs outside of the United States

- trip-cancellation coverage that protects the traveler's investment

- emergency evacuation needs

- life-insurance coverage for accidental death

Financial institutions are involved in financing travel and tourism businesses, such as loaning money for the construction of a large hotel or resort. Lawyers provide legal advice and guide travel and tourism businesses through the maze of paperwork and regulations. Travel and tourism publications are created and distributed throughout the world to promote destinations and events. Newspapers have weekly travel sections, and whole magazines are devoted to the topic. People like to read about potential travel opportunities and dream of a fantastic vacation trip.

Stopover

Name seven segments of the travel and tourism industry.

_____

_____

Marketing Myths

Federal and state legislators have not always noticed its major economic impact because travel and tourism is such a diverse and scattered industry. The industry, through professional organizations and public agencies, has recently made great strides in raising awareness of its "strength and diversity," according to Jonathan M. Tisch, chairman of the Travel Business Roundtable. Organizations such as the Travel Business Roundtable spend a great deal of time, effort, and money meeting with legislators to assure that laws are favorable to the industry.

THINK CRITICALLY

1. Do you think the travel and tourism industry should continue to promote itself to legislators? Why or why not?

2. Should the goverment be involved in promoting travel and tourism? Discuss your opinion with others.

ROLL OUT THE RED CARPET

All segments of travel and tourism are focused on customer service. Business and pleasure travelers alike have a level of expectation as to the quality of service they should receive. When discussing service and quality, a number of factors are considered across the industry, including

- quality performance standards
- a culture of service and quality
- measures of quality

Using these factors, managers seek to continually improve service and quality to the delight of their customers.

Setting Quality Performance Standards

Standards are the rules used for the measure of quality. Standards for cleanliness in restaurants and hotels are established and enforced by regulatory agencies, but a business decides what standards to use for quality service. Quality service is what guests most remember. Smart travel and tourism companies define their business, target their customers, and exceed their customers' expectations for quality service.

PRODUCT/SERVICE MANAGEMENT

It is expensive to set up a business and attract new customers. It then becomes important to maintain the relationships and retain them as repeat customers. One of the mainstays of repeat business is a consistent level of quality service. Each time a customer does business with the firm, he or she must receive the same, consistently high level of service 24 hours a day, seven days a week. Consistency requires planning, training, measuring, revising the plan, and retraining. This high level of service will keep the customer returning.

Creating a Quality Culture

Planning for quality service requires that the business have a clear picture of what the customer wants. Standards must be set in writing, and the standards must be shared with every employee. Each employee must be clear on his or her part in providing quality service to the customer. Quality service does not happen by chance. It requires management to model quality behavior and to provide training for employees on the exact behavior expected. Management must create a culture of quality within the establishment.

Major travel and tourism corporations have in-house training departments that prepare employees to provide quality service. Many professional organizations offer training for members and members' employees. Outside training companies may be hired to provide training as well. Hospitality Services Alliance (HSA) International is a company whose mission is to provide training and resources for the hospitality and tourism industry. For example, HSA offers an online training course that introduces students to the reservation sales process.

Measuring Quality

MARKETING–INFORMATION MANAGEMENT

The job of ensuring quality does not end with training. Management must set up a system for continuously monitoring the quality and level of service. Unless monitored and measured, no one can be sure that the standards taught in training are being implemented.

One outside agency that measures quality in the hotel industry is the American Automobile Association (AAA). AAA uses diamonds as its rating system. AAA employs full-time inspectors who rate the hotels based on industry-established criteria. A five-diamond rating from AAA means the ultimate in luxury and meticulous service that exceeds all reasonable expectations. A single-diamond rating means that the establishment is clean, comfortable, and priced for the budget traveler.

It is difficult for travel and tourism managers to determine if they are delivering the quality of service intended. Universities that offer degrees related to travel and tourism conduct research on ways to measure customer satisfaction. Most research models look at information from customers in three major categories.

Photodisc

- **Importance** The importance of a specific dimension of the customer's experience must be obtained from the customer. A dimension could be the accuracy of the information the customer received about a hotel before starting the journey or the way in which the customer was greeted upon arrival at the lodging. If a particular dimension is not important to a customer, then it may not matter if the hotel performs poorly in that dimension. The customer may still be completely satisfied.

- **Expectations** Customers arrive with a level of expectation for the quality of service. For example, customers may expect to be greeted promptly and that their reservations be found quickly and be correct. Customer expectations may vary according to a hotel's rating and price level.

- **Performance** The actual performance of service is the final test of customer satisfaction. If being promptly greeted is important to a customer, then the customer will likely expect a prompt greeting at the hotel he or she has chosen. If the customer has to stand in line and the reservation is wrong, then the customer will rank this dimension as below expectations and the facility as lacking quality service. If a customer has chosen a low-rated hotel in order to save money, then the customer may not have high expectations. If the performance is actually below average but higher than customer expectations, the customer may indicate high satisfaction. The accommodations will be perceived as high value for the money spent. It is important for a travel and tourism business to know its customers' needs and wants in order to fulfill their expectations.

Travel and tourism managers are responsible for customer satisfaction based on the established quality standards for their business. To assure quality service, clear standards must be established and communicated to all personnel. The personnel must then receive continual training. Finally, quality must be monitored and measured, and revisions made for continuous improvement.

Stopover

What three categories of information are measured when considering customer satisfaction?

_____

_____

Five-Star Traveler

GLORIA BOHAN

Gloria Bohan is president, CEO, and founder of Omega World Travel. Founded in 1972, Omega is currently the fifth-largest travel-management company and the largest female-owned travel business in the United States. Omega serves corporate, government, and leisure clients throughout the world.

Under Bohan's leadership, the company grew from a one-person travel agency into a major travel business with sales revenues of $1 billion a year. Omega has 200 offices in 15 states and four international offices in the United Kingdom, Guam, Japan, and Bahrain. It employs more than 1,100 people.

Bohan attributes Omega's success to her family of qualified employees. She is hands-on, and she believes in a personal touch and being accessible, as much as that is possible. To prove it, she travels regularly to various offices to get to know her agents and build team spirit. Her basic belief in treating others as she would like to be treated guides her management and service philosophy.

Bohan believes that flexibility and an ability to innovate are essential for success. Bohan is a leader in her industry and a role model for women and minorities. She has been honored by many national organizations, and Omega World Travel was recently recognized as one of the top diversity-owned businesses in the United States.

THINK CRITICALLY

Write a paragraph explaining how Gloria Bohan's personal characteristics have contributed to her success.

Understand Marketing Concepts

Circle the best answer for each of the following questions.

1. Which of the following is an example of a travel and tourism distributor?
    a. a professional organization
    b. a regulatory agency
    c. a law firm
    d. an online travel service

2. Examples of destinations are
    a. purchasing, distribution, promotion, and pricing.
    b. resorts and theme parks.
    c. planes, trains, and automobiles.
    d. all of the above.

Think Critically

Answer the following questions as completely as possible. If necessary, use a separate sheet of paper.

3. Why should a travel and tourism business have clear standards for quality?

    _____

    _____

    _____

    _____

    _____

    _____

    _____

4. **Communication** Think about the highest level of service you could possibly receive at a restaurant where you often eat. What dimensions of quality service are most important to you? Write a paragraph describing that service.

    _____

    _____

    _____

    _____

    _____

    _____

    _____

Chapter Assessment

Review Marketing Concepts

Write the letter of the term that matches each definition. Some terms will not be used.

_____ 1. Traveling for pleasure

_____ 2. The rules used for the measure of quality

_____ 3. When two companies are integrated into one company

_____ 4. Combines the right mix of products and services to correspond with customer wants and needs

_____ 5. Communicating to potential customers about the travel and tourism products and services

_____ 6. Moving the products and services from producer to consumer by the best means possible

_____ 7. Collecting and using data to make decisions for the business

_____ 8. Trips based on providing historical information about a location and its most prominent historical sites

_____ 9. The amount of money, from sales and services, remaining after all costs have been paid

_____ 10. Communicating directly with customers to determine, and then satisfy, their wants and needs with appropriate products and services

a. distribution
b. distributor
c. financing
d. heritage tours
e. marketing-information management
f. merger
g. pricing
h. product/service management
i. profit
j. promotion
k. selling
l. standards
m. tourism
n. travel
o. travel and tourism marketing

Circle the best answer.

11. People start travel and tourism businesses with the intent of
   a. becoming famous.
   b. traveling.
   c. making a profit.
   d. finding employment.

12. Tourism was originally available to only
   a. business people.
   b. marketing executives.
   c. explorers.
   d. the wealthy.

Think Critically

13. Spend five minutes discussing with another student how travel and tourism has changed within the last 200 years. Make a list of at least three changes that have occurred since the Industrial Revolution.

_____

_____

_____

14. A new bed-and-breakfast will accommodate six overnight guests and provide them hearty breakfasts. Make a list of possible expenses for this new business during the first six months of operations.

_____

_____

_____

_____

15. Choose one of the six core standards of marketing and describe how it would apply to the bed-and-breakfast in question 14.

_____

_____

_____

_____

16. Think about a trip you would like to take to somewhere you have never been. How did you become aware of this destination? How will you determine how to get there and where to stay?

_____

_____

_____

_____

17. Use the Internet or travel magazines to find promotions sponsored by a nearby state's tourism bureau. Name the state and list the major tourist destinations mentioned in the promotions. What dimensions of the destinations are the promotions emphasizing?

_____

_____

_____

_____

Make Connections

18. **Geography** Within the state you chose for question 17, find a location where you would establish a new tourist destination. Use online sources to research possible locations. Describe the location and list at least two reasons for your choice.

_____

_____

_____

_____

_____

19. **History** Use the Internet and other resources to learn about the economy and politics of Chile over the last 20 years. Why is it one of the most stable countries in South America?

_____

_____

_____

_____

_____

20. **Research** Your travel organization is hosting a group of visitors from Malta to help promote tourism in Malta. You need to learn some quick facts about the country before the guests arrive. Use the Internet and other resources and list the information you can find.

_____

_____

_____

_____

_____

21. **Marketing Math** A museum in your city wants to maximize its admission price and number of visitors. It normally has about 2,100 visitors per weekend and currently charges $25 per person. How many more people must visit the museum to earn the same amount of revenue if the price is lowered to $20?

_____

_____

_____

_____

22. **History** It is 1806, and you are responsible for marketing products related to the Lewis and Clark expedition. What products would you try to sell, and what media would you use?

_____

_____

_____

_____

_____

_____

23. **Communication** You are now responsible for marketing products related to the bicentennial celebration of the Lewis and Clark expedition. What products would you try to sell, and what media would you use?

_____

_____

_____

_____

_____

_____

_____

EXTENDED STAY

Project The island nation of Kiribati is located in the Pacific Ocean. It has a very weak economy. Currently, only about 3,000 to 4,000 tourists visit the island per year.

Work with a group and complete the following activities.
1. Use the Internet to learn about the economy of Kiribati.
2. Look at a map and determine the island's location and distance from Hawaii. What major nations are nearby?
3. Determine the major industries in Kiribati.
4. Using presentation software, make a short presentation about the history and current economic status of Kiribati. Include reasons why Kiribati is not more appealing to tourists, as well as suggestions for attracting more tourists to the island.

GREAT PLAINS NOT SO PLAIN FOR TRAVEL AND TOURISM

Seven states in the central United States make up the Great Plains. Many people relate the Great Plains to miles of flat grassland, wide-open spaces, fields of crops, and little else. Some individuals have been misled to believe that the central part of the United States does not have much to offer tourists. Many people who live in busy metropolitan areas desire an escape to a place where the pace is slower and life is simpler. The movie *City Slickers* shows a perfect example of how urban residents can escape the hustle of the city to experience a different lifestyle in the country.

Many farmers have diversified their business operations to provide more than crops. They have remodeled their Victorian-style farmhouses into bed-and-breakfasts, making the peace and quiet of the country available to city residents. In many bed-and-breakfasts, a private phone in a guest room is made available only on request. Most guests are there to get away from ringing phones and the demands of the city.

Many horse and cattle ranches have become guest ranches. Visitors may help work the ranch or simply relax and enjoy the peaceful atmosphere. Many city residents don't realize how dark it can get at night or how bright the stars can be until they vacation in the country. Activities may include horseback riding, calf roping, outdoor barbeques, sing-along campfires, swimming, fishing, and viewing the abundant wildlife. If you have never roped a calf or ridden a horse, private lessons may be scheduled at the ranch. Visitors can share a real farm or ranch experience with their families.

Vineyards, fruit orchards, and Christmas tree farms attract many visitors. Tourists may harvest their own fresh produce of pumpkins, strawberries, sweet corn, grapes, and delicious treats. Children may enjoy the excitement of helping to feed the farm animals or choosing a pumpkin to decorate for Halloween. The pumpkin patch provides a perfect setting for a hayride in the crisp autumn air. Families may choose their own Christmas trees to take home and decorate for the holidays.

Additional extensions to rural tourism businesses include gift shops, antique shops, restaurants, concession stands, and craft businesses. The Great Plains provide a perfect win–win situation for residents and tourists.

THINK CRITICALLY

1. What do many people associate with the Great Plains?
2. Why are the Great Plains a good vacation option for city people?
3. What does it mean to "diversify" the business operations?
4. What would be the best means to advertise the Great Plains for travel and tourism? Why?

TRAVEL AND TOURISM MARKETING MANAGEMENT TEAM DECISION MAKING

The Great Plains are not just for farming and ranching. Many residents of sprawling metropolitan areas yearn to take vacations where the pace is slower and the activities are unique.

Many farmers and ranchers in the Plains states have diversified their business operations to include travel and tourism. They have added bed-and-breakfasts or become guest ranches. Visitors can share a real farm or ranch experience with their families.

The Plains are also a place to experience unique wildlife, native culture, and pioneer history. You can see elk and bison grazing on open prairie that still bears the deeply cut grooves of pioneer wagon wheels. Follow the Oregon Trail or the course of Lewis and Clark. Experience native pride shows at the Cherokee Heritage Center. Visit the National Cowboy and Western Heritage Museum.

Many areas of the Plains states also have sections with scenic hills and rock formations, such as the Badlands area of North Dakota. State and national parks offer rock climbing, hiking, and fishing.

Residents will tell you that their state is not plain, it is "plain glorious." The governments of Iowa, Minnesota, Nebraska, Kansas, Oklahoma, and the Dakotas realize the value of attracting travel and tourism dollars. Your team has been hired by a tourism bureau (pick a Plains state) to promote tourism for the state. You have 30 minutes to develop your strategy, ten minutes to present to the tourism board (judges), and five minutes to field questions.

Performance Indicators Evaluated

- Design an advertising campaign for tourism in a Great Plains state.
- Develop a "tagline" (advertising slogan) for a vacation in the country.
- Explain what media will be used to advertise tourism to the Great Plains.
- Describe the target market for this travel and tourism destination.

Go to the DECA web site for more detailed information.

THINK CRITICALLY

1. What obstacles must the Great Plains overcome to increase tourism?
2. What themes might a television commercial emphasize for tourism in the Plains states?
3. List three advantages to vacationing in rural America.
4. Give two examples of effective advertising media to increase travel and tourism to the Plains states.

www.deca.org

Travel Regulations and Risk

Photodisc

CHAPTER 2 · CHAPTER 2 · CHAPTER 2 · CHAPTER 2

2

Point Your Browser

travel.swlearning.com

▶ ▶ ▶ ▶ ▶ ▶

Winning Strategies

Travel Business Roundtable

When the CEOs of 85 travel-related organizations joined together to form the Travel Business Roundtable (TBR), their unified voice moved Congress. TBR's mission was to keep elected officials informed about the economic and social importance of the travel industry to the United States.

This industry trade group formed in 1995 after The White House Conference on Travel and Tourism brought together the key players. Since TBR's inception, its members have visited more than 60 senators and 250 members of the House of Representatives. TBR has been able to bring together key members of every House of Representatives committee that is of interest to travel and tourism. Members of Congress and the media now recognize TBR as the leading voice on travel and tourism policy in Washington.

Homeland security issues have a major impact on the travel and tourism industry. TBR helps maintain a balance between promoting security and allowing travelers to freely visit and move about the United States. Jonathan Tisch is chairman of TBR, as well as chairman and CEO of Loews Hotels. He works hard to assure that the government helps promote the United States as an international destination of choice.

THINK CRITICALLY

1. Why does the travel and tourism industry need an organization like TBR?

2. What issues might TBR address with Congress in the future?

Governing Travel and Tourism

Goals

Describe public/private ventures to improve travel security.

Explain the role of government in travel and tourism.

All Aboard

Norovirus is the generic name for acute gastroenteritis, an inflammation of the stomach and intestines. It is also known as the 24-hour stomach flu. This highly contagious, but easily preventable, disease is passed from one person to another in confined spaces, such as cruise ships. Spread of the virus can be prevented by standard rules of sanitation. These rules include frequent hand washing and cleaning of common areas.

The U.S. Centers for Disease Control and Prevention (CDC) publishes a 244-page book entitled *Vessel Sanitation Program Operations Manual*. This book is the work of the cruise ship industry partnering with government for the protection of the public.

Work with a group. Discuss why the U.S. government should or should not be concerned with the level of sanitation provided by cruise ships. Why are cruise lines concerned about passenger health and sanitation? What can passengers do to protect themselves?

A BALANCING ACT

The goal of the U.S. travel and tourism industry is to attract both domestic and international visitors for business and pleasure. Balancing this goal with public health issues and security concerns is an ongoing project. Since September 11, 2001, homeland security concerns have brought about major changes in the way international travelers are screened for entry into the United States.

Public/Private Ventures

Travel and tourism is a major industry. It employs millions of people worldwide. Its size and its effect on the economy make the industry of interest to legislators. Protecting the industry from adverse laws, or lessening negative impacts of laws, is one part of the government's role. It is also the role of organizations that set industry standards.

Another important and visible role of government in travel and tourism is to provide for the health and safety of travelers. Protecting national security without hampering the travel industry is a balancing act. Input is requested from the travel industry as laws and regulations are developed and applied. Speaking at a joint summit of the Travel Business Roundtable and the U.S. Chamber of Commerce, Colin Powell, then secretary of state, declared, "We must continue to be a welcoming society, even as we take measures to secure our borders." When the TBR, Chamber of Commerce, and other private trade organizations work with government to jointly improve travel and tourism, these are known as **public/private ventures.**

Traveler Safety

A number of agencies within the U.S. government have travel and tourism segments under their jurisdictions. The Department of Transportation (DOT) oversees safety in all transportation-related industries. The Federal Aviation Administration (FAA), a part of the DOT, regulates both civil aviation and commercial space transportation safety. The FAA provides guidelines for air safety, from the manufacturing to the operation of an airplane. It is the licensing authority for U.S. pilots.

The Transportation Security Administration (TSA), a new department under the DOT, was created in 2001 after terrorist attacks in the United States. The TSA provides for airline safety, including passenger and luggage screening. It is also working to increase passenger safety in rail, water, highway, and mass-transit travel. Prior to the establishment of the TSA, private companies that were paid by the airlines conducted airline passenger safety screening.

Biometric Data

A **passport** is an internationally accepted document that verifies the identity and nationality of the bearer. A **visa** is an official authorization added to a passport, permitting entry into, and travel within, a particular country or region. The **Visa Waiver Program** (VWP) allows citizens of 27 countries to enter the United States for tourism or business stays of 90 days or less without obtaining a visa. The Enhanced Border Security and Visa Entry Reform Act of 2002 added a requirement for VWP travelers to have machine-readable passports (MRPs) that use biometrics. **Biometrics** are systems that measure biological features, such as the iris of the eye, fingerprints, or face. Biometric scans can be digitally stored on a chip that is imbedded in a passport. The scans can then be compared to those of the holder at an international entry point.

Marketing Myths

The long-time relationship between France and the United States hit a new bump when the countries disagreed over the war in Iraq. There was much talk by people in the United States about changing travel plans and avoiding France due to the squabble. U.S. tourism to France did suffer for several years, but probably not because of the political differences. Tourism in all of Europe hit new lows due to terrorism fears, the SARS virus outbreak, and a weak global economy.

In 2004, the number of U.S. tourists in France increased by 13 percent over the previous year. The 60th anniversary of the Allies' D-Day landings during World War II sparked a warmer relationship between the countries. The historical event helped rekindle an old friendship and tourism.

THINK CRITICALLY

1. Discuss with a partner how politics influences travel and tourism.

2. Should it affect U.S. citizens' travel when another country disagrees with the U.S. government? Why or why not?

The U.S. travel industry was concerned about the short implementation time of the new biometric requirement. In just five months, the 27 VWP countries were expected to obtain biometric recording equipment, train employees to use it, and provide all travelers with the new passports before they could enter the United States. There are approximately 13 million VWP visitors to the United States each year. The logistics of effectively launching the system were not possible. Deadlines were extended, due partly to lobbying by the travel and tourism industry. The impact of denying entry to some of the most frequent international visitors would have been severe to the travel and tourism industry, as well as to other U.S. commerce. Additionally, the United States would have been sending an unintended message that visitors were not welcome.

In addition to requiring biometric data from international travelers, all passports issued to U.S. citizens after late 2005 will contain biometric data about the holder. An electronic chip imbedded in a passport will hold the data as well as a digitized photo for facial recognition.

Privacy, Please

MARKETING– INFORMATION MANAGEMENT

A program entitled United States Visitor and Immigrant Status Indicator Technology (US-VISIT) is now used to screen almost all visitors to the United States. US-VISIT processing involves the collection of two index-finger scans and a digital photo. The biometric data is compared to the information on the visa or other travel documents of the international traveler. The process is performed quickly at the time of entry into the United States at airports, land borders, and major ports. Currently, Canadian citizens and most Mexican citizens are exempt from the process.

A number of countries and privacy advocacy groups object to the US-VISIT program. They claim it has an "enormous potential for error, invasion of privacy, and violation of international privacy laws and human rights standards." The Electronic Privacy Information Center (EPIC), a Washington, D.C.-based public interest research group, is one of the organizations in opposition. It is especially concerned about the adverse effects of incorrect data and the difficulty of confirming and correcting data errors.

In addition to the impact on international travelers, concerns were also expressed about the biometric addition to U.S. passports. Personal data could be electronically read by criminal "data skimmers" from as far as 30 feet away and used for a fake passport or identity theft. To combat this problem, each passport will contain an anti-skimming feature designed to prevent identity thieves from activating and reading the chip from a distance.

Stopover

Describe one way that government and private industry work together to improve travel and tourism.

_____

_____

OTHER GOVERNMENT ROLES

The travel and tourism industry contributes about 3.5 percent to the U.S. Gross Domestic Product (GDP). GDP is the output of goods and services produced by labor and property located in the United States. It is critical to the economy that the travel and tourism industry retains its high quality. In addition to homeland security, the government takes an active role in ensuring high standards of sanitation and service for U.S. visitors.

Traveler Health

The Environmental Protection Agency (EPA) tested the drinking water on 158 randomly selected airplanes. The results indicated that 12.6 percent of airplane water did not meet EPA guidelines. The test results were used to establish a baseline for testing frequency. Steps were recommended to help airlines clean up their water systems and bring the water up to acceptable, safe standards. Airlines are now required to test the drinking water on every airplane at least once a year.

Food safety is addressed by a number of federal, state, and local agencies. In Florida, where tourism is vital to the economy, four agencies join together to warn consumers and food-service establishments about the danger of improperly storing and handling food. The agencies include

- the Department of Business and Professional Regulation

- the Division of Hotels and Restaurants

- the Department of Agriculture and Consumer Services

- the Department of Health

The agencies make joint announcements regarding such topics as the thorough cleaning and cooking of imported fruits and vegetables to minimize the possibility of illness. Sanitation standards are critical to public health.

Traveler Service

MARKETING-INFORMATION MANAGEMENT

The quality of products and services offered by the travel industry is of interest to the federal government. The Office of Travel and Tourism (OTT) is part of the U.S. Department of Commerce. It works to ensure that a high quality of services is offered to travelers. The OTT also lends export assistance to service providers. **Export assistance** is provided in the form of gathered market-analysis data that may be used to attract more international travelers. The OTT is the only source of detailed information about international tourists in the United States.

Stopover

What are three major travel and tourism concerns that government addresses?

_____

_____

Understand Marketing Concepts

Circle the best answer for each of the following questions.

1. The Environmental Protection Agency tests airline
   a. pricing.
   b. marketing.
   c. water.
   d. tickets.

2. Biometrics include
   a. buildings and airports.
   b. digital facial photos and fingerprints.
   c. land ownership.
   d. public/private ventures.

Think Critically

Answer the following questions as completely as possible. If necessary, use a separate sheet of paper.

3. Why would privacy advocacy groups be concerned about the government collecting data from travelers? Does concern for security justify the collection of data? Why or why not?

_____

_____

_____

_____

_____

_____

_____

4. **Economics** What might be some positive and negative consequences of the United States making it difficult for international travelers to enter the country for business or pleasure?

_____

_____

_____

_____

_____

_____

_____

National and International Travel Infrastructure

Goals

- Describe the role of infrastructure.
- List economic resources for travel and tourism.
- Explain social, political, and environmental issues impacting travel and tourism.

All Aboard

The Chinese government is working hard to create the infrastructure necessary to allow the city of Shanghai to become a major tourist destination. Between 1994 and 2004, 16 five-star hotels were built. Additional hotels are being planned. A train that travels 260 miles per hour now moves passengers between the airport and downtown.

Dramatic infrastructure changes in Shanghai have transformed it from an ancient, mysterious Chinese city to a sterile imitation of a Western metropolis. Shanghai has lost its unique appeal, with McDonald's, Starbucks, and KFC replacing local eateries.

Work with a group. Discuss ways to add technology and modern conveniences to a city without destroying its unique, cultural charm.

STRUCTURAL SUPPORT

Tourist attractions require infrastructure, including transportation systems, lodging, and food services to support visitors. **Infrastructure** can be defined as the supporting structure beneath an industry. Government-provided infrastructure includes roads, water pipes, bridges, airports, and athletic stadiums. Privately provided infrastructure includes hotels and restaurants. A certain degree of infrastructure is required for an area to attract tourists. Even an area preserved as a natural attraction requires infrastructure. Roadways leading to the area, nearby lodging for its visitors, and a means of protecting natural habitat from tourists' impacts are all critical.

Photodisc

Some infrastructure may be provided by a partnership of public and private funding. An example would be a professional football stadium built to accommodate the Super Bowl. Both public and private infrastructure is needed for the travel and tourism industry to succeed.

Public Infrastructure

Efficient transportation helped create today's travel and tourism industry. It is also critical to maintaining it. In the United States, personal automobiles run on a publicly funded interstate highway system. Privately owned airlines take off and land at publicly financed airports. Cities and counties want their areas served by the highways and airports.

To operate at an appropriate level of service, additional runways are needed at many of the busiest airports. Runways are usually financed by a combination of federal and local public funds. The Government Accountability Office (GAO) estimates that it takes from 10 to 14 years from identifying the need to landing the first airplane on a new runway.

About five U.S. airports are scrambling to prepare for the new Airbus A380 jumbo jet to begin landing in 2006 and 2007. Airbus is headquartered in Toulouse, France, and is the number-one commercial plane manufacturer in the world. The A380 took 13 years to develop. The A380 will use 20 percent less fuel and will fly quieter, cheaper, and more environmentally friendly than the Boeing 747. The A380 will accommodate between 550 and 800 passengers, depending on the configuration of the seats. Airports must have wider runways and appropriate ground operations for the giant A380. Ground operations include catering and cleaning the double-decker plane, which is 79 feet, 7 inches high at the tail, compared to 63 feet, 8 inches for a 747. Other ground operations concerns are serving 550 to 800 passengers disembarking at one time and expecting their luggage and ground transportation to be accessible.

The giant airplanes were designed to help solve the problems created by overcrowded air space. Air travel is expected to grow, and the continued use of small planes making frequent flights will create larger air traffic jams at the airports.

Private Infrastructure

Land ownership restrictions hamper private infrastructure development in some Eastern European countries, such as the Ukraine. Independent from the former Soviet Union since 1991, the nation has had trouble closing a deal with an international hotel. Ukrainian laws prohibit private ownership of land. Thus, a hotel can be built only on land leased for 49 or 99 years. Private foreign investors are reluctant to take the risk of such a large investment. However, with so many old and run-down tourism facilities, opportunities for development are abundant.

The U.S. Commercial Service is a division of the Department of Commerce. It offers valuable assistance to help U.S. businesses increase exports of goods and services. A subsection of the U.S. Commercial Service helps promote development of travel and tourism infrastructure around the world. Architects, engineers, designers, construction firms, management companies, and finance companies are alerted to tourism opportunities for development in emerging areas, such as the Ukraine. The Service provides information to help U.S. companies understand what it takes to conduct international business and to gain a share of the potential business.

Stopover

Explain what is meant by *public infrastructure*.

_____

_____

ECONOMIC RESOURCES

FINANCING

In the United States, both state and federal agencies support travel and tourism through economic resources and services. In turn, travel and tourism businesses generate government funds through taxes and fees. The government then uses the revenues generated to support infrastructure, promote tourism, and provide direct loans that help travel and tourism-related businesses.

International Investments

The Overseas Private Investment Corporation (OPIC) was established over 30 years ago as a developmental agency under the executive branch of the U.S. government. OPIC helps U.S. businesses invest overseas and fosters economic development in new and emerging markets. OPIC provides assistance for projects such as a U.S. small-business group's expansion of an airline in a developing region.

Many U.S. travel and tourism businesses are **multinational corporations** with operations in many countries. Receiving economic resources and assistance from OPIC helps them compete in the global economy. OPIC provides information regarding business practices in other cultures to help smooth international operations. OPIC operates at no cost to taxpayers by charging market-based fees to its customers.

Financial Support

State tourism agencies are public/private partnerships that promote tourism in a state. They also conduct research about the economic impacts of travel and tourism. The Massachusetts travel and tourism industry suffered a major decline of about 20 to 30 percent following the

Time Out

The Overseas Private Investment Corporation (OPIC) has created 264,000 new jobs in the United States and $69 billion dollars in export business for U.S. companies. OPIC helps U.S. companies find international business opportunities in travel and tourism and other areas.

September 11, 2001, terrorist attacks. The two flights that struck the World Trade Center originated in Boston, a major tourist center for the state. During the next 12 months, the Massachusetts Port Authority Board eliminated a 25-person international marketing department and laid off about 150 other employees. Half of the members of the Boston Hotel and Restaurant Employees Union Local 26 were laid off. Several small companies went out of business, including an airport taxi service.

Due to the reduction in tourist-generated tax revenues, the state of Massachusetts wanted to reduce the amount of public funds available to its Office of Travel and Tourism. Employees and state tourism agencies worked hard to convince the government of the importance of the industry and the need for continued funds to promote tourism to potential visitors. By 2003, Massachusetts had recovered and was again growing as a tourist destination, generating over $3 billion in wages to employees in the industry.

Stopover What are two purposes of state tourism agencies?

_____

_____

SOCIAL, POLITICAL, AND ENVIRONMENTAL ISSUES

Tourism is generally supported by governments when it is seen as advancing government objectives. In the United States, there is continuous political debate about the degree and exact role of government in private businesses. Questions arise as to how much of taxpayers' money should be spent protecting and promoting the United States (or a state) as a travel destination. Some politicians fail to see the economic benefits of travel and tourism.

Economic and Social Development

When a governmental body focuses only on the costs of supporting and promoting travel and tourism, it is failing to recognize the benefits to economic and social development. Increases in travel and tourism generally have a broad effect, including increased jobs for the local workforce, more local business, and more government revenues.

Tim Tyrrell, of the Department of Resource Economics at the University of Rhode Island, suggested that, when talking with government officials about travel and tourism, the message should be targeted at their responsibilities. For example, "when talking with local financial officers, talk about new sources of tax revenue or offers from private business to share costs of infrastructure development." To justify the use of tax money, a return is required on the investment in the form of more tourists and travelers, more jobs, growth for existing and new businesses, and improvement in the standard of living for the citizens of the area.

Green Standards

PRODUCT/SERVICE MANAGEMENT

The U.S. Green Building Council is a coalition of building design and construction businesses. The group has developed the LEED (Leadership in Energy and Environmental Design) Green Building Rating System™. The system is focused on the construction of high-performance and environmentally responsible structures.

Airports, hotels, resorts, and tourist areas that are constructed using LEED standards save money over the life of the project. LEED encourages

- use of mass transit
- use of collected rain water for landscaping
- light-colored roofs
- occupancy sensors for lighting
- exterior lighting that limits light pollution of surrounding neighborhoods

These and other features for efficient use of resources save money. They also make a project friendly to the environment and to those who live nearby.

Sustainable Development Strategies

Sustainable development strategies have been defined by the United Nations as "development that meets the needs of the current generation without compromising the needs of future generations." Developing and maintaining tourist destinations as sustainable developments requires long-term thinking and planning. Allowing a lake to be over-fished to the point that fish no longer live in the lake will bring an end to pleasure and commercial fishing. Tourism may no longer be viable. A sustainable strategy would be to limit the number of fish an individual can catch, allowing fish to naturally replenish.

At both the state and federal levels, there is an ongoing obligation to protect wilderness areas and sites of natural beauty, such as the Grand Canyon. When infrastructure, such as a road, is built in a wilderness area, a balance must be achieved between protecting the area and allowing visitors access.

Missing the Boat

The beautiful Galapagos Islands are off the coast of Ecuador in South America. The islands are noted for their extraordinary ecosystem. The islands' giant tortoises are believed to be some of the oldest living animals in the world. There are 5,000 plant and animal species on the islands, and 1,900 of those are found only on the isolated Galapagos.

Tourism, overpopulation, over-fishing, illegal settlers, nonnative invasive plants, and 200,000 plant-gobbling, nonnative, wild goats are destroying the delicate ecosystem. The United Nations may classify the Galapagos as endangered, unless conservation efforts are dramatically improved. The Ecuadorian government limits the number of tourists who can visit the Galapagos. However, mainland Ecuadorians think they should be allowed to move there for jobs, including to fish the over-fished waters.

THINK CRITICALLY

1. Should tourism and migration be stopped on the Galapagos Islands? Why or why not?

2. Why are the islands of concern to the United Nations? Discuss your opinion with others.

Stopover

What is meant by a green system for building?

_____

_____

Understand Marketing Concepts

Circle the best answer for each of the following questions.

1. An example of travel and tourism public infrastructure is
   a. financing.
   b. marketing.
   c. a road.
   d. a plane ticket.

2. Growth in travel and tourism business increases
   a. jobs and government revenues.
   b. airport security.
   c. international tourism.
   d. privacy.

Think Critically

Answer the following questions as completely as possible. If necessary, use a separate sheet of paper.

3. **Ecology** Does using the LEED standards make good business sense? Why or why not?

   _____

   _____

   _____

   _____

   _____

   _____

   _____

4. **Economics** Is private ownership of land and businesses in conflict with sustainable development? Can privately owned businesses act in ways to protect the environment for future generations? Why or why not?

   _____

   _____

   _____

   _____

   _____

   _____

   _____

Travel Business Risks

Goals

Identify business risks.

Explain methods of controlling risks.

All Aboard

Allianz, a German insurance company, offers business-interruption insurance to travel and tourism businesses. It is one of only a few companies that continued after 2003 to cover losses due to outbreaks of SARS (Severe Acute Respiratory Syndrome). SARS was first reported in Asia in February 2003 and spread to North America, South America, and Europe. More than 8,000 people became ill, and 774 individuals died from the disease. The travel industry suffered severe losses when travel to Asia dropped to record low levels because of SARS concerns.

Major hotels had business-interruption insurance designed to provide funds to the business following a major disaster. The hotels received insurance payments to cover lost income due to SARS. Many, however, were unable to renew their insurance coverage for SARS for future years.

Discuss with a partner what a hotel could do to protect itself from loss of income due to disasters such as the SARS outbreak.

KNOW THE RISKS

When a travel and tourism business is started or expanded, there are risks involved. **Risks** are hazards or exposures to possible loss or injury. A travel and tourism business could spend millions of dollars to build a hotel that might catch fire and be destroyed. A natural disaster could occur, such as a hurricane or a tsunami, that might completely devastate a tourist area. A company could also fail to produce enough business to cover expenses and be forced to close. Identifying the potential risks and acting to limit them can lessen the negative impacts.

Photodisc

Categories of Risk

Risks can be sorted into three categories.

- risks resulting in gain or loss
- controllable risks
- insurable risks

Risking Gains and Losses Loss of income occurs when a business is no longer able to operate because of a catastrophe, such as a flood that closes a golf resort for weeks. This type of possible loss is called a **pure risk**, because there is no chance to gain from the event. When there is a chance for gain or loss, the risk is called a **speculative risk**. An airline that orders five new, multimillion-dollar airplanes that will not be delivered for three years is taking a speculative risk. There is a chance that business will increase and the new planes will generate a profit. There is also a chance that business will not increase, but the planes will still need to be paid for, causing a loss for the airline.

Controlling Risk When loss can be prevented or the frequency of loss reduced, the risk is a **controllable risk**. The potential loss of a hotel to fire can be controlled or reduced by providing safety training for employees and enforcing fire safety standards. If a tidal wave washes away a beachfront hotel, that is an **uncontrollable risk**. The hotel business could not have prevented the loss.

Insuring Risk Insurance companies and financial service companies will provide insurance against losses resulting from insurable risks. **Insurable risks** are pure risks for which the chances of a loss occurring are predictable. Additionally, the amount of the loss can be estimated for an insurable risk. The success or failure of a business is a speculative risk and uninsurable, because no one can predict the success or failure of the business.

Many U.S. companies that conduct business internationally can purchase political-risk insurance. The insurance protects them from *illegal expropriation*, where a foreign government takes their property. Other insurable political risks are *currency inconvertibility*, when a business is prevented from bringing the profits of the business back to the United States, and losses due to political violence. These risks can be covered by insurance purchased through the Overseas Private Investment Corporation (OPIC). Political risk insurance encourages travel and tourism investors to take a chance on establishing a business in a developing country that needs investment to grow its tourism industry.

E-Ticket

Electronic travel service providers like e-Travel must be able to protect their clients from external security risks. According to TruSecure, a provider of online security services, the major sources of external risk are electronic threats, viruses, piracy, physical security, and human factors. TruSecure protects the information assets and certifies that companies such as e-Travel are effectively managing their security risks.

THINK CRITICALLY

Look at the e-Travel web site. (When locating the site, note that *e-Travel* includes a hyphen.) What data does it collect from customers? Why is it important that these data assets are protected?

Marketing Risks

Most marketing risks can be classified into one of two categories—environmental risks and business-management risks. Environmental and business-management risks can overlap and interact as business is conducted.

Environmental Risks The level of safety of a travel and tourism facility dictates most of the environmental risks of the business. **Environmental risks** are usually pure risks that are preventable, predictable, and generally insurable. Since most accidents and fires are preventable, and the rate of such occurrences can be predicted, hotels can be insured against losses due to fires and accidents. Hotels must comply with local fire-safety codes. The exceptions are some older hotels built before the codes were established. Older hotels are exempt from compliance until they are renovated. However, not meeting the safety codes raises the cost of their insurance.

Business-Management Risks When a business makes decisions about what products or services to offer travelers, it is taking a risk. **Business-management risks** are risks that are speculative and uninsurable because the results are not predictable.

Time Out

Direct suppliers of travel products and services are affected by world events and the economy. For example, the war in Iraq and a sluggish global economy negatively impacted travel agencies such as Thomas Cook, due to a lower demand for international travel.

Stopover

What is meant by *pure risk*?

_____

_____

MANAGING RISK

To succeed, travel and tourism businesses must take every precaution possible to minimize risks that result in loss. Written guidelines, extensive staff training, and appropriate accident-reporting procedures help reduce the risk and protect the health and safety of customers and employees.

Reducing Environmental Risks

Training personnel to comply with fire safety standards is a critical part of reducing risks. When fire safety equipment in hotels is not properly maintained, frequent false alarms can result in guests and employees eventually ignoring the alarms. At a well-known hotel, when the piercing noise of a fire alarm sounded, no one started toward the exits. The hotel restaurant was full of guests eating breakfast. Most guests looked at the front desk staff for direction, but the staff did not take action. The guests found the noise an irritation, not a cause of concern. When no verbal directions were given to exit, the guests continued their breakfasts. Eventually the alarm stopped, and no explanation was provided. Guests were being unconsciously conditioned to ignore alarms. The hotel was not acting to limit future environmental risks of a real fire.

Good environmental risk management requires that businesses prepare to limit risks, such as fire or other hazards. Although the risk may be covered by insurance, the damage to the business and its reputation may not be repairable should harm come to employees or travelers.

Reducing Business Risks

Travel and tourism business owners make decisions every day that impact their businesses. They may take certain risks to help the business grow. They may borrow money to make improvements to their facilities or to buy additional sites to expand their business. By borrowing money, they are taking a risk that the intended improvements will generate additional income to pay back the loan and cover all additional expenses. New business owners may rely on guidance from financial institutions and professional organizations when making critical decisions that can affect the continuity of their businesses.

Stopover What are three precautions that businesses can take to minimize risks?

_____

_____

Five-Star Traveler

TOM LATOUR

Kimpton Hotel and Restaurant Group owns 38 properties in 16 cities, with plans to open properties in at least 14 more cities within the next five years. CEO Tom LaTour heads up the unique collection of boutique hotels. Kimpton doesn't build new hotels—it renovates old hotels that are historically significant. Each has a destination restaurant connected, where a number of famous chefs have launched their careers. LaTour personally stays in each of the locations under consideration for purchase before making an offer, and then stays a week in the newly renovated hotels to troubleshoot the details. Once a year, he personally conducts a reception at each Kimpton hotel and chats with guests. He learns about the locations to which guests frequently travel and uses this information to generate ideas for Kimpton's expansion.

LaTour joined Kimpton two years after it was founded in 1981. He has helped nurture the trendsetting services and amenities that set a standard for the industry. LaTour, CEO since 2001, wants his guests to feel at home and trains staff to be friendly, not aloof. Care, comfort, style, flavor, and fun are the five signature pillars of the hotels, described as having "style without attitude."

THINK CRITICALLY

Look at the web site for Kimpton Hotel and Restaurant Group and find examples of unusual marketing strategies. Make a list of how Kimpton hotels and restaurants are different from those of most hotel chains.

Understand Marketing Concepts

Circle the best answer for each of the following questions.

1. When a risk is a pure risk and predictable, it is also usually
   a. a business-management risk.
   b. a speculative risk.
   c. an insurable risk.
   d. an uninsurable risk.

2. To reduce environmental risks, a travel and tourism business should
   a. have safety procedures in writing.
   b. provide safety training to all staff members.
   c. report accidents.
   d. do all of the above.

Think Critically

Answer the following questions as completely as possible. If necessary, use a separate sheet of paper.

3. How can a travel agency help businesses limit travel risks for employees who must travel internationally?

_____

_____

_____

_____

_____

_____

_____

_____

4. **Research** Use the Internet to find information about how to stay safe in the case of a hotel fire. Write a paragraph about what actions guests can take to limit their risk of injury.

_____

_____

_____

_____

_____

_____

_____

Review Marketing Concepts

Write the letter of the term that matches each definition. Some terms will not be used.

_____ 1. Hazards or exposures to possible loss or injury

_____ 2. Businesses with operations in many countries

_____ 3. A chance of gain or loss

_____ 4. When private trade organizations work with government to jointly improve travel and tourism

_____ 5. The possibility of loss with no chance of gain

_____ 6. Allows citizens of 27 countries to enter the United States for 90 days without a travel visa

_____ 7. Providing market-analysis data that may be used to attract more international travelers

_____ 8. Systems that measure biological features, such as the iris of the eye, fingerprints, or face

_____ 9. Possible loss that can be prevented or the frequency of loss reduced

_____ 10. Pure risks for which the chances of a loss occurring are predictable

a. biometrics
b. business-management risks
c. controllable risk
d. environmental risks
e. export assistance
f. infrastructure
g. insurable risks
h. multinational corporations
i. passport
j. public/private ventures
k. pure risk
l. risks
m. speculative risk
n. state tourism agencies
o. sustainable development strategies
p. uncontrollable risk
q. visa
r. Visa Waiver Program (VWP)

Circle the best answer.

11. The Overseas Private Investment Corporation (OPIC) helps businesses
    a. build airports in the United States.
    b. keep airports safe.
    c. purchase land.
    d. expand into new and emerging overseas markets.

12. One of the purposes of state travel and tourism agencies is to
    a. enforce state food-safety laws.
    b. conduct research about the economic impacts of travel and tourism.
    c. serve as a state purchasing bureau.
    d. screen travelers.

Think Critically

13. How might jumbo jets help solve the problem of overcrowded air space and runways? What is the benefit of large planes over small planes? Where could the large planes be used most effectively? What are some problems that might arise from the use of the larger planes?

_____

_____

_____

_____

14. Why would the U.S. government help U.S. businesses invest in international travel and tourism opportunities? In what ways does the government help?

_____

_____

_____

_____

_____

15. What is meant by sustainable development strategies? Who do the strategies help? Why are they considered long-term strategies?

_____

_____

_____

_____

16. Using the Internet, find information about a recent natural disaster and its impact on tourism in the area. Write a paragraph about how the travel and tourism businesses were affected.

_____

_____

_____

_____

17. Find an example of public/private infrastructure in your community or state. How was the project funded? Is the community or state benefiting from the project? Discuss why or why not.

_____

_____

_____

_____

Make Connections

18. Ecology Use the Internet or your library to research the Mayan culture. Write a paragraph about what is speculated to have happened to the Mayan civilization and some of the suspected ecological causes.

_____

_____

_____

_____

_____

19. Geography Use the Internet to find information about the Galapagos Islands. Using presentation software, create a presentation about the location, history, and current conditions that impact tourism.

_____

_____

_____

_____

_____

20. Marketing Math You are starting a tourism business and have the following monthly costs.

Salaries, $5,000; rent, $2,045; utilities, $288; phone, $300; software lease, $325; business loan, $1,068; office supplies, $166; and other expenses, $432.

What are your total expenses per year? What percentage of your yearly costs are salaries?

_____

_____

_____

_____

21. Communication Look at the web site for your state tourism agency and determine the agency's main purposes. Learn how the agency benefits travel and tourism businesses in your state. Write a news article about the benefits to the taxpayers of having a state tourism agency.

_____

_____

_____

_____

_____

22. History Think of ways travel and tourism has changed since September 11, 2001. Make a list of both positive and negative changes that have occurred since that time. List at least one way these changes have affected travel and tourism in your area.

_____

_____

_____

_____

_____

23. Communication You work for the local tourism agency. Your boss is going to be giving a speech at a convention in another state. She wants to convince people to invest in tourism in your state. She wants you to help her by listing five major positive points about your state that would interest investors in developing privately funded infrastructure.

_____

_____

_____

_____

_____

EXTENDED STAY

Project The Amazon Rainforest, one of the most biodiverse regions on the earth, is being cut and burned at an alarming rate. The destruction is taking place for economic reasons, but the native people are not earning much from farming the cleared jungle.

Work with a group and complete the following activities.
1. Use the Internet or library resources to research what is happening to the Amazon Rainforest.
2. Brainstorm ways that travel and tourism can help improve the economic plight of the people living in the area while protecting the jungle.
3. Select one way that would create a sustainable development in the area.
4. Write a plan, with multiple ideas for promotion, for a sustainable development project that economically supports the people living in the Amazon Rainforest. Include creating a brochure as part of the plan.
5. Create a brochure meant to persuade the people currently clearing the jungle to support your project.

AIRLINE IMAGE PROBLEMS

The U.S. airports and skies cleared in 2001 as a result of terrorism and the ensuing recession, but congestion returned in 2004. The number of flights increased by seven percent to meet rising consumer demand. Runway delays returned to the peak levels experienced in 2000.

The airline industry is extremely fragile. When something goes wrong, the number of affected passengers, flights, and associated costs rise quickly in a domino effect.

Holiday travel pushes the airline industry to the limit. Add to the rush severe weather in the Midwest, prompting flight cancellations and the rescheduling of crews, and the result is disaster. In December 2004, Comair's computer system that handles crew scheduling became overloaded with the many changes and crashed. As a result, Comair canceled all 1,160 of its Christmas Day flights. Passengers were affected in over 100 cities.

Travel was also disrupted for thousands of US Airways passengers during the holidays due to a combination of bad weather and a high number of employees calling in sick. The airline canceled more than 350 flights and mishandled thousands of bags.

In a worst-case scenario, a scheduled 10-hour nonstop flight from Amsterdam to Seattle turned into a 28-hour nightmare for Northwest Airlines' passengers. The plane could not land as scheduled, due to fog at the Seattle–Tacoma International Airport. The plane circled the airport until fuel ran low and then was diverted to a central Washington airport. Passengers could not initially exit the plane because the airport was not set up to screen the unexpected international travelers in accordance with federal customs regulations. Passengers had to deal with backed-up airplane toilets, lack of food, and a near-riot when several passengers threatened to charge the cockpit.

When finally allowed to disembark, passengers were confined to a secure area of the airport. They had to wait further as a new pilot and crew were brought in to complete the flight. The original pilot and crew had exceeded the maximum work hours set by the FAA. Passengers said they felt like hostages.

Passengers filed 5,800 complaints in 2004—most related to delays, cancellations, missed connections, and mishandled baggage. Nearly 20 percent of all arrivals were late. The problems have made flying less desirable for many consumers. The airline industry has suffered a severe public-relations nightmare.

THINK CRITICALLY

1. Describe the current reputation of the airline industry. How has the industry acquired this reputation?
2. Why are travelers reconsidering travel plans and their mode of transportation?
3. What can airlines do to improve their image and reestablish consumer confidence?

TRAVEL AND TOURISM MARKETING BUSINESS SERVICES ROLE PLAY

The airline industry has suffered financial setbacks from rising fuel costs, the 9/11 terrorist attacks, and other safety issues. Many flights no longer include meals. On flights that do, most flyers are not impressed with the quality or quantity of food they receive.

You have been hired by a major airline to enhance its image. The airline wants to emphasize a record of on-time flights, excellent safety, and friendly associates who take good care of passengers.

Develop a strategy for the airline to offer meal service that customers can upgrade for an additional fee. The airline will provide a light meal for all passengers at no extra charge. Customers can pay an additional $5 on the purchase price of their ticket to receive a more substantial meal.

The ultimate goal of the airline is to increase its market share of business. This can be accomplished by convincing prospective customers that they will receive better service than competitors offer.

Your job consists of establishing an advertising campaign and promotional materials that describe the basic meal and the upgraded meal option. Your marketing strategy must emphasize personal service.

The airline has also asked you to develop additional customer service strategies that will set it apart from the competition.

You have ten minutes to develop a marketing strategy. You will then meet with an airline executive (judge) for up to ten minutes to present and discuss your plan.

Performance Indicators Evaluated

- Design a public relations plan for an airline.
- Write promotional messages that appeal to the airline's target markets.
- Differentiate your airline from the competition.
- Select advertising media.

Go to the DECA web site for more detailed information.

THINK CRITICALLY

1. What obstacles must the airline industry overcome to gain a larger portion of the market and make a larger profit?
2. What stereotype do most customers have about airline meals?
3. What type of promotional strategy will be the most effective to reach target markets?
4. Outline advertising and promotional strategies for the new and improved airline.

www.deca.org

Travel and Tourism Careers

Photodisc

CHAPTER 3

3.1 Employment Opportunities

3.2 Travel and Tourism Management

3.3 Developing a Career

Point Your Browser

► ► ► ► travel.swlearning.com

Winning Strategies

The Academy of Hospitality and Tourism

Why not start your career in a luxury setting at a fabulously hip beach location? Thirteen graduates of Miami Beach High School's Academy of Hospitality and Tourism are currently employed by Loews Miami Beach Hotel. Many other graduates have careers at prestigious travel and tourism organizations, such as the Greater Miami Convention and Visitors Bureau. All are former students of Dr. Lupe Ferran Diaz, the academy's lead teacher.

The academy was started in 1990 as a joint effort of the school district and the area's hospitality and tourism industry. The academy continues to have strong industry connections. It is a part of the National Academy Foundation (NAF). The NAF's network of hospitality and tourism academies includes 155 high schools nationwide.

The Miami Beach academy offers a college preparatory curriculum, including rigorous academics and a focus on travel and tourism. The administrators have arrangements with a number of colleges and universities. Students are awarded college credit for academy courses and receive advanced placement when they enter college.

Each year, Dr. Diaz takes opportunities to participate in teacher internships. She is the only high school teacher Marriott has accepted into its teacher internship program. Dr. Diaz's students benefit from her dedication and the time she spends outside the classroom learning from the industry's best.

THINK CRITICALLY

1. How can teachers benefit by participating in internships and other learning opportunities outside the classroom?

2. What are some ways Miami Beach High School's Academy of Hospitality and Tourism is tied into the travel and tourism industry? What are some other ways that schools can connect with industries?

0
100
200
300
400

Employment Opportunities

Goals

Identify opportunities for employment in travel and tourism marketing.

Describe convention and special event management careers.

All Aboard

Many people dream all year about taking a vacation. Travel and tourism professionals get to make those dreams come true. Anheuser-Busch Adventure Parks, including the Sea Worlds of Orlando, San Diego, and San Antonio, have numerous career opportunities. Many positions involve creating exciting vacations for thousands of guests.

The position of sales representative with Sea World in Orlando requires a bachelor's degree, preferably in marketing or business, and three to five years of experience in hospitality sales. Sales representatives work with hotels and destination management companies to ensure they are aware of current developments at Sea World. They also network with others in the industry at professional organization meetings and hosted events. Their primary job is to showcase the park and increase its number of visitors.

Work with a group. Brainstorm ideas about how a sales representative could increase the number of visitors to Sea World.

THE WIDE-OPEN WORLD

The travel and tourism industry is large and growing. The field is wide open for students interested in pursuing travel and tourism careers. Positions in the industry range from those requiring a high school education with no experience to those requiring advanced degrees and years of experience. Demand for travel and tourism professionals is projected to increase faster than demand in most other career areas through 2012.

Photodisc

The Segments

Within each segment of the travel and tourism industry, there are major international corporations; small, one-person businesses; and millions of other companies ranging in size between the two extremes. Each of these businesses has people who handle all six of the marketing core standards. In a small business, one person may juggle all of the activities. In large corporations, a team of people will divide the work of one activity into many smaller parts.

At the Philo Apple Farm in Philo, California, the owners do every job. Sally Schmitt takes your reservation for a weekend stay and helps teach the gourmet cooking classes. Her daughter, Karen Bates, takes orders for the organically grown apple products, provides information, and leads tours. Karen's husband, Tim Bates, runs the farm end of the business. In all, eight family members from three generations share the work of the farm, food processing, guest cottages, meal service, and cooking classes. At a large hotel, a number of people would be in charge of just reservations.

Career opportunities exist in travel agencies, hotels, resorts, theme parks, casinos, cruise ships, restaurants, and spas. Entry-level positions require little experience and provide modest pay, but they may lead to high-responsibility, high-pay management positions. The careers are perfect for people who love to help others relax and enjoy their surroundings.

Time Out

Large international travel corporations employ thousands of people in various locations around the world. For example, Hilton Hotels Corporation has more than 68,000 employees in more than 70 countries throughout the world.

Careers in Lodging

Large chain hotels have staff members at the corporate level as well as at each facility. Following are some of the management job titles in the lodging industry.

- **General Managers** usually have a college education and extensive experience. They oversee the entire hotel operations.

- **Front Desk Managers** generally have a college education and some management experience. They manage the front desk staff and the reservations process.

- **Sales Directors** generally have a college education and management experience. They manage the sales staff, who work on conventions, special events, and corporate accounts.

- **Human Resources Directors** generally have a college education and human resources experience. They recruit, hire, and arrange training for staff, as well as oversee employee benefit programs, such as health insurance.

- **Financial Managers** usually have a background in accounting. They are responsible for handling receipt of income and managing all expenditures of funds, including payroll and other expenses.

- **Communications Managers** usually have a college degree and related experience. They work for large corporations and serve as a liaison with the franchised hotel properties, to help them stay true to the corporate image. They are also responsible for writing and editing newsletters and other company publications.

E-Ticket

Online travel management programs are creating a dramatic change in how companies control employee travel. The driving force is budget savings on company-paid business trips. Corporate travel managers are looking for solutions that allow employee travel to be booked online and within the constraints of the company's travel policies. According to e-Travel, when employees use Aergo online software solutions, "they can easily plan, book, and purchase complete travel itineraries within company guidelines. With Aergo, corporations and travel agencies alike can integrate all the elements of their global travel programs, including travel policies, preferred suppliers, and negotiated rates."

THINK CRITICALLY

Do an online search for e-Travel Aergo. Look for information about how the product helps manage corporate travel. Discuss with a partner.

Similar job titles exist in other hospitality businesses, such as restaurants, cruise lines, resorts, and casinos. Almost all management-level positions require experience. Students and entry-level employees can gain needed experience by taking positions within the departments under the leadership of experienced experts. Internships and part-time jobs are excellent ways to gain experience while completing the educational requirements for the higher-paying jobs. **Internships** are work-based experiences usually connected to a high school or college course. The work is often unpaid but is rewarded with the valuable, firsthand experience gained in the desired career field.

Distributors and Travel Suppliers

Distributors are travel agents and travel suppliers who sell directly to consumers. **Travel suppliers** may be tour operators, cruise companies, airlines, hotels, and resorts that provide travel services. Their sales staffs work with travel agents and convention planners, as well as with individual consumers. The job of travel agents has changed dramatically in the last ten years. There will continue to be a demand for travel agents who establish relationships with customers and become specialists in a destination or a product, such as cruises.

Internet travel suppliers have become an enormous growth center for the travel industry. Information technology skills are critical to this important area of travel and tourism. People who can design and build technology systems to support travel and tourism business are in high demand.

Corporate Travel Management

The job of managing and purchasing travel services for large corporations is a special one within the travel industry. The responsibilities of a *corporate travel manager* include developing corporate travel policy, selecting the vendors or travel suppliers, and regulating employee business travel.

Some corporate travel personnel are part of the purchasing or finance department. They arrange for the travel of hundreds of employees. They book air flights, hotel rooms, and meeting rooms, and arrange for ground transportation or car rentals. Some large corporate travel departments work with full-service travel agencies. Others work directly with travel suppliers, such as airlines.

Travel Journalism

Writers who are interested in travel may find a career writing for travel guides, magazines, newspapers, and television and radio programs. There are over 500 travel magazines. Examples include *National Geographic Traveler* and Continental Airlines' in-flight magazine entitled *Continental*. Additionally, over 200 major city newspapers publish a weekly travel section.

A *travel journalist* must first be a creative writer. Some travel journalists may write full time for one publication as salaried employees. Others are **freelance writers** who submit articles to various publications and are paid for each article that is used. Articles must be so enticing that readers will want to visit the destinations. Many more travel articles are rejected than are accepted for publication. The articles submitted must meet the needs and interests of the publication's customers. Being a successful freelance writer may take years of practice and patience before articles are accepted for publication on a routine basis. It is a difficult area in which to earn a living.

Other careers related to travel journalism include photography, editing, film and electronic media production, and public relations.

Name three career fields in travel and tourism.

_____

_____

CONVENTION AND EVENT MANAGEMENT

Thousands of professional organizations have conventions each year. Millions of people travel to convention sites to attend. Every month, cities, counties, states, and organizations host events, such as festivals and competitions. Conventions and events take months of preplanning and preparation. Many people have successful careers in convention and event management.

Let's Meet

Dr. Richard Haught, an oral surgeon, was recently elected president of the 152,000-member American Dental Association (ADA). During his tenure, he played an active role in planning a number of meetings, including the ADA's annual conference and smaller meetings of the ADA Board. Dr. Haught worked with full-time paid staff of the ADA, whose primary responsibilities are to manage conferences and meetings. They work to make the meetings attractive and efficient to the well-educated, well-traveled, high-income members who will attend. The members want to benefit from the conferences and meetings, learn from the exhibits, and enjoy local attractions and restaurants. They expect everything to be professionally planned at a high level of quality.

© Getty Images/PhotoDisc

One position with the ADA is manager, Exhibition and Sponsorship. The person who fills this type of role is often referred to as the *exhibit manager*. For the ADA, this person will manage the budget for the trade show portion of the annual association conference. The exhibit manager must be knowledgeable about current trends and technologies in the meeting and exhibition industry. Technologies used to plan meetings include CAD/CAM exhibition management software. **CAD/CAM** is an acronym for Computer-Aided Design/Computer-Aided Manufacturing. It is used to design and control the manufacture of items for a trade show exhibit. Trade shows may encompass acres of floor space filled with vendor booths. For the 2004 ADA conference, about 35,000 members attended. They traveled, stayed in hotels, ate in restaurants, attended meetings, perused the trade show exhibits, and made purchases. The trade show segment of the ADA conference had over 700 technical exhibitors.

The sponsorship role of the exhibit manager position entails generating funding through sales of exhibit space and advertising. The exhibit manager is also expected to be a member of the International Association of Exhibition Management (IAEM) or the Professional Convention Managers Association (PCMA). The position requires a bachelor's degree and a minimum of ten years of industry experience, of which five must be at the management level. Those wishing to pursue a career in this area may begin by assisting an exhibit manager or by volunteering to help organize meetings for smaller groups. Advancing in the field requires the high levels of organization and planning skills that come with experience.

Hosting Major Events

Trade shows, sports competitions, concerts, and large organization meetings are examples of major events. They are usually held in publicly owned convention centers located in a downtown or park area. The city hosting the event generally will have a full-time staff person, sometimes called an *event coordinator*, who works with the group sponsoring the event.

An event coordinator usually needs a bachelor's degree in marketing or travel and hospitality management. The event coordinator's responsibilities may include concept development, marketing, project management, and post-event analysis. Providing attendees with an experience that exceeds their expectations is the goal of an event coordinator. An event coordinator might work with an exhibit manager when exhibits are part of the event.

Stopover List two or more characteristics needed by an exhibit manager.

_____

_____

Understand Marketing Concepts

Circle the best answer for each of the following questions.

1. Travel agents and travel suppliers who sell directly to consumers are
   a. interns.
   b. distributors.
   c. exhibit managers.
   d. travel journalists.

2. Corporate travel managers
   a. select travel suppliers.
   b. develop corporate travel policy.
   c. regulate business travel by employees.
   d. do all of the above.

Think Critically

Answer the following questions as completely as possible. If necessary, use a separate sheet of paper.

3. Why would it be important to network with people in the travel and tourism industry when you are starting your career in the field?

   _____

   _____

   _____

   _____

   _____

   _____

   _____

   _____

4. **Communication** Write a paragraph about the role of trade shows in the travel and tourism industry.

   _____

   _____

   _____

   _____

   _____

   _____

   _____

   _____

   _____

Travel and Tourism Management

Goals

Explain the role and functions of management.

Describe the purpose of labor unions.

All Aboard

The airline mechanic's union workers had a contract that specified their wages and benefits. The mechanics were highly trained, highly skilled workers who kept the planes safe for air travelers. The union had bargained hard with airline management to receive the pay scale and benefits the mechanics wanted, including health care paid by the company.

The airline fell into deep financial trouble. It had to reduce costs or declare bankruptcy. The largest cost to the airline was payroll. Airline management asked the mechanics to take a cut in wages and benefits. If they refused, they would be taking a chance that the bankruptcy court would reduce their wages and benefits. The alternative to filing bankruptcy was closing the airline. The union planned to ask members to vote for or against the wage and benefit cuts.

Discuss with a partner how you would vote if you were an airline mechanic. Would you vote for the cuts? Why or why not? What should management do?

IT'S THE PEOPLE

Becoming a manager requires knowledge, skill, experience, and the ability to lead people. **Managers** are creative problem solvers who plan, organize,

lead, and control business activities. Managing people means ensuring they know exactly what is expected of them, modeling desired behavior, and motivating employees to meet or exceed expectations. Managers in travel and tourism marketing also need to have mastered all six of the marketing core standards—distribution, marketing-information management, printing, products/service management, promotion, and selling—as well as the key skill of financing.

Photodisc

Making It Happen

Daryl Richardson owns the Dallas World Aquarium and Daryl's by Design, an event planning and catering business. Richardson is often away on business for weeks at a time. A trip might be to an exotic location to plan and execute a major exhibition and fabulous dinner/reception for Cessna Aircraft's key customers. In the meantime, the normal business of hosting thousands of tourists and catering wedding receptions and prom parties continues without a hitch. Hundreds of employees continue the perfect execution of their jobs. Richardson has provided them with the model of how things need to be done, clearly set targets for achievement levels, and positively motivated the staff to succeed. Richardson is an outstanding manager and motivator of people. Consequently, his employees do not need his constant supervision.

Management Functions

The specific responsibilities of a manager may vary considerably from one position to another, but there are four general functions of management that apply to most management positions. They are planning, organizing, leading, and controlling. A manager is expected to understand the four functions of management and use them effectively to reach company goals.

Planning is starting with the company goals in mind and mapping the best way to reach those goals. A manager must think about how the hotel front desk or convention exhibit will operate to exceed customer expectations. Then the manager plans how to achieve that ideal. Planning is not a one-time event, but a process that is continuously revisited and revised.

Organizing divides the planned activities and responsibilities among employees. A manager arranges the duties of each person under his or her responsibility. He or she delegates authority as necessary to each jobholder to accomplish the tasks. A manager generally has the authority to make decisions and is not closely overseen by a superior.

Leading is modeling behavior and influencing people to follow through and complete their assigned tasks in the most effective and efficient manner possible. A good manager will help people reach both the company's goals and his or her own personal career goals. A leader shares responsibilities with the staff and seeks from them ways to improve the process. A leader is an effective communicator who confirms the flow of information to and from the staff.

Controlling means setting standards, measuring and reporting the extent to which the standards are met, and revising the plan as necessary to meet standards. Without a control process, the best managers may fail to realize problems until it is too late to fix them. A standard may establish a timeframe in which every hotel guest should be greeted, registered, and escorted to their room. If guests are standing in long lines to register, the plan may need to be revised. Employees may know how to fix the problem and should have input into the revised plan.

Management Function Diagram

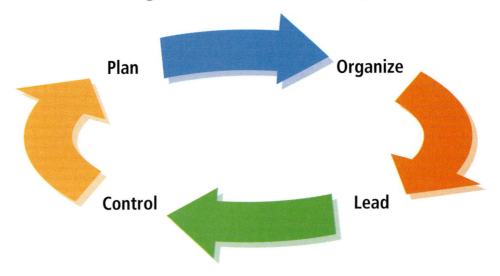

Plan → Organize → Lead → Control

The four functions of management form a *continuous improvement process*. When a control review shows the plan needs to be revised, the cycle starts again.

To stay in business, company goals must include making a profit. Managers must control the costs of their units of the business. They must be both effective and efficient, meaning they reach company goals using the least amount of resources possible. To use the least amount of resources, employees must be trained in the most efficient ways to perform each task. Employees must be motivated to accomplish much using the least amount of time and resources. In this way, the number of employees on staff, their associated salaries and benefits, the cost of supplies, and other expenses are kept at a minimum.

Stopover

What is meant by a continuous improvement process?

_____

_____

Time Out

It is against the National Fair Labor Act for a manager to restrict employees from wearing union insignia when they do not have customer contact.

UNIONS

A legal organization of workers that collectively represents the workers to management is called a **union**. A majority of workers for a company must consent to join the union in order for it to become operational in a company. When management makes an agreement with the union that only union members can be hired, the business is called a **closed shop**. Management cannot negotiate with employees individually regarding wages and benefits in a closed shop. The right of the union to be the sole negotiator for all employees is referred to as **collective bargaining**.

Managers are rarely members of unions. If the union cannot come to an agreement with management or non-union workers on issues over wages, benefits, or working conditions, the union members may vote to go on strike, or collectively refuse to work. The business may effectively shut down or continue operations with a skeleton crew made up of management or non-union workers until an agreement is reached.

The National Labor Relations Board (NLRB) is a federal agency that seeks to ensure that provisions of the National Labor Relations Act are followed. It investigates and remedies unfair labor practices by employers and unions. The NLRB has two main components—the board and general council. The board is made up of five members who hear labor dispute cases. The general council investigates and prosecutes unfair labor practices. The U.S. president, with Senate approval, appoints both the board and general council.

UNITE (Union of Needle-trades, Industrial, and Textile Employees) and HERE (Hotel Employees and Restaurant Employees) International Union merged in 2004 to become UNITE HERE. The newly formed union repre- sents about 50,000 fashion industry employees and about 265,000 hospitality workers. Hospitality industry members include room attendants, cooks, waiters, and hotel desk clerks employed in hotels, casinos, restaurants, airports, and other establishments. UNITE HERE was affiliated with the American Federation of Labor–Congress of Industrial Organizations (AFL–CIO). It left the AFL–CIO in 2005 to join a new federation called Change to Win Coalition. UNITE HERE's goals are not only to improve members' economic welfare, but also to win respect and dignity on the job and to achieve workplace democracy.

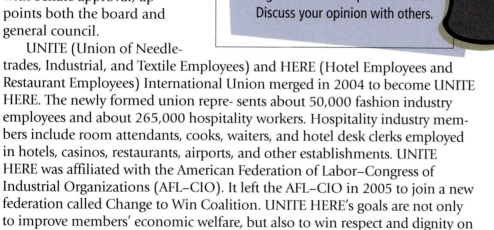

Marketing Myths

UNITE HERE and the Los Angeles Hotel Employer's Council were negotiating workers' contracts for eight upscale Los Angeles hotels. Sparks and accusations flew back and forth. The union wanted large pay increases amounting to as much as 18 percent in some instances. It also wanted a contract that would end at the same time as other hotel union contracts in many other major cities across the United States. The employers were totally opposed to the proposed contract expiration date. It would allow the union to coordinate strikes in major cities and provide national-level bargaining clout. The bargaining continued off and on for almost a year. The two groups had major differences and problems in reaching agreement.

THINK CRITICALLY

1. Why would the union want a contract that expired on the same date in many major cities? Why would the hotels oppose this?

2. Why would the hotel resist giving workers an 18 percent raise? Discuss your opinion with others.

What is the purpose of a union?

_____

_____

Stopover

Understand Marketing Concepts

Circle the best answer for each of the following questions.

1. Four functions of management are
   a. purchasing, pricing, placement, and promotion.
   b. planning, distribution, price, and advertising.
   c. creating, maintaining, satisfying, and financing.
   d. planning, organizing, leading, and controlling.

2. Controlling as a management function means
   a. setting standards, measuring them, and revising the plan.
   b. being the boss and making all the decisions.
   c. closely supervising everything employees do.
   d. knowing everything about the business.

Think Critically

Answer the following questions as completely as possible. If necessary, use a separate sheet of paper.

3. Think about some difficult decisions travel and tourism managers may have to make if business is slow and finances are low. Provide an example of a problem and two possible decisions that may be made to help solve the problem.

_____

_____

_____

_____

_____

_____

_____

4. **Communication** Discuss with a partner what gives unions power to negotiate with management. What gives management power over unions?

_____

_____

_____

_____

_____

_____

_____

_____

Developing a Career

Goals

- Identify educational and training opportunities in travel and tourism.
- Describe ways to get and keep a job in travel and tourism.
- Explain professional development for travel and tourism.

All Aboard

The Landmark Mandarin Oriental Hotel is an exclusive luxury hotel billed as "ultra chic." It boasts the largest average room size in Hong Kong and has LCD televisions in every room. The Mandarin Oriental Hotel Group has a company goal of exceptional customer satisfaction in each of its 21 hotels in 14 countries.

Six months before the hotel was set to open in Hong Kong, Cynthia Leong was named director of human resources (HR). Leong had been a director of HR at other Mandarin Oriental locations. She had gained experience by working in a number of hotel departments, including Front Office, Banquet Sales, and Guest Relations.

Leong's responsibilities include staffing the hotel. In a news release, she outlined the qualities she seeks in potential employees. Candidates must be service oriented, be stylish and refined, be familiar with foreign cultures, and understand luxury. Further, they must be flexible, caring, and considerate people with a high degree of initiative. "We will look at their abilities to solve problems creatively, work well in a team environment, interact socially, cope with pressure, and communicate effectively," stated Leong.

Discuss with a partner what a person might do to prepare for a career at the Landmark Mandarin or a similar hotel. Why is familiarity with foreign cultures important to this hotel?

WHAT SHALL I BE?

In the worldwide travel and tourism industry, the opportunity for careers is almost infinite. Careers within each of the marketing core standards require a wide range of education and experience. The best way to find a career that fits an individual is to research, gain experience in entry-level positions that give exposure to the industry while in high school and college, and then focus on a specific career path.

Digital Vision

Missing the Boat

The Charleston Place Hotel missed a valuable marketing opportunity when it failed to provide outstanding hospitality to Laura Landro. Landro is a travel journalist for the *Wall Street Journal.* According to her article "Convention Wisdom," Landro was attending a conference at the hotel. She booked her reservation weeks in advance and requested that the hotel arrange for her transportation from the airport.

Landro was miffed when she was not picked up at the airport. When she finally arrived at the hotel to make her opening session talk at the conference, the hotel's reservation manager said her reservation had been cancelled. Landro assured the reservation manager that she had confirmed the reservation the previous week. Landro eventually received a one-bedroom suite for $600 per night, just as she had originally booked, but was spoken to in a rude manner by the reservation manager. Although the balance of the stay was a positive experience, the start of the stay overshadowed it.

THINK CRITICALLY

1. What mistake did the reservation manager make? What could have been done differently?

2. Do you think a guest should expect every detail to be handled perfectly in a luxury hotel? Discuss your opinion with others.

Career Planning

If a career in travel and tourism sounds intriguing, then it's time to think about your interests and goals. By the time you are in your teens, you know that some activities are more interesting to you than others. You know whether being around people and helping them enjoy a vacation sounds like fun. If you have talent with numbers, you might enjoy managing the financial end of the business and dealing with budgets and payrolls. There is room for people of various talents and interests in travel and tourism. Many schools provide access to online testing that can help you evaluate your interests and aptitudes.

Researching careers has never been easier. You can use a search engine like Yahoo! or Google. Enter the name of a specific company for which you would like to work, or conduct a more general search for travel and tourism careers. With a quick online search for hospitality careers, you can find information about hotel and restaurant employment openings around the world. It should never be necessary for you to pay a fee to learn about jobs in travel and tourism. There is plenty of information available for free. Taking time to explore career options can help you find a path that leads to a satisfying career.

Education and Experience

Visualize yourself in the house where you want to live, in the car you want to drive, and wearing the clothes you want to wear. Determine what your lifestyle will cost by researching prices of housing, cars, insurance, and other expenses. People who reach their financial dreams do so by spending less than they make, saving and investing money, and planning for long-term goals.

There are many exceptions, but generally people with only a high school diploma earn less than people with a college degree. Your challenge is to make choices that lead to a career you will enjoy while providing a salary to support your lifestyle. Your level of education is one of the major choices you must make. A lack of education can cause you to be overlooked for advancement to higher-level jobs. Is finding the money to continue your education a problem? It can be solved by applying for scholarships, working part time, and discussing available financial options with school counselors.

In addition to your education, your work experience is an important factor in determining your salary and career potential. Work experience of any kind is valuable. Obtaining entry-level experience in your area of interest is more valuable for at least three reasons. The most important reason is that it gives you an opportunity to see the industry from the inside. You may not hold the job you ultimately desire, but you will have an opportunity to get to know people who are currently employed in your dream job. You will learn firsthand what they really do and how you can prepare for the job. A second important reason to work in entry-level jobs while still in school is that they give the employer an opportunity to look at you as an experienced employee with potential for full-time status. Paid or unpaid internships can be the ideal work experience for students. Internships should be taken advantage of at every opportunity. A third reason to obtain entry-level experience is that it is easier to get a job when you already have a job. This old adage is still true. There is less perceived pressure to jump into an unsuitable job, and you have work experience to offer the next employer.

Time Out

Many travel and tourism courses are aligned with college courses so that students can earn college credit while in high school. This allows students to begin their college degree and not have to repeat course material already learned.

Stopover

Why is work experience (paid or unpaid) acquired during school years valuable?

_____

_____

YOU'RE HIRED!

To hear those magic words, "we want you to work for us," takes preparation on your part, even for your second, third, or fourth job. The application, interview, and follow-up take practice to be perfect.

Paperwork

For most jobs, you will need to complete paperwork as part of the application process. You will want to start by presenting yourself in the best light possible with a resume. A **resume** is a written summary of your education, accomplishments, and work experience, including unpaid or volunteer work. A resume is your opportunity to begin sharing with the employer the reasons you should be hired. Resumes should be laid out in a neat, organized, easy-to-read format using a word-processing program on a computer.

Photodisc

The resume should reflect your skills and accomplishments, not just list previous job titles and duties. For example, include under "Work Experience" such things as "Exceeded the sales quota by 25 percent for the senior class fundraiser." The resume is sent to the potential employer with a cover letter. At the time of an interview, you should offer a copy of the resume to the interviewer.

A **cover letter** accompanies a resume. It is the first written document the employer will see. It needs to be crafted with care so as to make a good first impression. The employer may be a caring person but does not need to know that you need a job to pay your car insurance. The employer is looking for an applicant to fulfill a need of the business. Your cover letter can present you as that person.

The cover letter should be one page containing at least two paragraphs. It should create a desire to look at your resume and call you for an interview. If an employer has received hundreds of resumes and cover letters, yours needs to stand out. Like your resume, the cover letter should contain all the information needed to contact you. Your full name, full address, and phone number should be at the top of the cover letter in the return address position. Grammatical errors and misspellings are not acceptable. They will cause your cover letter and resume to make a quick trip to the trash can. Proofread your work as if your job offer depended on it, because it does! Do not trust a spell checker, as the word "manger" is a correctly spelled word, but not the correct spelling for "manager."

An **application** is a data-collection form the employer provides to a potential employee. It is used to gather the information an employer needs to consider before hiring you. Ask the employer for two blank copies of the application form. This will allow you to complete a draft and then a final, clean form. Have you ever written your last name in the wrong blank on a form? Take care and read the form before beginning, fill in all blanks, and proofread your work. Consider it a test of your ability to read and follow directions.

Selling Yourself

A job interview is the face-to-face time for you and the employer to decide if the job is right for you. The employer wants to know that you can do the job, be there on time every day, and get along with supervisors and other employees. You want to know if this job will provide what you need, such as added skills and funds to pay your bills.

During interviews, employers ask questions and you give answers. You can anticipate what the questions may be and practice your responses. Questions may include, "Why do you want to work here?" or "What experience do you have?" Be prepared to talk about your accomplishments, including your volunteer work. You will also be given a chance to ask questions. Use this opportunity to clarify anything that is unclear regarding the job. Make sure you truly understand what the job entails and if it is what you are seeking.

Dressing carefully and neatly for an interview is important. Avoid wearing extreme or flashy clothing and strong fragrances. Be sure to shower, comb your hair, brush your teeth, and use deodorant. Get started early and allow yourself plenty of time.

Be at least ten minutes early for the interview. Being late can kill the interview before it starts. When you first meet, the interviewer will probably extend a hand to shake. Your handshake presents a critical part of the interviewer's first impression of you. You should firmly grasp the interviewer's hand with your right hand while making eye contact. State that you are glad to be there. Practice handshakes that are firm but don't crunch the person's hand.

Photodisc

Interviewing skills take practice. Ask a teacher or other person with experience to help you. Stand in front of a mirror and interview yourself. Keep your answers short and to the point. Look at the interviewer when either of you are speaking. Smile, relax, and practice breathing.

After the interview, write a thank-you letter to the interviewer. A thank-you letter is a professional way to keep your name on the interviewer's mind. It is a courtesy that shows you have manners and are polished. It can set you apart from other applicants.

What are some steps you can take to prepare for an interview?

Stopover

PROFESSIONAL DEVELOPMENT

Getting hired is not the end of the career story. It is only the beginning of a new phase. Staying current with the industry and moving up to a higher level of responsibility and pay are the next challenges.

Mastering the Job

Learning how to do your new job and function as a team member takes time. Respecting others and taking directions from experienced workers can help you ease into your job. One major reason people lose jobs is that they cannot get along with coworkers. Getting along does not mean going along with something that is unethical. It does mean treating others with the same respect you would like from them.

Once you have mastered your job, you can look for ways to advance to the next job level. Observe what people at the next level are doing. Offer to assist them when you have a chance. Show initiative by doing more than is expected of you. Let your supervisor know you would like to spend your own time shadowing those in the positions you desire for the future.

Lifelong Learning

Continuing to grow and learn is important at every phase of your career. One way to do so is to belong to professional organizations associated with the industry. There are 125 travel and tourism-related trade organizations listed at the Black Hills State University web site. Each one has opportunities for continued growth in the profession. Most of the organizations encourage young people to join by offering student memberships at a reduced fee. Joining trade organizations is an excellent way to network with many professionals. You may find leads for opportunities that fit the vision of your dream job and the lifestyle you seek.

Stopover   What does "showing initiative" mean?

_____

_____

Five-Star Traveler

TIM CAHILL

"It's not about travel. It's about writing. Think about readers first," states Tim Cahill, a man who has lived out his dream of being a writer. Cahill is famous for writing engaging and humorous tales set in obscure locations. He has written seven books, including *Lost in My Own Backyard* about Yellowstone National Park.

Cahill has a master's degree in English and creative writing. After starting his career in freelance writing, he accepted a position as a writer for *Rolling Stone* magazine. He claims he was the only writer there who was interested in going outdoors. As a result, he was assigned to a new magazine, *Outside*, where he is a founding editor. Cahill writes adventure-travel stories. He decided "people are scarier than mountains or rivers" after Colombian rebels joked about kidnapping him.

The Society of American Travel Writers named Cahill as the 2003 Lowell Thomas Gold Award winner. His collection of writings was judged as best in a variety of categories.

Travel journals rarely get published. Cahill's success as a travel writer comes from his style of writing like a novelist rather than a journalist. An article that reads like a novel has continued to be his winning trademark.

THINK CRITICALLY

Read two travel articles, one by Tim Cahill and one by another travel writer. Discuss the writing styles. How is Tim Cahill's style of describing a destination different from other travel journalists'?

Understand Marketing Concepts

Circle the best answer for each of the following questions.

1. A reason to gain work experience while in school is
   a. it gives you an opportunity to see the industry from the inside.
   b. it gives the employer an opportunity to look at you as an experienced employee with potential for full-time status.
   c. it is easier to get a job when you have a job.
   d. all of the above.

2. Paperwork involved with getting a job includes
   a. goals, objectives, and standards.
   b. essays, paragraphs, and brochures.
   c. cover letters, resumes, thank-you letters, and applications.
   d. textbooks and magazines.

Think Critically

Answer the following questions as completely as possible. If necessary, use a separate sheet of paper.

3. A young woman has a job interview with an upscale hotel. If hired, she will work part time assisting in the lobby area. What should she wear to the interview? Would what she wears to a party on the weekend be appropriate? How can she find out what to wear? Can what she wears influence her job chances? Why or why not?

   _____

   _____

   _____

   _____

   _____

   _____

4. **Communication** Describe how to prepare for a job interview. Where could you find information about the company? How can you practice for an interview? Why should you practice?

   _____

   _____

   _____

   _____

   _____

   _____

Review Marketing Concepts

Write the letter of the term that matches each definition. Some terms will not be used.

_____ 1. Modeling behavior and influencing people to complete assigned tasks

_____ 2. Paid or unpaid work-based experiences usually connected to a high school or college course

_____ 3. Dividing the planned activities and responsibilities among employees

_____ 4. Starting with the company goals in mind and mapping the best way to reach the goals

_____ 5. Providers of travel services, including tour operators, cruise companies, airlines, hotels, and resorts

_____ 6. Journalists who submit articles to various publications and are paid for each article that is used

_____ 7. A written summary of your education, accomplishments, and work experience

_____ 8. The right of the union to be the sole negotiator for all employees

_____ 9. Creative problem solvers who plan, organize, lead, and control business activities

a. application
b. CAD/CAM
c. closed shop
d. collective bargaining
e. controlling
f. cover letter
g. freelance writers
h. internships
i. leading
j. managers
k. organizing
l. planning
m. resume
n. travel suppliers
o. union

Circle the best answer.

10. Items found on a resume include
    a. contact information.
    b. education.
    c. accomplishments.
    d. all of the above.

11. A thank-you note following an interview
    a. keeps your name in the forefront of the interviewer's mind.
    b. is a courtesy that can set you apart from other candidates.
    c. shows you have manners and are polished.
    d. does all of the above.

12. When managers control, they
    a. set standards, measure progress, and revise plans accordingly.
    b. keep others from having new ideas.
    c. use electronic devices.
    d. do all of the above.

Think Critically

13. In pairs, discuss the purpose of travel and tourism magazines. Do they provide useful information for travelers, or are they just advertisements? What careers are associated with them?

_____

_____

_____

_____

_____

14. Visit the Conrad N. Hilton College of Hotel and Restaurant Management web site. Click on the Prospective Students link. What are the requirements for admission for undergraduate students? When is the admissions application due? The college is a part of what university?

_____

_____

_____

_____

_____

_____

_____

15. List ways a manager can lead employees to reach company goals and at the same time help employees reach their own career goals.

_____

_____

_____

_____

_____

16. Why should high school students be looking at requirements for jobs they might not get for five to ten years from now?

_____

_____

_____

_____

_____

Make Connections

17. **Marketing Math** You have an opportunity to work full time right after high school, making $20,000 per year. You plan to take college courses part time. It will take you ten years to finish a college degree. An alternative is to work part time and earn $8,000 per year while attending college full time. You will finish college in four years. Most jobs you will be eligible for with a college degree start at $32,000. Not taking into account possible raises, which alternative would net the most money after ten years?

_____

_____

_____

_____

18. **Geography** You want to see some of the world before you choose a place to live. You would like to work in travel and tourism. What are some careers that would allow you to travel as part of your work?

_____

_____

_____

_____

19. **Career Connection** What skill do you personally think you need to develop most to have a successful career in travel and tourism? Write a short plan on what you will do to improve that skill while in school.

_____

_____

_____

_____

20. **Sociology** What does networking within the travel and tourism industry mean? What are the advantages of doing so? How can you gain opportunities to network with people in the industry?

_____

_____

_____

_____

_____

21. Economics In a group, discuss the conflict between workers' rights and management decisions. How can a balance be reached?

_____

_____

_____

_____

_____

22. Research Call the Human Resources (HR) Department of a large hotel chain. Tell the HR representative that you are conducting a survey for your class. Ask about the preferences for the education and experience of potential managers. Do the managers of the hotel chain require a specific level of education? If yes, what is that level of education? What kinds of internships or work experience do they want candidates to have? Share your answers with the class.

_____

_____

_____

_____

_____

_____

EXTENDED STAY

Project An extensive amount of information about careers is available online. Excellent information is available from trusted sources, such as industry organizations and America's Career Information Network (ACINET), a web site sponsored by the U.S. Department of Labor.

Work with a group and complete the following activities.
1. Do an online search for "resume tutorials."
2. Spend some time exploring all of the information available on the resume tutorial web sites.
3. Use the information to create your own resume using a word-processing program. Your teacher may provide sample formats that you may follow.
4. Write a cover letter to accompany your resume. Address it to a travel and tourism business with which you might like to intern.

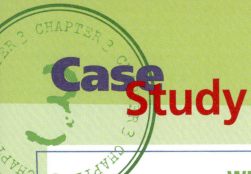

Case Study

WHAT HAPPENED TO OUR ROOM RATES?

Hotels are very interested in convention business. Major student conferences such as DECA, FBLA, and FFA fill hotel rooms and conference centers. Not only do conferences earn money for hotels and convention centers, they also have a positive financial impact on the local economy.

When an organization plans a conference with a large hotel, the hotel blocks out a certain amount of rooms to accommodate the attendees. The rooms are restricted from being rented to other guests up to a certain date. Conference participants have until the specified date to confirm reservations. A discounted rate is also usually given to the group members.

DECA is a popular student organization in Texas. The state's membership is so large that it is divided into 12 districts. Each district has a DECA competition to determine which students are eligible for state competition.

District III is located in southeast Texas and includes the greater Houston area. The district III competition can involve between 700 to 1,000 students. The J.W. Galleria Marriott Hotel was recently chosen to host the conference. The hotel liked the January timing of the event and was happy to offer rooms at a special rate of $89 per night. Normal room rates were $199 per night.

The district III DECA director and the hotel group reservations director met well before the January conference to block a number of rooms at the $89 rate. Their agreement was that the block of rooms would be held until the first Friday in January. After that date, all rooms reserved would go for the usual $199 per night. If all of the blocked rooms were booked before the first Friday in January, the higher rates would apply to any additional DECA reservations.

A larger-than-usual number of DECA members from district III decided to participate in the conference. On the final day to book rooms at the discounted rate, ten schools were notified that no more $89 rooms existed. They could reserve rooms for $199 per night. The schools could not afford the $199 rate, and DECA advisors were extremely upset. They had been under the impression that the $89 rate was guaranteed if they booked by the deadline.

THINK CRITICALLY

1. Was the hotel justified in charging $199 per night for the additional rooms? Why or why not?

2. What should the district III DECA director do for next year's conference?

3. Explain how a block of hotel rooms works for a conference.

4. The hotel wants the district III DECA conference to return to its hotel. What can the hotel do to repair the relationship?

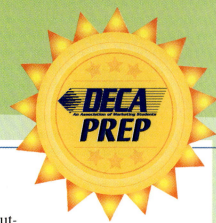

TRAVEL AND TOURISM MARKETING MANAGEMENT TEAM DECISION MAKING

A new luxury hotel recently opened in a major suburb of Houston, Texas. It is a gorgeous, 300-room facility located in a beautiful setting close to shopping and many tourist attractions.

The human resources director and her assistant recently moved from Florida to Texas. They were hired as a team, due to their success with a major hotel in Florida. Together, they hired the rest of the professional staff. Each employee has shown personal dedication and a good work ethic.

During the first few weeks of operations, the hotel evaluations have been less than satisfactory. In particular, staff responses to customers' special requests have been slow. Rooms have not always been ready at check-in time, causing some guests to have to wait. Some rooms have not been supplied properly for the number of guests.

The hotel must achieve higher customer service ratings in order to win repeat business and remain competitive. The human resources department has set priorities to increase teamwork and employee ownership of customer satisfaction.

You and a partner have been hired to plan training and development sessions for hotel employees. You have been asked to develop an incentive program for employees who reach a customer satisfaction rate of 90 percent or above.

You have 30 minutes to outline your strategy. You may use a laptop computer and presentation software to prepare and give a ten-minute presentation to the human resources team (judges). The judges will have five minutes to ask questions about your plan.

Performance Indicators Evaluated

- Define customer expectations in the hotel industry.
- Design training and development for customer service.
- Coordinate activities to increase teamwork.
- Create incentives for employees to increase customer service.
- Create a family atmosphere among hotel staff.

Go to the DECA web site for more detailed information.

THINK CRITICALLY

1. What are the hotel's existing strengths?
2. Why is teamwork essential for customer satisfaction?
3. What are some of the best motivators for superior hotel employee performance?
4. Why should the new hotel be concerned about customer feedback?

www.deca.org

Travel and Tourism Industry Segments

4

4.1 Diverse Travelers

4.2 Culture, Language, and Religion

4.3 International Organizations

Courtesy, National Museum of the American Indian, Smithsonian Institution. Photo by Leonda Levchuk.

Point Your Browser

travel.swlearning.com

Winning Strategies

National Museum of the American Indian

"The National Museum can be a point of departure for a cultural reconciliation between those who were here and those who came," stated W. Richard West. West is the founding director of the National Museum of the American Indian (NMAI) and a citizen of the Cheyenne Nation. He spoke with writer Lyric Willwork Winik for an article published in *Parade*. He stated that he wants the museum to help native people reconcile the tragic past and move into the future. The museum will also remind visitors that native people have been in the Americas for over 20,000 years. The museum is part of the Smithsonian and is located on the National Mall near the Capitol in Washington, D.C.

"Well before the opening, we had a major public relations campaign to inform the public and Indian Country about the new museum," stated Thomas W. Sweeney. Sweeney is a citizen of the Potawatomi Nation and Director of Public Affairs for NMAI. The media were separated into categories such as arts and architecture, Indian press, national press, specialty press, and foreign press. According to Sweeney, the goal of all of the outreach was to "introduce the museum to varied media and thus audiences worldwide." By selective use of media, NMAI targeted the visitor audience it hoped to attract. The promotional efforts have paid off in an active museum membership of over 90,000 people and thousands of visitors per day.

THINK CRITICALLY

1. In what ways can the National Museum of the American Indian contribute to the understanding of diverse groups of people?

2. Why is it important for individuals to understand diverse cultures?

3. Why is it important for travel and tourism marketers to understand diverse cultures?

Diverse Travelers

Goals

Describe the needs of challenged travelers.

List ways to target specific age groups in marketing travel services.

All Aboard

Travel writer Jeremy Schmidt met a young girl through her Girl Scout troop, where he is an adult sponsor. Inspired by her accomplishments, Schmidt wrote about her in a *Universal Press Syndicate* article entitled "Few Limits Put on Adventures for Disabled." She is an outdoor adventure traveler and athlete. She began rock climbing at age 7, won an alpine ski race at age 8, and skied into the wilderness on winter camping trips at age 9. She also enjoys canoeing, rafting, and horseback riding. An upbeat, positive person with a natural athletic ability, she is now age 12.

She does more with the one leg she was born with than many people do with two legs.

People sometimes underestimate the possibilities for the disabled. Wilderness Inquiry, an outdoor adventure travel company based in Minnesota, plans adventures for the physically challenged along with their friends and family. All can enjoy the adventure together, rather than sending the challenged family member off to a specialized camp for the disabled only. Everyone has some shortcoming—Wilderness Inquiry figures out ways to focus on people's strengths.

Work with a partner. Discuss ways to focus on people's strengths rather than disabilities when planning vacations. Make a list of your ideas and share with the class.

WIDENING VIEWS

Photodisc

When people are different than we are, we are sometimes leery of them. We sometimes judge them by stereotypes that limit our thinking. We may feel uncomfortable and not know how to act around them.

Helping customers who are different than we are is a great way to grow personally and to discover others' abilities. In marketing, it is also the way to learn to serve a diverse population. Those we perceive as different could become our best customers.

A World View

We must look beyond our own comfort zone to discover the world. Travel can broaden our perspectives. According to population projections made by the U.S. Census Bureau in 2002, there were about 6.2 billion people in the world. The table that follows displays the geographic distribution of the population.

Geographic Region	Population
Asia	3,518 million
Africa	839 million
Europe and the New Independent States	803 million
Latin America and the Caribbean	539 million
North America	320 million
Oceania	32 million
Near East	6 million

The growth rate of the world's population is not expected to slow down for the foreseeable future. China is the most populous country in the world, but India's population is projected to exceed China's by 2037. The life expectancy of people varies greatly from developed to undeveloped countries. Developed countries are those that are technologically advanced, highly urbanized, and wealthy. According to the U.S. Census Bureau, the current disparities among countries in levels of life expectancy are expected to decrease over the next 50 years. Life expectancy worldwide is projected to increase to an average of 76.6 years.

The impact of world population changes on travel and tourism will be significant. An important change will be that people of developing nations will benefit from the growth as owners of travel and tourism businesses, rather than just as workers with outsiders reaping the profits. As countries develop, there will be increased travel and tourism from those nations as well. Travel among nations will encourage understanding and tolerance of each other's cultures. Tailoring travel services and products to people of various cultures will be the challenge for marketers.

Sensitivity to Diversity

How boring the world would be if we all looked, acted, and thought alike. Instead we are **diverse**, with each individual distinguished from others by a unique set of physical, mental, and cultural qualities. People who are physically or mentally challenged want and need to travel. Smart travel marketers will find ways to help them do so in a comfortable and affordable way.

In a *Wall Street Journal* article entitled "Disabled Travelers Say Discrimination Is Still a Problem at Airlines," author David Armstrong tells of a father who was traveling with his 13-year-old daughter. He warned US Airways that his developmentally disabled daughter might act out during boarding, but that "he could handle her." The child was not allowed to board the plane. The mother and son flew home while the father and daughter ended up taking a bus. They arrived home 34 hours later. A US Airways spokesperson stated, "It appears we didn't handle it as sensitively as we could have."

The Air Carrier Access Act addresses discrimination by airlines against disabled travelers. Airlines are not held to the same standards as other forms of transportation. Only large airplanes with two aisles are required to have restrooms for the physically disabled, making accessibility to air travel for the disabled severely limited.

Unleashing the Limits

PRODUCT/SERVICE MANAGEMENT

Accommodating physically and mentally challenged travelers can open a new **target market**, or specific group of potential customers. The characteristics of a target market, such as age, gender, ethnic group, income, physical or mental disability, and level of education, are referred to as **demographics**.

About 54 million people in the United States are disabled. The Americans with Disabilities Act (ADA) prohibits discrimination on the basis of disability in employment, government services, public accommodations, commercial facilities, transportation, and telecommunications. Under the law, a person who has a physical or mental impairment that substantially limits one or more major life activities is considered **disabled**. The law applies to travel and tourism businesses and specifies what must be done to accommodate the disabled traveler. Businesses that target the disabled as potential customers look for ways to go beyond the minimum standards of the law.

Businesses like Wilderness Inquiry target both disabled and abled adventure travelers. Its web site states, "The unique thing about Wilderness Inquiry is that we make the outdoors accessible to everyone, including persons with disabilities." Wilderness Inquiry helps families with disabled members experience an outdoor adventure together.

Kindergarten teacher Mary Beth Sheward has to plan carefully every trip she takes. She must spend three hours every other day connected to kidney dialysis equipment. Her special needs can now be met on cruises with care provided by companies like Dialysis at Sea Cruises. Cruises are available to Hawaii, Mexico, Alaska, and more. The cruise ships are equipped with dialysis machines and staffed with licensed medical professionals.

Travel suppliers now accommodate many health and physical disabilities. Stories of people who need a wheelchair for mobility but can repel off the side of a mountain on an outdoor adventure trip are no longer uncommon. The limits of what disabled people can experience in travel and tourism continue to expand.

E-Ticket

Online travel companies have added features to their web sites to make hotel selection easier for customers. Sites such as Orbitz and Travelocity offer maps of the hotel search areas for major cities. A customer may click within a city map and receive a list of hotels in a specific neighborhood. Room descriptions may include "room is accessible," which means the room is set up for wheelchair access and for physically disabled people.

THINK CRITICALLY

Visit the Orbitz web site and look up hotel information to see what is available for disabled travelers. Can you find information for a traveler who is blind? What would you need to know?

Provide an example of how to accommodate a disabled traveler.

_____

_____

_____

BABY BOOMERS AND BEYOND

Baby boomers, people who were born between 1946 and 1964, represent the largest and best-known population of the United States. The baby boom began at the end of World War II, when hundreds of thousands of soldiers returned home and started families. The boomer generation, about 76 million people, has created a bulge in the demand for goods and services and has had a major impact on the economy. The generation is projected to reach its prime spending capacity by 2010. Smart marketers will find ways to target the aging boomers' raging appetite for travel.

Active Travelers

MARKETING-INFORMATION MANAGEMENT

Baby boomers may continue to work past the usual retirement age, at least on a part-time basis, and are expected to remain active throughout their lives. As a group, they are conscious of health and fitness issues and know that exercise helps keep them young. Baby boomers like entertainment and travel, and many have the income and leisure time to enjoy both. Smart travel and tourism marketers will target the baby boomers and challenge them to remain actively engaged in travel.

Photodisc

According to *Domestic Market Travel Report*, baby boomers are traveling more than people in any other age group, both for pleasure and for business. Baby boomers are in the most affluent age group, having an average salary above $75,000. Most boomers are not tied to the school calendar for vacations, like younger families are. Boomers often take trips with their parents, adult children, and grandchildren. Smart marketers will not refer to older baby boomers as senior citizens, since they consider themselves youthful and healthy. Baby boomers will change travel and tourism, just as they have changed business and economics in the United States for the past 60 years.

Senior Travelers

The parents of the baby boomers are also active travelers who may need a few more special accommodations and services to continue traveling. Since the baby boomers do not want to be considered seniors, their parents, ranging in age from 65 to 80, are now considered seniors. These active seniors are often retired and have the time and money to travel. Some studies refer to people in their mid-60s and older as elders. For this text, those 80 and older are called elders. This age designation may need to be pushed further out as the health and longevity of people in general continue to improve.

Senior Traveler Characteristics

Megan Cleaver Sellick was assistant professor of business administration (marketing) at Central Washington University in Ellensburg, Washington. While there, she conducted research to determine seniors' motives for traveling. Her article entitled "Discovery, Connection, Nostalgia: Key Travel Motives" was published in the *Journal of Travel & Tourism Marketing*. According to Sellick, the senior travel market can be targeted by "psychological characteristics" such as

- the persons' motives for traveling
- the extent to which they see travel as a risk to themselves
- their cognitive age

    Cognitive age is the age with which a person most closely identifies. Sellick further defines age according to a senior's activity level. **Activities age** is a measure of one's "cognitive age related to the age a person identifies with while enjoying travel activities." In other words, actual age may not be the major factor to consider when preparing to market travel to seniors.

    Within the senior market, Sellick categorized travel motives into four segments.

- **Nostalgic travelers**—The largest group (30 percent) of senior travelers in Sellick's research was motivated by nostalgia. This group often brought several generations of the family along with them as they revisited places of importance to their past or to their family's heritage.

- **Discovery and self-enhancement group**—About 25 percent of the seniors traveled because of their excitement for learning and were labeled the discovery and self-enhancement group.

- **Enthusiastic connectors**—Another 20 percent of the senior travelers, the enthusiastic connectors, responded that their motives for travel were for a variety of reasons that included learning and nostalgia.

- **Reluctant travelers**—About 25 percent of seniors were not motivated to travel and were called the reluctant travelers.

    Sellick recommends that when developing products and services for seniors, consider the seniors' motives and focus on their cognitive age and activities age, not their actual age.

Focusing on the Customer

With a few added amenities, such as shuttle buses or ramps, even active elders can be welcomed on most travel adventures. Many seniors and elders have concerns about their health. They feel more confident about traveling when they are assured that medical attention will be available nearby. This special need must be considered when planning tours for seniors and elders.

Some organizations such as SOLO-NET are strictly targeted at seniors who travel. SOLO-NET is a free, private e-mail service for single recreation-vehicle and camping enthusiasts. Members must be widowed, divorced, or single and old enough to belong to a senior group. The group specifically targets people who travel alone and offers support and companionship while on the road, primarily via e-mail.

Seniors can also be enticed by *travel protection plans* that insure that a tour operator is in sound financial condition. Seniors have heard stories of paying for a trip in advance and finding the company has gone bankrupt before the trip starts.

Well-known tour operators like Eldertreks offer outdoor adventure travel for people over 50. There are three levels of Eldertreks trips—light, moderate, and demanding—based on the activity level required to complete the adventure. An example of a trip of moderate activity level is the 24-day trip to Pakistan and Kyrgyzstan, which includes a drive over the world's highest paved mountain pass—the Khunjerab Pass into China. The trip includes individual hikes of up to two hours, some slopes and steep stairs, and at least two days at elevations over 9,000 feet. A "demanding" activity level would require even more physical activity.

Photodisc

Stopover

What should you consider when marketing to baby boomers and seniors?

_____

_____

Understand Marketing Concepts

Circle the best answer for each of the following questions.

1. To be diverse means
   a. departing from normal.
   b. being separate and apart.
   c. having a unique set of physical, mental, and cultural qualities.
   d. being troubled or stressed.

2. The broad, legal definition of *disabled* is
   a. unlike or dissimilar to a majority of the population.
   b. incapable of living on one's own.
   c. having a physical or mental impairment that limits the performance of one or more major life activities.
   d. none of the above.

Think Critically

Answer the following questions as completely as possible. If necessary, use a separate sheet of paper.

3. **Communication** Visit the Wilderness Inquiry web site. Read about the ways people of all ages and abilities can be accommodated. Write a paragraph about how you would market Wilderness Inquiry's services.

   _____

   _____

   _____

   _____

   _____

   _____

   _____

4. The Kidney Dialysis Foundation web site is sponsored by the Carlton Hotel in Singapore. Why would a hotel want to sponsor this web site?

   _____

   _____

   _____

   _____

   _____

   _____

   _____

Culture, Language, and Religion

Goals

Describe the impact of culture, language, and religion on tourism.

Explain how to market to a specific target group.

All Aboard

The first civilization of Cambodia existed from the first to sixth centuries in a state called Funan. Liv Saa Em is a silk collector by trade but has made it his avocation to preserve artifacts of ancient culture in Cambodia. He has amassed one of the largest collections of ancient Cambodian art, sculpture, fabrics, and jewelry. Liv Saa Em has been a collector since childhood. He considers it his mission to help preserve the heritage of Cambodia.

Liv Saa Em's collection is kept in his home, which now serves as a museum. Visitors from around the world find his collection amazing. He personally displays the artifacts and frequently rearranges them. Movie companies have used his home as the background for scenes calling for traditional Cambodian homes. Liv Saa Em would like to see tourism in Cambodia built around the ancient artifacts and temples in his country.

In a group, discuss the reasons why someone like Liv Saa Em might want to preserve the heritage of a particular region. What are the benefits to the community and culture?

MUTUAL APPRECIATION

The predominant attitudes and behavior of a group of people are referred to as their **culture**. Culture includes language, religion, ethnicity, food, clothing, and politics. A cultural group shares common beliefs and values. Respecting the culture of others is a learned behavior and a must for success in travel and tourism.

Sing Diversity

Singapore is an island nation with people from diverse backgrounds, including Chinese, Malaysian, Indian, and European. The number of religions is also a reflection of the diversity of the population. In general, the people with Chinese backgrounds

Photodisc

are followers of Buddhism, Taoism, Shenism, Protestant Christianity, or Catholicism, or they are not religious at all. People from Malaysia are most often Muslims and people with an Indian heritage are usually Hindus, Muslims, or Sikhs. People with European heritage are mostly Jews, Protestants, and Catholics. With this mix of backgrounds and religions, tolerance and understanding are requirements of life in this prosperous nation.

There are four official languages in Singapore—Mandarin, Malay, Tamil, and English. Most Singaporeans speak English and at least one other language. They also may speak Singlish, a mix of English with other languages. The travel industry brings people together, much like occurs in Singapore. People in the industry should have a knowledge of the cultures, languages, and religions of the people they serve.

Missing the Boat

There has recently been phenomenal growth in the number of children's museums throughout the country. Dozens have opened in the last five years. The Association of Children's Museums in Washington, D.C., at one point had a list of 70 children's museums that were under construction. EdVenture, located in Columbia, South Carolina, is one of the largest children's museums in the South. It drew more than 250,000 visitors during its first year.

The concept of children's museums has been around since the first one opened in 1899 in Brooklyn. The Chicago Museum of Science and Industry has always drawn a large number of children since its opening in 1933.

The current trend of creating more children's museums is focused on attracting tourism. The museums are promoted to parents as a way to provide education to children in an unstructured way. Parents who struggle to find leisure time to spend with their children are targeted, and the museums are offered as a place that makes that time count.

THINK CRITICALLY

1. Should children's museums promote themselves to parents as a good way to spend time with their children? Why or why not?

2. What should a museum offer children and parents? Discuss your opinion with others.

Cultural Tourism

According to public radio celebrity Garrison Keillor, culture is really what tourism is all about. Tourists travel to see the culture of the place they are visiting. **Cultural tourism** is tourism focused on the culture of the region, including its heritage, art, food, clothing, geographic points of interest, historic sites, and museums.

MARKETING-INFORMATION MANAGEMENT

A survey conducted by the Travel Industry Association of America for the National Endowment for the Arts showed that about 65 percent of travelers include a cultural, art, heritage, or historic activity as part of their trips. Up to 32 percent added extra time to their trips in order to experience a cultural activity. Cultural travelers tend to spend more money on trips than noncultural travelers.

When an area has an interesting cultural attraction, large travel suppliers may identify the area as a location for development. When the area also has high unemployment, attracting tourists to improve the economy can be a local reason for development. Care must be given so that mega tourist developments do not cloud the culture and character of the original attraction. Too much development can lead to cookie-cutter destinations that no longer attract the cultural tourist. Tourism that involves locals and protects the culture and the environment can bring long-term benefits to residents and developers.

Language

English has become an almost universal language of business. Even so, people are most comfortable with their own languages and appreciate the efforts of others to communicate with them using their languages. Travel and tourism is a service industry and must cater to the customers. Efforts in learning to converse with foreign visitors in their own languages will result in repeat business. Travel and tourism professionals who know multiple languages are in high demand.

The Adelaide Institute of TAFE (Technical and Further Education) is in Australia. Its Center of Tourism and International Languages provides training in European languages. Standards for proficiency are based on the needs to converse in travel and tourism situations, as described by the Council of Europe's "Threshold 90" specifications. At Threshold 90 standards, according to Lingocity.com, the "users should be able to cope linguistically in a range of everyday situations which require a largely predictable use of language." Threshold 90 is the minimum level needed for tourism work.

Religion

Religion has long played a role in travel and continues to do so today. International research is conducted about the interrelationships among religious pilgrimages, consumers, and culture. A **pilgrimage** is travel undertaken for a religious purpose. In *Travels in Asia and Africa: 1325–1354*, the reader learns about the Islamic need to make a pilgrimage to Mecca. In the 1300s, Muslim pilgrims traveled in caravans that increased in size every few miles as more and more people joined the group. In *The Canterbury Tales,* Chaucer wrote a series of short stories told through the eyes of 30 people making a religious pilgrimage to Canterbury, England, in the mid-1300s.

Sensitivity to religious beliefs and customs is necessary when serving a diverse, worldwide group of customers. There are about 12 major religions in the world. Within each of these religions, there are many branches of varying beliefs and customs. Many religious groups have strict guidelines regarding the proper handling, preparation, and consumption of food. Sensitivity does not require an extensive knowledge of a particular religion. It does require an ability to inquire, listen, and respond in a respectful manner to the needs and wants of people. Traveling guests with religious food requirements should be treated just as guests with food allergies would be. You would not question them or make any attempt to change them to another way of thinking. Their needs should be sought out and graciously met in the most unobtrusive manner. How guest requests are handled can determine the success or failure of the business.

Stopover

Why is respecting the culture of others so important to tourism?

TARGETING A GROUP

Most travel and tourism businesses focus on a target market of potential customers. The target may be people of similar tastes, lifestyles, or demographics. A target market may be divided into **market segments,** or subgroups based on demographics or psychographics. **Psychographics** are ideologies, values, attitudes, and interests that a group has in common. When grouping people, care must be given not to assume that all members of a group have the same tastes or values. Everyone in a high school marketing education class may be close in age and education level. Within the class, there may be varying tastes of where and how to travel, as well as a wide range in the discretionary income available to pay for travel.

Grouping People

Income level is an important demographic indicator for travel and tourism marketers. The amount of discretionary income of a traveler is a good indicator of the level of service the traveler may want and expect. Young travelers just starting out in their careers may want to stay in basic lodging that meets their minimum needs while not exceeding their budgets. Baby boomers who have invested well may be willing and able to afford luxurious accommodations. Corporations that pay for employee business travel generally set a limit on the amount they will reimburse an employee for a hotel room.

Photodisc

PRODUCT/SERVICE MANAGEMENT

Most hotels are owned, franchised, or branded by a management corporation. Building a **brand** is establishing an identity or image for the product or service based on the target market. The major lodging-management companies reach out to a variety of target groups by offering varying levels of lodging at stair-stepped pricing. For example, Marriott International, Inc. offers lodging to travelers under 12 different brand names, including The Ritz-Carlton, JW Marriott Hotels & Resorts, Renaissance Hotels and Resorts, Courtyard, and Fairfield Inn.

Sometimes hotels target specific groups, such as extreme-sports enthusiasts. eXtreme Hotel is a property in Cabarete, Dominican Republic. Owner Bill Lee hopes it is the first of many such hotels. Located on a beach, the hotel offers kiteboarding, surfing, and skateboarding experiences. On-site instructors are available for beginners. A successful travel business will design products and services around specific target markets.

Stopover   What is a *market segment*?

_____

_____

Understand Marketing Concepts

Circle the best answer for each of the following questions.

1. Culture includes
   a. finance, pricing, and distribution.
   b. hotels, restaurants, and cruise ships.
   c. target markets.
   d. language, religion, food, and clothing.

2. Psychographics include
   a. ideologies, values, attitudes, and interests.
   b. age, gender, ethnic group, disability, education, and income.
   c. purchasing, planning, advertising, and distribution.
   d. language, religion, food, and clothing.

Think Critically

Answer the following questions as completely as possible. If necessary, use a separate sheet of paper.

3. What approaches can be used to develop cultural tourism, employ local people, and preserve the environment and culture?

_____
_____
_____
_____
_____
_____
_____
_____

4. **History** Do people today still take religious pilgrimages? How are religious pilgrimages today different from those of the 1300s?

_____
_____
_____
_____
_____
_____
_____
_____

International Organizations

Goals

- Explain the purposes of international travel organizations.
- Describe the advantages of association memberships.

All Aboard

Between May 1 and September 1 each year, life in France centers on vacations and leisure-time activities. There are four public holidays in May, and many people bridge the holidays with vacation time.

A 35-hour workweek was adopted in France in an attempt to create jobs. Now only an option to French employees, it has done more for increased leisure time and vacations than for unemployment. People in France tend to take 12 to 14 weeks of vacation per year.

French workers may sell part of their vacation time back to employers in exchange for more paid workdays. U.S. employees, in contrast, usually work more than 40 hours per week. Americans receive two to four weeks of paid vacation per year, depending on length of employment, plus about ten paid holidays. Just as people in different countries speak different languages, different cultures have different perspectives on vacation and leisure time. One perspective is not right or wrong, just different.

Work in a group. Discuss the differences that culture might make to the way you would market travel services to a person in a country other than the United States.

AROUND THE WORLD

As travelers from around the world increasingly impact each other and their destinations, the study of travel and tourism increases in importance to the industry. The social and economic impacts of travel and tourism, as well as the environmental and cultural impacts, cause professionals in the industry to join together to effect improvements.

Photodisc

World Tourism Organization

The World Tourism Organization (WTO), headquartered in Madrid, Spain, is a specialized agency of the United Nations. The WTO's membership is comprised of 144 countries and 300 affiliate members representing private sectors, educational institutions, tourism associations, and local tourism authorities. Its mission is to promote "sustainable and universally accessible tourism, with the aim of contributing to economic development, international understanding, peace, prosperity, and un-iversal respect for, and observance of, human rights and fundamental freedoms." Since tourism is a major factor in employment and economic development, the WTO focuses on eliminating poverty while sustaining the social, cultural, and environmental aspects of a region.

The WTO also shares travel and tourism know-how among its 144 member countries. The countries with strongly developed travel and tourism industries are able to help the developing nations create plans for promoting tourism that benefit the local regions.

Since 1994, the WTO has worked with Asian and European countries to open the Silk Road Project, which promotes and develops tourism opportunities. The Silk Road refers to the route traveled between Asia and Europe by traders, missionaries, conquerors, and now tourists. This effort involves multiple countries as well as travel suppliers such as hotels, transportation providers, tour operators, and travel agents. Together, they have created a comprehensive marketing plan. The WTO spearheaded the task of developing a comprehensive list of tourism resources along the Silk Road, including attractions, facilities, accommodations, transportation, and information centers.

Travel and Tourism Research Association

The Travel and Tourism Research Association (TTRA) is a professional organization of travel research providers and users. It has as its purposes to

- provide access to numerous sources of information in order to support research efforts

---

Marketing Myths

Many upscale hotels are now trying to enhance the cultural experiences of guests with music. The music may be chosen according to the tastes of targeted customers. Music may also be selected to match the theme of the hotel or the cultural heritage of the area that tourists are visiting. Music via compilation CDs plays throughout the property, including the guests' rooms, the lobby, and the lounge. Copies of the CDs may be available for sale or given to customers as complimentary souvenirs.

At the Conrad chain, Hilton's upscale property, the music is selected by a survey of guests. At the Wild Horse Pass Resort & Spa, a Sheraton property outside of Phoenix, a selection of Native American music is played.

The intent of the music is to improve guest relations. Since music is personal, the hotels hope to extend the relationship beyond the walls of the hotel. If guests take the music home, they may be pleasantly reminded of the hotel and return as repeat customers.

THINK CRITICALLY

1. Should hotels try to make a personal connection with guests? Why or why not?

2. Do different cultures enjoy different music? Can hotels target customers with music? Discuss your opinion with others.

- educate members in research, marketing, and planning skills through publications, conferences, and networking

- encourage professional development and recognize research and marketing excellence through its awards program

- create opportunities for members to interact with their peers throughout the industry

- help set international standards for travel and tourism research

The standards established by the TTRA help ensure that research is valid and useful to the industry. The international association has about 800 members who are actively engaged in conducting or using research on travel and tourism.

Convention and Visitors Bureaus

Convention and visitors bureaus (CVBs) are nonprofit organizations focused on promoting travel and tourism in the areas they cover. CVBs are membership organizations bringing together businesses that rely on tourism and meetings for revenue. The funds for CVBs are generated from membership dues and hospitality taxes assessed on hotel rooms and car rentals. CVBs are some of the most important travel and tourism marketing agencies, because they directly promote to the public. Their primary goal is to market a destination as an area to visit and spend the night.

The International Association of Convention and Visitors Bureaus (IACVB) is, as its name implies, an organization of professionals who direct state, regional, and local convention and visitors bureaus. Its mission is to improve the "professionalism, effectiveness, and image of destination management organizations."

The association conducts research and compiles data on such things as the economic impacts of convention attendees on local economies. For example, the IACVB has determined that the average expenditures of a convention attendee are $266 per day. About 77 percent of the expenditures are for lodging and food. The average attendee stays 3.6 nights and spends a total of $957.60 per event.

In addition to research, the association is a source of education and training for professionals in the industry. It offers seminars through annual conferences and online training courses. The association helps provide the convention and visitors bureaus with opportunities to network and share best practices.

Stopover

What are the benefits of belonging to a professional travel organization?

_____

_____

ASSOCIATION POWER

By working together, travel agencies and travel suppliers can operate their businesses more efficiently and offer better service. The power of multiple businesses joining together for a common cause gives strength to the travel and tourism industry.

Agent Consortiums

SELLING

When selling travel services to seniors who are not experienced travelers, a travel agent must use caution about the quality of the tour operator contracted to conduct the tour. The agency can screen tour operators through a *member-driven consortium*, or an organization of small travel agencies. Most small travel agents belong to a consortium of agents so they can receive a higher commission from tour operators based on the volume of sales of the consortium.

One of the travel agent consortiums is MAST (Midwest Agents Selling Travel) Vacation Partners (MVP). MVP offers its members alliances with travel suppliers and access to electronic booking. MVP can provide a small travel agency with access to data and reputable tour operators.

Aiding Travelers

The International Association for Medical Assistance to Travellers (IAMAT) is a nonprofit organization. Its mission is to advise travelers about health risks, geographic distribution of diseases worldwide, and immunization requirements for all countries. It also maintains a network of Western-trained physicians in order to make medical care available to travelers worldwide. IAMAT is an organization with free membership open to all, but it asks for donations to support its efforts.

On its web site, IAMAT lists health risks and outbreaks of disease by location throughout the world. The web site also contains links to other health organizations, such as the World Health Organization and the U.S. Centers for Disease Control and Prevention. This information is valuable to travelers as they prepare to visit areas where they may be at risk. For

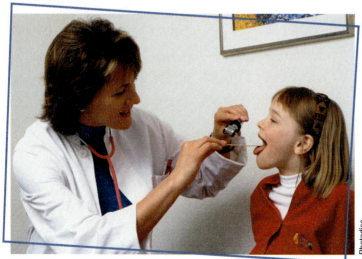

Photodisc

example, the West Nile Virus, a mosquito-borne illness, has infected people in all areas of the United States except Alaska, Hawaii, and Washington. This information would alert international travelers to the United States to wear mosquito repellent when outdoors. Additionally, IAMAT puts out climate charts for major cities around the world and information about foods to eat and avoid.

Stopover What is the purpose of the International Association for Medical Assistance to Travellers?

_____

_____

Five-Star Traveler

WILLIAM TALBERT III

Promotion of Miami and its beaches as a premier visitor destination is the job of the Greater Miami Convention & Visitors Bureau (GMCVB). William Talbert III is the president and CEO of GMCVB. Under his leadership, the bureau's advertising base has doubled, and an increasing number of tourists and conventions have been attracted to the area.

Talbert served as the bureau's chief operating officer for eight years prior to stepping into the CEO role. He has prepared two successful Super Bowl bids and promoted the passage of a food and beverage tax that provides funds for the GMCVB advertising budget.

Talbert has a bachelor's degree in business administration and a master's degree in public administration. He is an officer and/or active member of many travel and tourism organizations and local associations, including the

- International Association of Convention and Visitors Bureaus

- Meeting Planners International

- Greater Miami Chamber of Commerce

THINK CRITICALLY

1. Is it important that the CEO of a convention and visitors bureau belong to professional, trade, and community organizations? Why or why not?

2. What makes a convention and visitors bureau a success?

Understand Marketing Concepts

Circle the best answer for each of the following questions.

1. The purpose of the Travel and Tourism Research Association is to
    a. educate members in research, marketing, and planning skills.
    b. provide access to numerous sources of information.
    c. set international standards for travel and tourism research.
    d. do all of the above.

2. Convention and visitors bureaus are
    a. organizations of convention attendees.
    b. nonprofit, promotional organizations.
    c. travel suppliers.
    d. none of the above.

Think Critically

Answer the following questions as completely as possible. If necessary, use a separate sheet of paper.

3. Why would the World Tourism Organization (WTO) focus on ending poverty through travel and tourism? How might this be possible?

    _____

    _____

    _____

    _____

    _____

    _____

    _____

    _____

4. **History** Research the history of the Silk Road. In what century was it most used? How did it get its name?

    _____

    _____

    _____

    _____

    _____

    _____

    _____

    _____

    _____

Chapter Assessment

Review Marketing Concepts

Write the letter of the term that matches each definition. Some terms will not be used.

_____ 1. The age with which a person most closely identifies

_____ 2. Focuses on heritage, art, food, clothing, geographic points of interest, historic sites, and museums of a region

_____ 3. The characteristics of a target market, such as age, gender, ethnic group, income, physical or mental disability, and level of education

_____ 4. Differing in physical, mental, and cultural qualities

_____ 5. A specific group of potential customers

_____ 6. Subgroups based on demographics or psychographics

_____ 7. A person who has a physical or mental impairment that substantially limits one or more major life activities

_____ 8. The predominant attitudes and behavior of a group of people

a. activities age
b. brand
c. cognitive age
d. cultural tourism
e. culture
f. demographics
g. disabled
h. diverse
i. market segments
j. pilgrimage
k. psychographics
l. target market

Circle the best answer.

9. Airlines are prohibited from discriminating by the
   a. customers.
   b. local police.
   c. Interstate Commerce Act.
   d. Air Carrier Access Act.

10. The law that requires hotels to accommodate disabled travelers is
    a. the Interstate Commerce Act.
    b. the Civil Rights Act.
    c. the Americans with Disabilities Act.
    d. none of these.

11. Baby boomers are
    a. senior citizens and elders.
    b. the largest generation in the United States.
    c. the parents of many children.
    d. all of these.

12. A brand is
    a. the established identity or image of a product.
    b. the company that produces the product.
    c. when people buy the same product.
    d. all of these.

Think Critically

13. Name two or more challenges facing travel and tourism marketing due to changing demographics. What is a solution to one of the challenges?

_____

_____

_____

_____

14. Why are baby boomers important to travel and tourism marketing? What can travel and tourism businesses do to attract them?

_____

_____

_____

_____

15. How are seniors' cognitive ages and activities ages more important than their real ages? Does their attitude and image of themselves affect their travel? How can travel marketers capitalize on this?

_____

_____

_____

_____

_____

_____

16. You are a convention and visitors bureau executive for your area. Develop a brochure about your area that is aimed at a specific target market. Who is your target market, and why?

_____

_____

_____

_____

17. Look at the web site for your state's convention and visitors bureau. What areas of your state is it promoting? To what target market segments is it trying to appeal? Why has it chosen those segments?

_____

_____

_____

_____

_____

Make Connections

18. **Marketing Math** Assume the following.

    Your destination can accommodate 550 travelers per day.
    Baby boomers on average spend $500 per day and stay 2.2 days.
    Convention attendees on average spend $266 per day and stay 3.6 days.
    Young adults on average spend $186 per day and stay 5 days.

    To which market (baby boomers, convention attendees, young adults) should you target your promotional efforts in order to maximize tourist spending per stay at your destination?

    _____

    _____

    _____

    _____

    _____

19. **History** Wars impact travel and tourism. Baby boomers predominately made up the military units that fought in the Vietnam War. Use the Internet to research the Vietnam War. What was the timeframe of the war? What age were the baby boomers during the war? Why is Vietnam now becoming a tourist destination?

    _____

    _____

    _____

20. **Communication** You want your community to be more sensitive to diverse travelers. Write a one-page news article that describes actions that can be taken to encourage sensitivity to diversity.

    _____

    _____

    _____

21. **Geography** Look at the world population chart on page 81. Where are the largest populations? Are they potential markets for travel and tourism? Why or why not? What might limit the potential of the largest populations?

    _____

    _____

    _____

    _____

22. **Science** Why is disease control an important issue in travel and tourism? How has the speed at which people can move around the world changed the dynamics of contagious diseases? Why is hand washing such a powerful issue in disease control?

_____

_____

_____

_____

_____

_____

23. **Research** Why would travel and tourism professionals want to know how much convention attendees or tourists of a certain age spend? What can be done with this kind of information? How would a non-profit convention and visitors bureau use the information?

_____

_____

_____

_____

_____

_____

_____

EXTENDED STAY

Project Find someone in your community who grew up in another culture. Ask the person if he or she would be willing to answer questions for your research and serve as a mentor for cultural understanding.

Work with a group and complete the following activities.
1. Determine what continent and country your mentor is from and the current type of government of that country.
2. What are the dominant culture, religion, and language in the country? How are the native food, clothing, and entertainment different from that in your community? Prepare a chart to compare the mentor's country with your community.
3. What would a visitor to the country need to know to get along there? What are the major attractions of the area?
4. Write a one-page report about your findings. Share the information with the class.

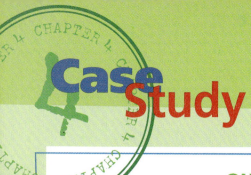

OLYMPICS—BOOM FOR INTERNATIONAL TRAVEL AND TOURISM

Sports and entertainment events have a great financial impact on the travel and tourism industry. Crowds drawn to the events will book hotels, eat in area restaurants, shop, and use transportation services. Large events like the Olympic Games can bring millions of dollars into a local economy.

Cities throughout the world compete for the opportunity to host the Summer and Winter Olympics. Cities go through a complicated bid process and are reviewed by an International Olympic Committee (IOC) Evaluation Commission.

When deciding which city will host the international games, major issues to be reviewed include whether the city has up-to-date sports facilities and sufficient lodging to accommodate all the participants and spectators. The area must have a suitable climate for the seasonal games, a transportation infrastructure, and the ability to manage appropriate levels of security.

The ideal city will also have a diverse population. The Evaluation Commission visits potential cities looking for multicultural acceptance. Cities that demonstrate a respect for different cultures receive higher approval ratings.

Host cities are chosen several years in advance. In preparation for the Games, hospitality businesses may need to make adjustments to ensure their international guests will have a great experience. Hospitality businesses may hire employees who speak more than one language. A hotel restaurant menu may be expanded to include a greater variety of ethnic foods.

Hospitality employees need to be aware of, and trained to respect, a variety of religious and social practices unique to different cultures. Studying a culture in advance will help customer service associates better serve the needs of international guests. Travel and tourism businesses that demonstrate patience and understanding of other cultures will reap financial benefits.

THINK CRITICALLY

1. Why is a multicultural image important to a city wishing to host the Olympic Games?
2. List two adjustments that a hospitality business can make to better accommodate the needs of international guests.
3. What would be a good U.S. city to host the Summer Olympics? The Winter Olympics? Explain your answers.
4. Why is it important to study other cultures before hosting guests from those cultures?

HOSPITALITY SERVICES MANAGEMENT TEAM DECISION MAKING

Success in the travel and tourism industry depends heavily on making a good first impression. Repeat customers and word-of-mouth promotion are important factors for ongoing business operations. Additionally, travel and tourism professionals must understand the importance of catering to the needs of different cultures. International guests want to feel at ease when traveling to other countries.

Your city has been selected to host the 2012 Summer Olympics. You and a partner have been hired as marketing managers for an upscale hotel. The owners of the hotel have decided to promote most heavily to Japanese and Australian visitors. The hotel's general manager has asked you to develop a marketing strategy that will appeal to the target markets.

Your assignment includes

- researching your target markets' psychographics
- developing a marketing tagline (advertising theme or slogan) for each of the countries
- recommending any needed adjustments to the accommodations and services offered by your hotel to make your international guests feel at home

You have 30 minutes to develop your marketing strategy. You may use a laptop computer and presentation software to prepare and give your ten-minute presentation to the general manager and hotel owners (judges). The judges will be allowed five additional minutes to ask questions about your plan.

Performance Indicators Evaluated

- Develop a marketing strategy for international guests.
- Demonstrate a respect and understanding for other cultures.
- Recommend necessary adjustments for international guests.
- Present a viable hospitality offer to guests from two totally different countries.

Go to the DECA web site for more detailed information.

THINK CRITICALLY

1. Why should a hotel in the selected Olympic city be concerned about other cultures since it is guaranteed to be full during the Games?
2. List two good sources of information about other cultures.
3. How can you determine the services and amenities that guests from Japan and Australia might want from a hotel?
4. What theme (tagline) will you use for each country?

www.deca.org

Transportation and Tour Management

5

Photodisc

Point Your Browser

▶ ▶ ▶ ▶ travel.swlearning.com

Winning Strategies

Continental Airlines

Continental Airlines serves 122 international destinations—more than any other U.S. airline. The more-than-60-year-old airline is headquartered in Houston, Texas. Its location on the Gulf Coast and midway between the East and West Coasts makes it strategic for international travel. About 2.5 million international customers travel via Continental through Houston each year.

The City of Houston and Continental Airlines have a public–private partnership to make travel to Houston a pleasure. To ensure Continental's success, the city added a new airport terminal with upscale restaurants and shops. International travelers are sped through with new passport readers at self-check-in kiosks and 50 ticket counters. More than 4,500 people per hour can be cleared through international processing. Continental has the largest international inspection center in the United States.

According to Holden Shannon, Continental's senior vice president, "Working together, the city and Continental have positioned the airline to be the premier gateway to Mexico and Latin America."

THINK CRITICALLY

1. Why would a city spend money to help improve the services that a private airline offers its customers?

2. How might the experience in an airport influence an international traveler's choice to return to the area in the future?

0

100

200

300

400

Business Travel, Conventions, and Incentives

Goals

- Describe the significance of business travel to the industry.
- Explain what attracts conventions to a city.
- Identify incentives for volume business.

All Aboard

Bruce Schechinger is president and CEO of BHS Marketing, a chemical distribution corporation headquartered in Salt Lake City, Utah. He travels about 80 percent of his 65- to 80-hour workweek. His company has suppliers and customers around the world. The extent of his travel makes him a sought-after customer by airlines, hotels, and rental car companies. During his most intensive weeks of travel, Schechinger flies to a different major city every day, hitting both coasts of the continental United States. One week's travel may involve six flights and security screenings, five hotels, and five car rentals.

Schechinger's international travels have increased steadily in the past five years as the company has grown. He believes it is important to establish face-to-face relationships with both vendors and customers. He and all of the company account executives plan to continue to travel, but they are cost-conscious and use mid-range hotels and car rentals.

BHS Marketing staff members are high priority for travel suppliers. Airlines upgrade them to first class based on their high level of frequent-flyer status. They get priority treatment at hotels and car rental businesses. These benefits help take the hassle out of business travel.

Work with a partner. Discuss ways a hotel might provide a hassle-free check-in for priority customers. Make a list of your ideas and share with the class.

BUSINESS TRAVEL

According to the Travel Industry Association (TIA) and the National Business Travel Association (NBTA), business travel represents about one-third of all travel expenditures in the United States, but only 18 percent of travel volume. Business travelers spend more per trip than leisure travelers. The amount of expenditures makes business travel a key component to the travel industry.

Travel Trends

Business travelers took 245 million business trips in 1998. By 2003, the number of business trips dropped by 14 percent, to 210.5 million, because of a slow economy. During the five years of decline, business travelers changed their spending habits. The changes continue to cause concerns for the travel industry, even in an improved economy.

Although the volume of business travel has improved and is projected to continue to increase, the expenditures per trip are remaining flat or decreasing. The trend is attributed to tightened company travel policies that are slow to be relaxed as the economy improves. Restrictions are placed on the amounts that can be spent and the type of hotel and airfare that can be purchased. Many companies no longer allow business travelers to purchase first-class airline tickets without regard to the length of the trip. Prior to the tightening of restrictions, some companies allowed upper managers to always fly first class, and other employees could fly first class if their flight was longer than six hours.

The Cost of Business Travel

SELLING

The travel industry maintains a close watch on revenue based on volume and ticket price ranges. Service providers try to maximize prices and volume, whereas business travelers try to limit the cost of travel. Some companies use online booking services. These services may report employees to supervisors if they do not purchase the cheapest ticket available.

When the economy is strong and employers are having a difficult time filling positions, first-class travel may be offered as a perk. A **perk** is an added benefit that may be used as a means to attract and keep good employees. When economic times are lean, travel becomes an area targeted for cost control. Large corporations have written travel policies that control who travels and how much they can spend.

Corporations frequently have to rethink their travel policies when they become detrimental to business. For example, FMC Corporation gave its sales personnel the same travel budget, no matter where they were located in the United States. Sales personnel were required to attend quarterly sales meetings at the headquarters in Philadelphia. The sales staff based in California frequently ran out of travel funds sooner than staff in other locations because it spent a large percentage of its budget flying to the meetings.

Some companies place restrictions on the amount of money a business traveler can spend on a hotel room and for meals. Classifications of hotel rooms are often divided into luxury, upscale, deluxe, tourist, standard, economy, and budget, based on the amenities offered. The same rating may have different meanings in various parts of the world. A clean room with a private bath may be a deluxe room in many places, but a budget room in other places. Experienced, frequent business travelers, such as Bruce Schechinger, choose hotels based on a mid-range price, the convenience of the location, and the benefits of the loyalty-reward program.

Time Out

Some customer loyalty programs provide tiers of rewards, based on the cost of the product or service provided. When businesses tighten travel budgets, employees often lose their VIP status with airlines.

Managed Travel

Major corporations have in-house travel managers or may contract with outside services to manage employee travel as a specialized business function. Travel managers work to balance employee travel needs with the company's financial goals. Travel managers help the company find ways to cut travel costs, oversee compliance with travel policy, collaborate with suppliers for quantity discounts, and ensure that employees have safe and effective trips.

Travel is one of the top three controllable expenses for corporations. Because travel expenses are generally significant for most companies, controlling them can be financially beneficial. According to the NBTA, one-third of all travel managers report to the finance department of the business. Travel managers working for large companies can negotiate discounts and preferred rates based on the volume of business they do with any one supplier, such as an airline. The supplier then becomes a **preferred vendor**, or one with which there is a negotiated agreement for discount prices based on volume.

For the negotiated preferred-vendor rates to effectively benefit the company, employees must be compelled to make travel arrangements through the company's travel department and use the preferred vendor. The preferred-vendor discounts with an airline are generally based on a contractual agreement stating the company will meet at least a minimum number of bookings between two key cities. When the contracted number is met, the company will receive an incentive payment from the preferred vendor called an **override**.

Many large corporations are considering discount airlines for cost savings. **Discount airlines** make frequent stops and do not offer food or reserved seating, making boarding a first-come, first-to-get-seated rush. Many of the discount airlines, such as Southwest Airlines, offer businesses web-based tools to monitor business travel. Southwest's SWABiz program tracks ticket purchases, travelers' locations, and average one-way fares.

An efficient and effective travel management department will collect and compile data for the corporation. Data regarding the average cost per trip and the total travel costs within each department of the company will be reported. Just as with the costs of manufacturing and salaries, travel costs are included in the cost of doing business and should be monitored and controlled.

Photodisc

Stopover   What must business travelers consider when choosing suppliers?

_____

_____

CONVENTIONS AND EVENTS

Attracting conventions and major events to a city brings added revenue to the community's retailers, hotels, transportation companies, and restaurants. To attract repeat conventions and events, professional meeting planners and attendees must be satisfied with the event.

Meeting Professionals

The many people who converge on a single location to attend a convention have high expectations for service and quality. Acquiring the knowledge and skills required to manage thousands of people takes years of education and practice. **Convention and meeting professionals** are people who effectively plan, organize, budget, publicize, and manage group events of any size. Frequently thought of as having a logistical and tactical role, a meeting professional plans how to attract and move people through a convention center.

The Convention Industry Council (CIC) is an association made up of 30 organizations. The CIC represents over 98,000 individuals and 15,000 businesses involved in the meeting, convention, and exhibition industry, as well as oversees the convention industry certification program. To become a **certified meeting professional (CMP)**, you must demonstrate the standard of knowledge and skills needed in the convention industry. One qualification to be considered as an applicant for the certificate is three years of experience in meeting management. After you are accepted as an applicant, you must successfully complete an examination before being awarded the certificate.

A major event like the Super Bowl is planned at least six years in advance. It requires that the host city meet the NFL's minimum for hotel rooms and transportation. Jacksonville, Florida's plan for hosting Super Bowl XXXIX included the use of several cruise ships to make up for the shortage of hotel rooms needed in the mid-sized city. The cruise ships were docked around the city, and transportation was provided from the ships to the related events. Jacksonville learned it was the successful bidder for the 2005 game five years in advance and almost a year before the September 11, 2001, terrorist attacks. The subsequent increased need for security introduced new challenges for city event planners. The U.S. Coast Guard imposed restrictions on all boats and water vehicles in the area. All vehicles were subject to search. Boats docked near the stadium on game day were banned from moving, beginning at noon until the game ended. The Jacksonville convention and event planners demonstrated the flexibility to problem-solve and adapt to a changing environment.

E-Ticket

Bill McGee, a consultant to *Consumer Reports WebWatch*, conducted research on 20 U.S. and European travel web sites. The research found that a Belgian site turned up the lowest airfare 49 percent of the time. Although some European sites use euros as currency, aren't offered in English, and don't offer e-tickets, good deals can be found, especially when booking travel within Europe.

THINK CRITICALLY

Visit *Consumer Reports WebWatch* and find discounters that fly between Agadir, Morocco, and Frankfurt, Germany. What airlines fly this route? Do the airlines offer online information in English?

Business-to-Business Shows

Most conventions that are directed toward a specific industry require meeting rooms and a trade show area. The trade show area consists of booths set up by vendors who wish to make attendees aware of their products and services. Attendees visit the trade show area to network and discover new products and services that can improve their businesses.

Attracting business attendees to conventions requires special skill. According to Michael Hughes, associate publisher and research director for *Tradeshow Week,* business travelers must ask themselves two important questions before they decide to attend a trade show.

1. How will this event help me in my job function and career?

2. Is attending this event worth the time away from the office, family, friends, and other interests?

Show planners must promote convention attendance as a valuable experience for the attendee. Promotions are often focused on the educational and networking opportunities available at the conference. Attendees may be enticed with *appointment and matching services.* For example, when international real estate broker Ed Boen attended the MIPIM in Cannes, France, his main objective was to make contact with potential customers. (MIPIM is the French acronym for Europe's largest international commercial property conference.) Boen was able to use the conference database provided to him as a member of the National Association of REALTORS®. He sent e-mails to attendees who subsequently met with him during the conference to discuss future business.

Location, Location, Location

The location of a convention is often a strong consideration in a person's decision to attend. When convention and event planners choose a city in which to hold a convention, they know the image of the city will influence travelers. According to Michael Hughes, the price and quality of hotel rooms in a city is the number-one factor a convention planner considers. The number of available rooms and the quality of the area near the hotels and convention center are also important factors. An open date and service costs are secondary issues.

A major concern of convention and meeting planners centers on labor issues. In most cities, hotel employees, transportation workers, and the people who deliver and set up the materials needed for a trade show are all members of a union. A labor dispute can disrupt service and leave a negative image in the mind of convention planners and attendees.

Stopover   What must business travelers ask themselves before deciding to attend a trade show?

_____

_____

FREQUENT-USER PERKS

In 1981, American Airlines began offering rewards to flyers who were repeat customers. The rewards were free travel through a mileage-points award system. Today, nearly every airline, major hotel corporation, and rental car company has a frequent-user reward system.

Traveler Rewards

Frequent-user programs are designed to reward customers for repeat business. The programs generally award points based on use of the service and grant free services after a number of points are collected.

Most airlines award points per flight or per mile flown and require a minimum of 25,000 mileage points to receive a free flight. At this level, the points may be redeemed for **restricted domestic flights** within the United States that are available only on certain dates and at certain times. Airlines set aside only a few seats on each flight that may be redeemed for 25,000 mileage points. The restrictions can make the flights difficult to reserve.

Hotel frequent-user programs are usually based on the number of nights stayed at a hotel property. More expensive hotels in a chain will earn a higher number of points, but will also require more points to claim a free night's stay.

Travel reward programs often offer additional perks to travelers as they reach tiered levels of membership. For example, the Continental Airlines program, called OnePass, has three levels above the initial membership—Silver, Gold, and Platinum Elite. The Platinum Elite status offers

- priority check-in, boarding, and baggage handling

- unlimited upgrades to first class

- mileage bonuses

- priority security screening

Most award programs require re-earning of membership status each calendar year. Account executive Chuck Elkers obtained lifetime Continental Airlines Platinum Elite status by flying more than 75,000 miles per year for five years in a row.

For jobs that require travel, frequent-user programs are considered a perk. After more than a decade of debate, the Internal Revenue Service (IRS) clarified in 2002 that business-travel award miles earned through employer-paid travel would not be taxed as income. However, some award programs allow award miles to be converted to cash, and cash received must be reported to the IRS as income.

Auto Perks

Car rental companies have joined forces with hotels and airlines to attract repeat customers. Repeat customers' business costs much less per transaction than new customers' business. The cost of promotion to attract new customers and the extra time spent setting up and verifying customer information in the system make new customers more expensive to serve.

Photodisc

Car rental companies reward frequent users with free days of car rental and upgrades to higher-quality cars with no increase in price. Additionally, frequent users are rewarded with no-hassle check-in.

At National Car Rental, Emerald Club members earn a free rental day for each seven paid rental days. All levels of membership enjoy the "counter bypass" service with an intermediate-size car rental. Counter bypass means that the rental car shuttle van picks you up at the airport and drops you on the Emerald Aisle, where you select your car. The keys are already in it, and there is no standing in line or paperwork to complete. You make a quick stop at a security gate for an identification check, and then you are on your way. Upon returning to the airport or pick-up location, an employee meets you at the car with a handheld terminal that prints your receipt. The highest level of Emerald Club membership is Executive Elite. It requires 25 or more rentals per year, but provides a free rental day for each five paid rental days. Executive Elite members gain added benefits and can choose from full-size or luxury cars. Travel agents who refer customers to National earn a five percent commission on the base rental rate. Other rental car companies have similar programs to reward frequent customers and travel agents.

It Pays to Be Loyal

Travel and tour managers use loyalty programs to steer travelers to specific services, such as flights between selected cities. When British Airways decided to focus marketing efforts on passengers based in North America, it offered passengers making one round-trip transatlantic flight from the United States or Canada enough bonus reward points for two free tickets to anywhere in North America. Continental Airlines matched the loyalty offer with bonus reward points for flights from the United States to London.

Hilton HHonors upped the ante in the competition among frequent-user programs by allowing members to carry over stays from one calendar year to the next to meet HHonors VIP membership status. Most hotels only count stays within one calendar year for a member to qualify for elite status.

Stopover Why do travel service providers give priority to frequent users?

_____

_____

Understand Marketing Concepts

Circle the best answer for each of the following questions.

1. The most important factor that a meeting planner considers when choosing a location for a convention is
   a. an available convention center.
   b. airline service to the location.
   c. nearby attractions.
   d. price and quality of hotel rooms.

2. An added benefit that may be used as a means to attract and keep good employees is called a(n)
   a. business trip.
   b. perk.
   c. raise.
   d. override.

Think Critically

Answer the following questions as completely as possible. If necessary, use a separate sheet of paper.

3. Why are business travelers so important to travel suppliers?

_____

_____

_____

_____

_____

_____

_____

4. **Communication** Why do travel suppliers provide rewards for repeat customers? Write a paragraph about business travel and customer loyalty rewards.

_____

_____

_____

_____

_____

_____

_____

_____

_____

Luxury Travel, Budget Travel, and Ecotourism

Goals

Explain ways to target a market based on price points and level of service.

Describe travel that is sustainable and environmentally friendly.

All Aboard

When the economy is slow, luxury hotels offer bargains that open their posh surroundings to people on a budget. When the economy picks up again, the bargains disappear, but savvy travelers can still stay in luxurious surroundings. Choosing the second-best hotel in an area can provide luxury and savings.

Most luxury hotels are name-brand facilities that are well known to affluent travelers. The best-known luxury hotels spend millions of dollars to promote their amenities and remain a name brand, often overshadowing lesser-known hotels. The level of service and amenities in some of the lesser-known hotels may be close to the luxury standard, but for a much lower price.

For example, the George V in Paris has a fabulous lobby and consistent outstanding service for about $719 per night for a standard room in September. The Hotel du Louvre, located directly across from the Musée du Louvre in Paris, was built in 1855 on orders of Napoleon III. The grand staircase and marble floors in the entry provide a luxury setting, but at a more reasonable price of $299 per night for a standard room.

Look at the web sites for the George V hotel and the Hotel du Louvre. Make a list of the amenities of each. Discuss the differences in amenities with a group. Do the differences justify the wide gap in prices? Why or why not?

PRICE RULES

PRICING

People who have discretionary funds to spend on leisure travel or who work for an employer that allows first-class business travel enjoy the best that travel suppliers have to offer. Luxury is available to everyone—for a price.

The Lap of Luxury

The expectations of people who can choose luxury travel are high. Luxury travel generally means more space, whether in a private jet, a commercial airliner, or a hotel room. The amount and quality of the amenities offered through luxury travel increase with the cost.

Name-brand recognition is often a significant part of defining luxury. Ritz-Carlton has been known for many years for its luxury hotels and destination properties. The Ritz-Carlton Hotels are five-star hotels that are considered traditional. When Ritz-Carlton partnered with the luxury Italian jewelry firm Bulgari to open a chain of hotels, the properties were named the Bulgari Hotels and Resorts. The Ritz-Carlton name was completely omitted. The Ritz-Carlton group operates the hotels, but without any name recognition. In Milan, Italy, the soothing, muted tones of Bulgari's décor are simple and elegant. It features black Zimbabwe marble in the interior public spaces, suites with magnificent baths carved entirely into a solid block of Turkish Bihara stone, a personal trainer, a personal shopper, a Lamborghini, and a helicopter. The Bulgari is a twenty-first century version of Roman Empire excess.

The merging of the two top-name brands is an interesting experiment. You may wonder why Ritz-Carlton would be willing to do the work without the name recognition. The Bulgari hotels are seeking a new target market willing to pay higher price points than typical Ritz-Carlton customers. **Price points** represent the range between the top price and the bottom price customers are willing to pay. The merger of Ritz-Carlton and Bulgari provides an opportunity to attract ultra-premium customers and charge ultra-premium prices.

The Mass Affluent

In the past, marketers thought the majority of households in the United States earned a similar amount of money, with a few ultra-rich people on one end of the scale. Marketers directed products to two groups of people—the mass market and the luxury market. Between the 1970s and 2000s, the distribution of income in the United States changed dramatically. A large increase occurred in the number of people earning between the average and top incomes, creating a center level of people large enough to be called the **mass** affluent.

Within the mass affluent market are consumers ready to travel. In *Mass Affluence: Seven New Rules of Marketing to Today's Consumer*, authors Paul Nunes and Brian Johnson indicate that this particular group of consumers is not finding products that fulfill its wants and needs. New market opportunities are available to travel and tourism providers willing to create products and services for the large, new, affluent middle class.

Marketing Myths

A luxury resort may sometimes create an image in its advertisements that is over-promising and under-producing. The Carlisle Bay Resort in Antigua charges almost $1,000 per night during peak season for its beach suites and ocean suites. The beautiful photographs and descriptions on its web site showcase the hotel's contemporary design, original art, library, screening room, and gift shop.

Wall Street Journal reporter Laura Landro wrote about her disappointment when she stayed at The Carlisle. She had booked an ocean suite that turned out to be a single room with a sitting area. Because a suite is generally thought to have more than one room, Landro asked to be moved to a beach suite. Upon entering the new suite, she found that it had not been cleaned. Landro cut her visit short and was charged for only three nights instead of the six she had booked.

THINK CRITICALLY

1. Should The Carlisle call a single room with a sitting area a suite? Why or why not?

2. Should guests expect a clean room and much more from luxury hotels? What level of service should be provided? Discuss your opinion with others.

Photodisc

Copper Mountain, a ski resort in Summit County, Colorado, offers an advantage lift ticket to upscale skiers that costs about twice the regular price. The ticket, called the Beeline Advantage, is like a VIP pass that allows a skier to skip lines and go directly to the skier's own lift to make "first tracks" by starting to ski 15 minutes earlier than regular admission. Theme parks have also begun selling VIP treatment in tiered pricing for the more affluent customer. Special passes allow customers to move to the front of lines, receive special seating at shows, and take behind-the-scenes tours. Targeting the mass affluent market means selling status that is above the normal treatment but below the highest level of service.

A Hostel World

PRICING

Luxury travel is out of the question for many people's budgets. A large market exists for travel products and services offered at the lowest possible rate. Many people are looking for clean, safe, efficient service at a minimal price.

A **hostel** is an inn that provides the budget tourist a minimal sheltered place to sleep for a minimal price. Generally, only basic amenities are provided and guests must share bathrooms. There are more than 9,000 hostel properties in 155 countries.

Many hostels include related opportunities to learn about the community or participate in an activity such as surfing or diving. Seven Suns, a hostel in Chiang Mai, Thailand, is just a few minutes walk from the city's nightlife and offers a Thai cooking course. At The Secret Garden Hostel in Quito, Ecuador, guests can learn Spanish.

For as little as £59 (British pounds) or $112 (U.S. dollars) per day, travelers can board the easyCruise and sail around the western Mediterranean. The base price does not include food, and the tiny cabins are minimally furnished. Young Greek business owner, Stelios (his last name is never used), designed easyCruise. While traditional cruises usually start and end on a fixed date, easyCruise customers may board on any day and stay for only two days or cruise for longer periods. Offered as an alternative to hitchhiking, the ship is a way to move from one Mediterranean port to another.

The first hotel Stelios owned is easyHotel. It offers rooms for as little as £5 (less than $10). The earlier a traveler books a reservation, the cheaper the price. Stelios is targeting a customer who is between 20 and 30 years old and wants or needs to travel as inexpensively as possible. The traveler can expect minimal services and amenities.

What is a hostel? How is it different from a hotel?

_____

_____

ECOTOURISM

The International Ecotourism Society defines ecotourism as "responsible travel to natural areas that conserves the environment and sustains the well-being of the local people." Ecotourism can be budget or luxury travel, depending on the level of service provided.

Minimizing the Impact

When hordes of tourists descend into an area, they impact the environment and local people. Tourists sometimes introduce disease and often leave behind litter and pollution that contribute to the destruction of a natural area. The local people, plants, and animals can all be irreversibly harmed.

Major corporations headquartered thousands of miles away often develop resorts in remote locations that are naturally beautiful and attractive to tourists. If the corporations then bring in people from outside the area for all of the high-skill, high-pay positions that are created, the local people do not benefit financially. Leaving only the minimum-wage, low-skill jobs for local people builds resentment and can create problems that lead to social deterioration.

Missing the Boat

Hotels and tour operators in Maasailand areas of East Africa tout the Maasai people as one of the attractions of the area, but then treat them with disrespect. Mass-produced replicas of Maasai cultural products are sold to tourists as real Maasai artifacts, thus undermining the value of the original artwork. Additionally, this act undercuts the community-based entrepreneurial activities of the Maasai to sell their handicrafts.

Some tourism lodges have built replicas of Maasai villages that compete with the real villages' ability to attract tourists. The tourism lodges rarely hire Maasai people, except for their use in completing the most menial, low-wage jobs. The Maasai Environmental Resources Coalition (MERC) is working to stop the sale of fake products and improve the participation of the Maasai in area tourism.

THINK CRITICALLY

1. What part should Maasai people play in the tourism industry in their area?

2. What can tourism operators do to show respect for the Maasai people? Discuss your opinion.

Wildland Adventures, headquartered in Seattle, Washington, provides travelers to Tanzania with lodging in campsites leased from local Masaai communities. Masaai locals lead the travelers on bush walks and provide information about the Masaai culture.

The Maasai people have lived in East Africa for centuries and have existed by grazing herds of cattle and goats. They do not eat or hunt wild game, and thus wildlife have benefited from their stewardship of the land. In the late nineteenth century, British colonials forcefully removed the Maasai to make way for national parks and private ranches owned by European settlers. Over the years, the Maasai continued to be squeezed by the development of ranches and parks. In 2004, drought in the dry, barren, overpopulated areas left to the Maasai caused them to seek grass and water for their livestock in the ranches and rare game preserves. The Maasai were arrested for trespassing. Additionally, unregulated tourism in Maasailand has contributed to forest depletion, water pollution, soil erosion, habitat destruction, and economic exploitation.

Responsible Development

PRODUCT/SERVICE MANAGEMENT

Responsible development of ecotourism sites means respecting and working with the local people so that they benefit financially from the increased commerce. Additionally, the damage to their environment should be minimal, and there should be direct financial contributions to conservation of the region. Community-based ecotourism ventures reach out to partner with developers who seek to bring tourism to a region so that both the developer and the region benefit.

The Targhee National Forest is located in eastern Idaho and western Wyoming. It is situated next to Yellowstone and the Grand Teton national parks. The Nature Conservancy is a nonprofit conservation group.

Photodisc

It purchased a 133-acre ranch in eastern Idaho to connect the Targhee National Forest and the Conservancy's Flat Ranch Preserve. Connecting the two areas allows Yellowstone National Park's wildlife to migrate to their wintering area. The additional property adds to the popular Flat Ranch wildlife viewing area. By working to understand the people, cultures, and economic activities of the area, the Conservancy has broadened the meaning of conservation.

Stopover

Why is ecotourism so important?

_____

_____

Understand Marketing Concepts

Circle the best answer for each of the following questions.

1. Luxury hotels spend millions of dollars on marketing to
   a. maintain their name-brand status.
   b. improve amenities.
   c. influence culture.
   d. raise prices.

2. The mass affluent want
   a. ultra-luxury service.
   b. the least expensive service available.
   c. mid-level service.
   d. none of the above.

Think Critically

Answer the following questions as completely as possible. If necessary, use a separate sheet of paper.

3. What can be done to respect local people and provide them with economic benefits from tourism?

_____

_____

_____

_____

_____

_____

_____

_____

4. **Geography** Look up Tanzania on a map. On what continent is it located? What is the climate of the area? How might the climate impact tourism?

_____

_____

_____

_____

_____

_____

_____

_____

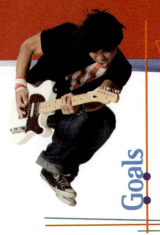

Sports and Adventure Travel

Goals

Explain sports travel management.

Discuss an emerging type of adventure travel.

All Aboard

Being first, or one of the first, is a thrill that many adventure travelers seek. Being the first to see uncharted areas of Earth, climbing to the top of the highest mountain, or flying solo around the world creates history and a sense of accomplishment. Dennis Tito purchased his way into history when he became the first tourist to visit the International Space Station. After paying a reported $20 million and receiving 900 hours of training, the 60-year-old Tito flew aboard a Russian supply spaceship with two veteran cosmonauts.

Tito was a scientist employed by the North American Space Administration (NASA) in the 1970s. He left NASA to open an investment management firm, but space travel was an adventure he continued to dream about. In 2001, Tito rocketed to a week's vacation in zero gravity, where he watched the Earth from a point of view only 415 others had seen before.

In a group, discuss other adventure travels that are available now. What new adventure travels may be available in the future? Why do you think the first space tourist traveled as part of the Russian space program and not as part of the U.S. program? Would you like to vacation in space? Why or why not?

TRAVEL LEAGUES

Each year, the Amateur Softball Association (ASA) conducts over 90 national championships in which 30,000 players compete. The ASA requests bids for the group's tournaments. Representatives from potential destinations make three-minute presentations in front of 250 league administrators. The administrators choose the locations by voting via electronic pads. The competition for hosting amateur sports events, such as ASA championships, is fierce. The number of hotel room rentals generated by amateur sports spectators can be greater than the number generated by hosting the Super Bowl.

Waiting to board a flight out of Orlando, travelers began to discuss the length of the security lines. One cause of the long lines was the 2005 National All Star Cheerleading Championship being held that weekend at Disney's Wide World of Sports complex. One traveler commented on how full the viewing stands had been at all of the week's events. Parents and other family members of the competitors had purchased tour packages to accompany the cheerleaders to Orlando. They watched the competitions and also took advantage of the area's tourist attractions. Adults, some who are normally reluctant to travel, will often purchase tour packages to watch their children's sporting events. The tours are managed by travel suppliers and can provide a level of comfort to infrequent travelers.

Sports associations work in conjunction with convention and visitors bureaus, host facilities such as Disney, and travel suppliers to package and manage the tours. The packages include airfare, ground transportation, lodging, and tickets to the sports event as well as to local attractions. Some sports travel packages offer a volume discount to lower the prices below standard travel costs. Team members, as well as their parents, family members, and friends can take advantage of the savings.

Photodisc

Stopover

How are travel suppliers benefiting from youth sports?

OUTER LIMITS

When some think of adventure travel, thrill-seeking maniacs come to mind. Those adventure travelers who are deficient in judgment may push the limits by slipping into war zones or skiing in avalanche areas. They risk their lives and the lives of those who must rescue them. Real adventure travelers push themselves through physical activity and take risks without doing harm to others or the environment.

The Final Frontier

PRODUCT/SERVICE MANAGEMENT

The driving motivation for adventure travel may simply be curiosity—wanting to see what is over the next horizon. The final frontier is space. Many fantasize about the opportunity to explore beyond the gravitational pull of Earth. That fantasy is already becoming reality for private citizens, and entrepreneurs are working to have the accommodations ready for tourists.

Budget Suites of America owner Robert Bigelow has announced a $50-million prize for the first adventurers to achieve successful flights of a five- to seven-person orbital spacecraft. The winning spacecraft will dock with Bigelow Aerospace's inflatable space habitat, bringing guests to Robert Bigelow's orbiting hotel, tentatively scheduled to open in 2010. An article on the *Popular Science* web site deemed Bigelow's future lodging "The Five-Billion-Star Hotel."

Time Out

Zero-G Corporation sells rides on a Boeing 727 to anyone who wants to try two hours of 10,000-foot-high, roller-coaster-like arcs called parabolas. At the top of the arcs, the passenger becomes weightless for about 25 seconds. The largest demand for the flights is from companies giving the rides as employee awards.

Biking on the Edge

In Bolivia, mountain bikers can take riding literally to the edge on the "Road of Death," a one-lane, 40-mile road that drops 12,000 feet down a mountain outside La Paz. The main tourist street in La Paz has a number of agencies that will arrange a ride down the "Road of Death," which is declared to be the world's most dangerous road. The quality of service varies, however, and care is needed to avoid renting poor-quality bikes with unqualified guides. A mountain bike trip package includes transportation up the mountain and back into La Paz, a guide, a bike, and food to eat on the ride. For travelers looking for a less risky adventure, there are other excellent mountain bike routes around La Paz. La Paz offers a wide range of accommodations, from hostels for $3 per day to upscale hotels. It is an excellent destination for the budget-minded adventure traveler.

Stopover Which demographic group might be the target for mountain bike riding?

_____

_____

Five-Star Traveler

MARILYN CARLSON NELSON

After graduating from Smith College with a degree in international economics, Marilyn Carlson Nelson began her career at Paine Webber, an investment banking firm. She was asked to use her initials to disguise her gender until customers were confident that she could do the job. Today, Nelson is considered one of the most powerful businesswomen in the world. *Fortune* lists her as one of the top-ten women leaders in the United States.

After she joined her family business, the Carlson Companies, Inc., Nelson was instrumental in adding many brand names, including Radisson Hotels and Resorts, Carlson Wagonlit Travel, Park Plaza Hotels and Resorts, SeaMaster Cruises, T.G.I. Friday's, and Carlson Marketing Groups. Nelson became president and CEO of Carlson Companies, Inc. in 1998 and chair of the board in 1999. She is the leader of one of the largest privately owned corporations in the world, with more than $31 billion per year in gross sales and 188,000 employees worldwide. Nelson is a member of the World Travel and Tourism Council, and at the invitation of Bill Clinton, was a delegate to the White House Conference on Tourism in 1996.

Nelson is considered a role model for those in the travel industry and for all women in business. She has worked to create "A Great Place for Great People to do Great Work," and her company is included in most lists of "Best Places to Work." Employees of Carlson Companies tend to stay for many years. Nelson has received hundreds of awards for her achievements, including the Hospitality Industry Lifetime Achievement Award and the Woodrow Wilson Award for Corporate Citizenship.

THINK CRITICALLY

What personal characteristics would you expect from the CEO of a large corporation? Does Marilyn Carlson Nelson fit that model? Why or why not?

Understand Marketing Concepts

Circle the best answer for each of the following questions.

1. Travel destinations compete for amateur sports events because
    a. of the volume of travelers the events attract.
    b. they want to encourage fitness.
    c. local people attend the events.
    d. none of the above.

2. Prizes are being used to
    a. encourage NASA to allow tourist space travel.
    b. encourage private development of space travel.
    c. encourage adventure travelers to push the limits of sound judgment.
    d. do all of the above.

Think Critically

Answer the following questions as completely as possible. If necessary, use a separate sheet of paper.

3. What amenities would you offer in a space hotel? How might this be possible? What limits might there be on the amenities that can be offered?

    _____

    _____

    _____

    _____

    _____

    _____

    _____

4. **Communication** Why are some people fascinated with adventure travel? What can travel suppliers do to help ensure that adventure travelers keep themselves, as well as others and the environment, safe? Write two paragraphs that answer these questions.

    _____

    _____

    _____

    _____

    _____

    _____

    _____

    _____

Chapter Assessment

Review Marketing Concepts

Write the letter of the term that matches each definition. Some terms will not be used.

_____ 1. An incentive payment from a preferred vendor

_____ 2. A large number of people earning between the average and top incomes

_____ 3. The range between the top price and the bottom price customers are willing to pay

_____ 4. An added benefit that may be used as a means to attract and keep good employees

_____ 5. Responsible travel to natural areas that conserves the environment and sustains the well-being of the local people

_____ 6. A supplier with whom there is a negotiated agreement for discount prices based on volume

_____ 7. One who has demonstrated the standard of knowledge and skills needed in the convention industry

_____ 8. An inn that provides the budget tourist a minimal sheltered place to sleep for a minimal price

a. adventure travelers
b. certified meeting professional (CMP)
c. convention and meeting professionals
d. discount airlines
e. ecotourism
f. frequent-user programs
g. hostel
h. mass affluent
i. override
j. perk
k. preferred vendor
l. price points
m. restricted domestic flights

Circle the best answer.

9. Responsibilities of meeting planners include
   a. buying products and services.
   b. establishing policies.
   c. developing an image.
   d. planning, organizing, and budgeting.

10. The number of hotel rooms generated by amateur sports spectators can be
    a. less than 1,000.
    b. greater than the number generated by hosting the Super Bowl.
    c. disappointing to the event's host city.
    d. none of the above.

11. Ecotourism involves
    a. protecting the environment.
    b. including local people in the financial benefits.
    c. respecting local people and customs.
    d. all of the above.

Think Critically

12. What is meant by the statement "a meeting planner's role is logistical and tactical"? Describe the role of the meeting planner.

13. Look at the web site for the Convention Industry Council (CIC) and find the process for becoming a certified meeting professional (CMP). List the steps other than gaining experience and taking an exam.

14. In a group, discuss why some travel veterans insist that smaller, locally owned properties may have atmosphere but cannot match the service of the big-name luxury hotels. List services the large hotels might offer that exceed those of smaller facilities.

15. What rewards can be offered to loyal customers of a hotel? What incentives can be offered to the mass affluent? Make a list of each.

16. How would you promote the items listed in question 15. What media would you use? What would be your message?

Make Connections

17. **Marketing Math** Your company has 12 people who travel between Seattle and St. Louis 15 times per year and average two overnight stays per trip. The corporate travel manager has two options for travel contracts. Travel Supplier A is offering airline tickets, hotel rooms for one night, and rental car packages for $350 per person plus $155 per person for each additional night. Travel Supplier B is offering each two-day trip at $645 per person, with a 5 percent discount once total company travel expenditures reach $100,000. Who is offering the better deal—Supplier A or Supplier B?

_____

_____

_____

_____

_____

18. **History** In the early 1900s, why did the British remove native people of Africa from areas, under the guise of setting up parks to protect the wildlife? Why were the British in Africa?

_____

_____

_____

_____

_____

19. **Technology** Create a spreadsheet that compares the services and amenities of two luxury, two mid-range, and two budget hotels. Include the standard room prices and services featured on each hotel's web site.

_____

_____

_____

20. **Geography** Select a remote location with natural attractions. Write a persuasive paragraph on why it should or should not be developed for tourism.

_____

_____

_____

_____

21. **Science** Use the Internet to determine how tourism impacts water depletion and water pollution in remote areas. Write one page about your findings.

_____

_____

_____

_____

_____

_____

22. **Research** Using the Internet, determine hotel prices in your area or a large city nearby. What is the most expensive hotel, and what amenities does it offer? What is the second most expensive hotel? Compare the offerings and determine why one is more expensive.

_____

_____

_____

_____

_____

EXTENDED STAY

Project You have been hired to attract youth sports events to your area. Choose a specific sport and complete the activities below based on that sport.

Work with a group and complete the following activities.

1. Determine what facilities would be needed and how many teams could be accommodated.
2. Determine what groups would need to be involved in the planning. How would the city or county government be involved? Would the school district be involved?
3. Discuss factors that would cause the team association to choose your area. Is there anything needed that your area is lacking? If so, what new development to your area would you recommend to city leaders to attract future events?
4. What are the major attractions of the area? Describe travel packages you might put together to market to team members' families.
5. Write a page about your findings and share the information with the class.

SMALLEST HOST CITY ACCOMMODATES SUPER BOWL

Host cities for the Super Bowl can expect nearly 100,000 visitors. Revenues between $250 million and $300 million can be expected to flow into the host's local economy. The exposure received from hosting the event can also produce long-term benefits. According to NFL research, 81 percent of Super Bowl visitors intend to revisit the host city again within two years. Further, 65 percent of Super Bowl visitors are key decision makers in their companies, and 60 percent of those companies host meetings outside their corporate headquarters. Local sports also benefit from the Super Bowl. The NFL builds practice fields at local high schools that rival the nation's best professional fields. You can see why cities with travel and tourism facilities want to host such an event.

The NFL has 20 pages of requirements that a city must meet in order to be selected as a Super Bowl host. Ideally, 29,000 hotel rooms should be available, 17,500 of which will be set aside for NFL-related groups. In addition, there should be 65 limousines available for exclusive NFL use, 1,000 buses for transporting fans, and many private and public golf courses for fan use.

Jacksonville, Florida, was a surprise selection for Super Bowl XXXIX. It is the smallest city chosen to host the United States' largest annual sporting event. Downtown Jacksonville has only 1,800 hotel rooms, and only 15,000 rooms are available in the entire greater Jacksonville metropolitan area.

Jacksonville increased the number of hotel rooms by docking several cruise ships on the St. Johns River that served as floating hotels for NFL guests. The cruise ships provided an additional 4,000 rooms to the city. Water taxis shuttled people around downtown. The cruise ship rooms were a creative solution to the lack of lodging. However, small, cramped rooms did not appeal to some wealthy attendees.

Some visitors to the Super Bowl rented homes and condominiums in Jacksonville or chose yachts on the river. Local real estate agencies collaborated with local residents who were interested in renting out their homes to Super Bowl fans. In addition, many fans who paid thousands of dollars for game tickets booked hotels more than 100 miles away in Savannah, Georgia, and Orlando, Florida.

THINK CRITICALLY

1. Why would a city want to host a Super Bowl?
2. How is the Super Bowl related to travel and tourism?
3. Why does the NFL set minimum standards for a city to host the Super Bowl?
4. How much could the owner of a four-bedroom home charge per night to rent his or her house to Super Bowl fans? Explain.

TRAVEL AND TOURISM MARKETING MANAGEMENT TEAM DECISION MAKING

Country Fest USA is a national music event that draws country music fans from all over the United States and around the world. Many of the biggest names in country music perform at various times throughout the four-day festival. Opportunities are provided for fans to meet with the artists to ask questions, capture photographs, and obtain autographs.

For a city to be selected as the host of Country Fest USA, there must be 2,000 hotel rooms available to accommodate visitors. The festival is planned to be held outside, but there must be a facility available to hold a minimum of 10,000 people in the case of inclement weather. In addition, there must be an international airport nearby and sufficient transportation services to shuttle fans to and from the event.

Assume that your city has a population of 200,000, sufficient transportation services, and 2,500 hotel rooms. It is the home of the state fairgrounds, with an outdoor grandstand for entertainment. A local university has an arena that seats 14,000 people. A major amusement park, a water park, a zoo, a children's museum, an antiques mall, and an outlet mall are all nearby.

You and a partner have been hired by the city's tourism bureau to develop a marketing proposal for your city to host Country Fest USA.

You have 30 minutes to develop your proposal, ten minutes to present it to the tourism bureau and Country Fest USA representatives (judges), and five minutes to field questions.

Performance Indicators Evaluated

- Develop a marketing strategy to attract an entertainment event to a city.
- Demonstrate an understanding of the economic importance of travel and tourism.
- Highlight key economic factors for event planners to consider when selecting a location.
- Present a clear plan to host a major entertainment event that is financially beneficial to the city's travel and tourism industry.

Go to the DECA web site for more detailed information.

THINK CRITICALLY

1. What are the economic benefits for the city hosting Country Fest USA?
2. Why should the marketing proposal highlight facilities and number of hotel rooms?
3. Why do cities of all sizes have tourism bureaus?
4. What promotional items could be given to Country Fest USA representatives at your presentation? Why?

www.deca.org

Business and Leisure Travel Markets

Photodisc

CHAPTER 6 • CHAPTER 6 • CHAPTER 6 • CHAPTER 6

6

6.1 Product Planning

6.2 Transportation and Accommodations

6.3 Food and Hospitality

Point Your Browser

▶ ▶ ▶ ▶ travel.swlearning.com

Winning Strategies

Carey International, Inc.

Assume a partner in a Wall Street financial investment firm needs to fly to Chicago to make three presentations. All of the presentations must be given on the same day, in three different locations 30 miles apart, on a tight schedule. A rental car may not be the best transportation choice in this situation, especially if the traveler is not familiar with the area. Business travelers or tourists who need more than minimal ground transportation look to Carey International to provide chauffeured services. Carey is the industry leader and has set the standard for exemplary chauffeured service since 1921.

Using late-model luxury vehicles, the Carey fleet includes sedans, limousines, SUVs, minibuses, vans, motor coaches, and a specially built Carey Edition Lincoln Town Car. The Town Car is an extended sedan with extra leg room for the rear seat. It is equipped with mobile office capabilities, including a cellular phone, satellite radio, DVD player, pull-down writing/laptop desk, and powerful reading lamps. The highly trained chauffeurs can provide information about the city's sites and restaurants.

Carey offers "customer-directed" service, which means customers can change plans, times, or destinations with no advance warning, allowing total flexibility. Carey reservations are available 24 hours a day, 365 days per year, and the services are available in thousands of cities in over 40 countries. Whether it is airport pickup, city-to-city transportation, special occasions, or sightseeing, Carey will ensure the chauffeured vehicle is "where you need it, when you need it."

THINK CRITICALLY

1. What are some of the customer-oriented services offered by Carey?

2. Why would the quality of service offered by a company like Carey determine the success of the business? How important would repeat customers and positive opinions be to the business?

Product Planning

Discuss how to develop a successful product mix.

Explain quality standards.

All Aboard

The city of Soap Lake, Washington, is located in the Columbia River basin at the edge of the mineral-filled lake for which the town is named. Soap Lake has served as an attraction for the area, beginning with the first store and hotel built in the early 1900s. By 1919, Soap Lake was a busy resort and spa, with four hotels and many businesses catering to campers. The medicinal attributes of the mineral lake initially brought most visitors, but the social attractions soon rivaled the lake. Big bands from Seattle played for large dance crowds and attracted honeymooners and tourists. During the Great Depression, Soap Lake fell on hard times. The area has never regained the level of tourism it attracted years ago.

Brent Blake is a semiretired architectural design consultant, magazine publisher, and artist. He wanted to help Soap Lake once again become a tourist destination. Blake spent several years working to have the world's largest lava lamp placed in the city. In 2005, Target Corporation donated a 60-foot mechanical lava lamp and moved it from Times Square in New York to Soap Lake. The lamp was stored pending private funding to restore and assemble it in Soap Lake.

Work with a group. Discuss why destinations go out of favor with tourists. What should be done to encourage growth and repeat business?

THE PRODUCT MIX

When a new travel or tourism business is established, its founders must first decide on a target customer. The new products and/or services offered must be designed to meet the wants and needs of that customer. The contrast between leaving an airport on a crowded shuttle bus that stops at every hotel in the area and being chauffeured directly to your destination in a luxury car provides an idea of how related products and services can differ. The variety of products and services offered is referred to as the **product mix**.

"LAVA®, LAVA LITE®, and the configurations of the LAVA® brand motion lamp and its base and globe are trademarks used under license from their owner, Haggerty Enterprises, Inc., Chicago Illinois, and are registered in the United States and other countries." Brent Blake, Originator of the Giant Lava Lamp Concept for Soap Lake, WA.

Targeting the Customer

PRODUCT/SERVICE MANAGEMENT

Product/service planning means determining the combination of product or service classifications and price points within a company's product or service mix. Before deciding on the mix, the company needs to understand what the target customer is willing to pay and the cost of providing that product or service. Because the purpose of operating a business is to make a profit, the cost of providing the product or service must be less than what the customer is willing to pay. Promotional activities, salaries, taxes, insurance, and all other costs must be more than covered, with a percentage left for profit.

Choosing luxury travelers as target customers means offering many high-quality amenities. Luxury travelers expect to pay for and receive extra privileges and services. Ultra-premium luxury accommodations include more than just a lovely suite. For example, the Brussels, Belgium, Royal Windsor Hotel offers a package that includes

- 1,001 roses in a choice of colors in the room

- limousine ground transportation

- a visit to a famous jeweler and a specially selected diamond

- a lavish dinner cruise on a yacht

- a helicopter ride to a Formula One racetrack

- personal driving instructions and a trial run in a two-seat Formula One race car and in a Gillet Vertigo, one of the world's fastest cars

- a special tour of the Gillet factory

- a romantic dinner with an extravagant fireworks display

This package offers a product mix that is not for the average traveler. It costs almost $2 million for a four-day, three-night stay. Ultra-premium travelers are willing to pay the price for packages that offer unusual, one-of-a-kind amenities.

Business travelers will be attracted by a different product mix. Many who must travel regularly strive to keep up with their fitness routines. A number of mid-level hotels offer in-room fitness equipment, such as treadmills or stationary bicycles, and a television channel dedicated to exercise. Omni Hotels offer a fitness kit that includes a radio headset, dumbbells, an exercise mat, an elastic exercise band, and an exercise booklet. These services may be attractive to frequent travelers who prefer not to exercise in a more public fitness center.

Mixing It Up

MARKETING-INFORMATION MANAGEMENT

Airlines, tour operators, and hotels must determine what extras will be offered to guests and what prices must be charged to pay for all of the additional amenities. **Marketing research** is the process of gathering and using information about potential customers. Marketing research must be conducted to determine what customers want and expect from the travel service provider.

Time Out

Resorts and vacation destinations across the United States are squeezed by a shortage of workers available for short-term, seasonal jobs. Many of these jobs are offered to foreigners with H-2B visas. H2-B visas are temporary visas issued to non-immigrants for U.S. employment. When the economy is good, the 66,000 H2-B visas granted each year are not enough to cover the thousands of seasonal jobs open in restaurants and hospitality businesses.

Selecting the target customer means focusing on the price points. To focus on the mass affluent, for example, means establishing price points that are higher than average but less than luxury. The services provided for those price points will be somewhere between the 1,001 roses offered to the ultra-premium guest in a luxury suite and a clean room offered to the budget guest. Offering status, such as a privileged tier of services, can attract customers who value the extra amenities enough to pay for them. Successful travel and tourism operators think creatively and listen carefully to their customers' reactions to the product mix offered.

Rethinking the **exchange model**, the way the service is paid for, is one way to change the product mix. Vacation lodging used to be offered in two ways—either you temporarily rented a hotel room or vacation cabin, or you bought vacation lodging. Equity ownership, or fractional ownership, is a recent model that provides privileged ownership to a new group of customers. Often referred to as a *timeshare*, the **fractional ownership model** means the customer has part ownership of the property, with access to it for a period of time each year based on the percentage of ownership. The fractional owner's share may be resold just as a condominium or house may be resold. A mass-affluent customer may not be able to afford complete ownership of a beachfront condominium in the tranquil bliss of St. Thomas. Ritz Carlton Club of St. Thomas offers fractional ownership that makes multiple-week stays at the property affordable. The service provided by Ritz Carlton takes the hassle out of second-home ownership. The service appeals to mass-affluent customers who have little time to care for a vacation home. The facility is maintained in the owners' absence and prepared for their arrival. The model has been successful enough for Ritz Carlton that additional clubs are being added to existing properties.

Placing money into a property that will retain value as well as provide vacation enjoyment is considered an investment. Positioning the travel and tourism product as an investment is an additional way to appeal to the mass affluent who want to hang onto their money and have it grow in value.

Marketing Myths

Cruise lines often advertise cruises at unbelievably low prices, such as five nights in the Western Caribbean from $359 per person with double occupancy. The cost does not include meals, beverages, admissions to shows, boarding/debarking taxes, or land excursions. The guest, once aboard, is captive and must purchase all services and products from the cruise ship, and they may be priced unreasonably high. A $359 cruise may cost $800 to $1,000 when meals, fees, and taxes are counted.

THINK CRITICALLY

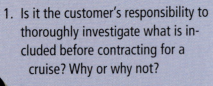

1. Is it the customer's responsibility to thoroughly investigate what is included before contracting for a cruise? Why or why not?

2. Should travel and tour operators be more forthcoming with information for inexperienced travelers? Discuss your opinion with others.

Service, Please

PRODUCT/SERVICE MANAGEMENT

The travel and tourism industry is largely involved in service marketing. With **service marketing**, the work or acts sold to customers are without physical attributes that they can touch or take home with them. For example, a cruise includes many *intangible* services, such as safe travel and the convenience of not changing hotel rooms to see beautiful ports or the open ocean each day.

Photodisc

Part of the challenge of service marketing is presenting for sale something that the customer cannot touch, feel, or see. Service marketers must help customers visualize the benefits of purchasing the tour or cruise. Customers do consider the cruise ship and the meals provided aboard ship as tangible attributes. They expect the ship to be clean and well maintained and the meals to be delicious. The image of a dirty, run-down ship would not attract customers at any level. Additionally, cruise ships compete to offer the best destinations, the best entertainment, and the best food. Selecting the specific product/service mix to offer to target customers takes knowledge of the customers' needs and wants and the skill to provide them in a satisfying way. Service providers get only one chance to make a good first impression. They must have high standards to surpass the expectations of consumers and ensure repeat business.

Stopover

Define service marketing.

_____

_____

QUALITY STANDARDS

Competition is fierce among travel and tourism providers. The rivalry to achieve a larger market share helps keep quality standards high. A provider's **market share** is the percentage of business received compared to the total market. For example, if it is determined that your area receives one million overnight visitors per year and 100,000 of those visitors stay in your hotel, then your hotel has ten percent of the market share. **Service quality** is the degree to which the service meets the needs and expectations of the customer. In travel and tourism, service quality must be consistent to maintain a proven reputation and ensure repeat business.

Customer Satisfaction

Three ways to measure service quality are

1. compare reality against written performance standards

2. compare service to that of competitors

3. survey customer satisfaction

Although most effective businesses have performance standards that define the level of service they will provide, they also research what the competition is doing and try to match or exceed that level of quality. When one mid-level hotel offers fitness kits, another will jump to offer in-room fitness equipment. The final measure is determining what the customer thinks of the service. Repeat business is an excellent indication that the service is meeting customers' expectations. But, a business must recognize a problem before it keeps customers from coming back. Marketing research is used to determine customer satisfaction while there is still time to retain the customer.

Until recently, hotels haven't always been a favorite place to sleep. Beds were often of poor quality and saggy. Locations near a freeway made rooms noisy. Often, draperies had major gaps that let bright parking lot lights shine into the room. Guests who were anxious about staying in a strange place or concerned about waking up on time didn't sleep well. After listening to customers, hotel chains finally realized their primary function was to provide a comfortable place to sleep away from home, and they began to address the problems. They upgraded mattresses and pillows used in rooms to a quality closer to what guests would have in their own homes. Guests at Crowne Plaza Hotels and Resorts are offered a sleep kit that includes a clip to keep drapes closed, a nightlight, earplugs, a CD with muscle-relaxing techniques and soothing music, and lavender spray. Guests are responding well to the product mix improvements.

Rating the Service

The "gold standards" for quality service in the lodging industry are the rating systems of the *Mobil Travel Guide* and the American Automobile Association (AAA). Mobil and AAA use inspectors who actually visit hotels and rate them based on tightly defined criteria. Mobil only recommends about 9,000 out of 50,000 hotels in the United States.

Online travel sites like Orbitz use a star rating system, but admit that their inspection teams are also their sales teams who negotiate discount room rates for their online services. This situation could create a conflict of interest if ratings are negotiated rather than earned.

Stopover   What are three ways to measure service quality?

_____

_____

Understand Marketing Concepts

Circle the best answer for each of the following questions.

1. When a new travel or tourism business is established, it must first decide on
   a. a target customer.
   b. a name.
   c. a location.
   d. a product mix.

2. With fractional ownership,
   a. the customer has part ownership of the property.
   b. the customer has access to the property for a period of time each year based on the percentage of ownership.
   c. the owner's share may be resold.
   d. all of the above are true.

Think Critically

Answer the following questions as completely as possible. If necessary, use a separate sheet of paper.

3. What are the intangible benefits of fractional ownership of a vacation home? Why would someone be interested in this form of ownership?

   _____

   _____

   _____

   _____

   _____

   _____

4. **Product/Service Management** You are the owner of a small start-up airline that will travel between three U.S. cities. Only one of the cities has over one million residents. Choose the three cities, and make a list of the product mix you will offer. Why should passengers choose your airline?

   _____

   _____

   _____

   _____

   _____

   _____

   _____

Transportation and Accommodations

Goals

- Describe the importance of transportation infrastructure and services to the economy.
- Define front-of the-house and back-of-the-house lodging operations.
- Describe characteristics of destination marketing.

All Aboard

South Fork is destined to be a premier resort facility on the southern coast of Vietnam, near the city of Phan Thiet. The area has spectacular beaches, an ideal climate, and beautiful scenery, making it the perfect location for a five-star resort complex. A number of successful resorts are already operating in the area. Vietnam is rapidly becoming a vital tourist destination. South Fork plans to catch the wave of tourists who are discovering Vietnam's beauty.

The government of Vietnam began to recognize the economic potential of tourism in the 1990s, but it still has some cumbersome processes for approval of new development. The plan to build South Fork took 11 months to approve. The lengthy process has been discouraging to many would-be investors. The resort will generate supporting businesses, but requires additional transportation infrastructure to make it convenient for visitors.

Work with a group. Discuss who the potential target customers might be for South Fork. From what countries and economic groups would they come?

BY AIR, SEA, AND LAND

DISTRIBUTION

Transportation systems are a critical piece of the distribution channel for travel and tourism. Until a creative inventor figures out how to beam people from one location to another, mechanized vehicles will be needed to move people quickly and efficiently. Transportation systems require a publicly funded infrastructure consisting of an airport, roadways, and/or a port. Some cities operate mass-transit options, such as bus lines or subways, that serve a specific region. However, most transportation businesses are privately funded.

Photodisc

Taking Off

Depending on the destination, travelers may choose to fly, drive, take a train, cruise on a ship, or hike. In North America, the interstate highway system is set up to accommodate coast-to-coast travel by car. In most European countries, travel by train is fast and economical. The passenger train system in the United States does not compete with traveling by car or plane.

The United States has more airlines than any other nation. Most nations have only one airline. From 1938 through 1978, the Civil Aeronautics Board (CAB) provided economic regulation of the U.S. airline industry. An airline could not go into or out of business, or do anything in between, without the permission of a majority of the five presidentially appointed CAB members. This all changed with the Airline Deregulation Act of 1978. The driving force behind deregulation was the perception that regulation by the CAB had resulted in reduced competition and higher fares. After deregulation, prices of fares decreased and productivity of the airlines improved. Deregulation allowed the airlines to fill empty seats by offering discounted fares. A number of airlines failed to reset their company goals to address the new, deregulated business environment. The subsequent failure and bankruptcy of these airlines can be blamed on their failure to change strategies to meet the new reality of competition.

Airlines continue to face major challenges, including enormous competition, ticket price wars, union pressure for salary increases, and the rising cost of fuel. Discount airlines like Southwest Airlines are competing head-to-head with the major carriers—and winning. Southwest Airline's vice president of finance, Laura Wright, stated, "The industry's low-cost provider is keen on finding innovative ways to keep our operating costs in check so we can continue to provide low fares to millions of Americans." Southwest is a no-frills airline that offers no in-flight food and does not assign seats to passengers. To get a seat next to a companion means getting to the airport early to be in the first group boarding the plane. Southwest also does not allow passengers to change to an earlier flight without a charge, even if the earlier plane is leaving with many empty seats. While other airlines are negotiating with their union employees to lower salaries, Southwest has maintained a reputation as a great place to work. Southwest's pilots' salary contract ties raises to the profitability of the airline.

Missing the Boat

Mechanical trouble aboard an airplane can be costly. If shortly after takeoff a plane must turn around and fly back to the point of origin, it must dump tons of expensive jet fuel, because planes have trouble landing with full tanks. If passengers cannot continue on to their destination, the airline is responsible for the cost of their lodging. Additionally, under a 2005 European Union rule, if passengers arrive at their destination more than five hours late, the airline must pay them €600 (euros) or about $780 (U.S. dollars) each.

In February 2005, an engine failed on a British Airways 747 during takeoff from Los Angeles bound for London. The plane, with 351 passengers aboard, flew ten hours with a dead engine, until finally making an emergency landing in Manchester, England. The pilots' union stated the new EU rule was forcing pilots to take risks in order to save money. On its next round trip, the same aircraft lost use of an engine three and one-half hours into an 11-hour flight and continued, landing on time in London.

THINK CRITICALLY

1. In U.S. dollars, what is the total the airline would have had to pay passengers on the delayed flight under the EU rule?

2. Is the amount significant enough to warrant taking a risk? Explain your answer.

Asia has joined the United States and Europe in airline deregulation, opening the way for low-cost Asian airlines. A growing middle class of customers with interest in traveling is attracted to the new, Asian low-cost providers. These airlines are creating interest in secondary destinations by offering much lower fares than full-service airlines. Most of the newer Asian airlines, just like Southwest Airlines, do not offer assigned seats. Tickets on low-cost airlines usually cannot be purchased through online discounters, such as Orbitz or Travelocity. Some charge extra for luggage that exceeds very low weight limits.

The importance of the airlines to the travel and tourism industry, as well as to the U.S. economy in general, is significant. According to Laura Wright, "Aviation represents about 10 percent of all economic activity in the United States. In the state of Nevada, aviation is about 19 percent of the economy." The success or failure of airlines can have a major impact on the national economy. Continued mergers of airlines are expected. The reduced competition among fewer airlines may result in higher ticket prices.

Cruising Along

Photodisc

During the 30 years between 1970 and 2000, the cruise industry evolved from an exotic, point-to-point service for the rich to a fun vacation for the middle class. By 2005, the number of North American passengers sailing on Cruise Lines International Association member ships was 11.1 million. The Caribbean region has 52 percent of the worldwide passenger capacity for cruises. Carnival Cruise Line is the largest cruise line, with nearly 40 percent of the Caribbean passenger capacity. Miami, Florida, serves as the busiest cruise ship port in the United States and has long been known as the "Cruise Capital of the World." More than three million cruise ship passengers pass through the Port of Miami every year. Travel agents are often specialists in selling fly/cruise packages that include airline tickets to the cruise port city.

Cruising with a theme is a growing trend. For example, country music-themed cruises may feature top singers and songwriters from Texas and Nashville. Other themes include Disney characters on family cruises and famous chefs teaching cooking classes. Children's activities are a high-growth area for cruise ships and include roller blading, rock climbing, snorkeling, foreign language classes, and video games. The cruise industry considers land-based entertainment centers such as Las Vegas as its competition.

Over Land

Economic need, national defense issues, and the love of the independence provided by private automobiles has spurred the impetus in the United States for the creation of the National Highway System and, in particular, the Eisenhower Interstate System. Proposed during the administration of President Eisenhower, the interstate system crisscrosses the United States from east to west and north to south, connecting states for commercial and private travel. Use of the interstate system is powered by fuel.

The price of fuel is a common denominator across the travel industry. It impacts all forms of transportation, from airlines to rental car companies. When fuel costs are high, fewer people can afford to travel and the economy slows down. Rental car companies are trying to offset the costs by offering hybrid cars that have both a gasoline-powered engine and an electric motor. The hybrid cars can often get up to 20 or 30 more miles per gallon than a standard car.

Photodisc

Rental car companies come in all sizes, from major corporations to small independents. They provide the link for travelers between airports and final destinations. Most rental car companies offer a similar product, so each company must struggle to differentiate itself from the competition. Customer service and price are the two biggest distinctions. The major factors in customer service are the speed, accuracy, and courtesy with which customers are handled. Customer loyalty programs also help keep customers coming back.

Rental car companies contract with airports for the privilege of running private shuttles that transport passengers to a central rental car location. Some airports limit the number of rental car companies that can drive their own shuttles through the airport, forcing customers of smaller rental car companies to use the time-consuming communal bus. Either way, the airport receives a fee for allowing access to the rental car company. Most airports require a guaranteed volume of business for a rental car company to have counter space within the airport. Rental car companies pass on the cost of leasing airport space to their customers, but the convenience is considered worth the cost.

Rental car companies have grown to provide service far outside the airport. Most major companies now have locations in or near car dealerships and retailers, as well as in suburbia, where insurance companies contract with them for temporary replacement cars for accident victims. The costs of doing business away from the airport are much lower and more within the control of the rental car agency. Airport fees add about 26 percent to the cost of renting a car.

Over the last 30 years, how has the target customer of cruise lines changed?

Stopover

LODGING

DISTRIBUTION

The lodging industry in the United States employs almost two million workers and generates over $13 billion in pretax profits, based on Smith Travel research. According to the American Hotel and Lodging Association (AH&LA), 48 percent of business travelers are female. About 40 percent of business travelers spend one night per trip in a hotel, 24 percent spend two nights, and 36 percent spend three or more nights. The typical business traveler makes reservations and pays about $91 per night. More and more business travelers are including family time on their trips. Hotels are making accommodations for these additional family travelers.

AH&LA describes typical leisure travelers as being two adults, ages 35–54, traveling by car, making their own reservations, and paying about $87 per night. Forty-seven percent of leisure travelers spend only one night per trip in a hotel. Almost 14 million travelers from outside the country visit the United States each year, and 53 percent of them are leisure travelers.

Front of the House

In the lodging industry, the places of contact with customers are called the **front of the house**. The front of the house includes all areas to which the public has access, such as the lobby, guest rooms, fitness center, meeting rooms, restaurants, and gift shop. People who work in these areas must exhibit enthusiasm and professionalism to have effective constant contact with the public. The front-desk agents who register guests and the bell-station employees who transport luggage set the tone for the hotel by welcoming customers to the property.

The **guest cycle** includes all the events that occur between the time a guest initially makes a reservation and finally checks out of the property. The front-desk agent is responsible for obtaining the information from the guest for the registration record, establishing credit for payment, attempting *upselling* by informing the guest about higher-quality rooms and services available, fulfilling the guest's special requests, and assigning a room.

Back of the House

Behind the scenes in a major hotel are all of the support personnel who keep the facility running. The areas out of the view of customers are called the **back of the house**. The behind-the-scenes positions include those of engineering/facilities staff who take care of the building and equipment, such as air-conditioning systems. The human resources (HR) department handles recruiting, hiring, training, compensation, benefits, employee evaluations, and separations and terminations from jobs. The accounting department keeps track of revenue, cash flows, and financial procedures. The sales and marketing department personnel work with meeting or event planners rather than individual guests. Others in the back of the house are security and loss-prevention personnel and information-technology and audio-visual staff. The security and loss-prevention personnel keep the hotel property and guests safe. The information-technology and audio-visual staff maintain all of the technology in the hotel.

What is the difference between the front of the house and the back of the house?

Stopover

_____

_____

MARKETING DESTINATIONS

Tours, resorts, and theme parks are some of the destinations for leisure travelers. Knowledge of target customers and focused promotional activities are necessary to attract tourists to a destination and draw repeat business.

On Tour

A **tour** is usually a guided or escorted travel product that bundles several elements, such as transportation, hotel room, sightseeing, admission to local attractions, and possibly meals. A **package** may include the same elements, with the exception of a tour guide. People who do not travel frequently or who are visiting an area for the first time may be more comfortable with a guided tour. Additionally, a tour guide can provide fascinating information about the destination that the individual tourist may miss.

SELLING

The cost of a tour or package can be less than the total cost of purchasing the individual products and services separately. Packages allow a travel agent to cross-sell to customers. **Cross-selling** means offering the additional products of a package to a customer who may have called to purchase only one element, such as a plane ticket. The customer may not have thought of purchasing all of the additional items, such as ground transportation, through the agent, or may not have known about the wonderful museum nearby. Both the customer and the travel agent benefit from cross-selling. The customer can have a more efficient trip with fewer worries, and the travel agent can make a larger profit from the client's entire trip. Some tours and packages are assembled for an individual client. Others are packaged by a national or international travel provider who has reached an agreement with all of the key players, such as the airline and the hotel.

Relaxing Resort

Resorts can be a whole city or a specific hotel that has a number of activities and leisure attractions, such as golf courses and spas. The intent of resorts is to provide the whole vacation experience in one place. Resorts that include conference centers provide a double benefit to business travelers. The conference attendee can add a personal weekend stay to the business trip and play a few rounds of golf.

When resorts overbuild or during low- or off-seasons, they sometimes have to broaden their target market in order to fill rooms. For example, an upscale resort originally designed for adults may try to attract families by adding supervised children's activities. The children's activities may run the gamut from swimming lessons to digging for fossils and can sometimes cost as much as the room. By adding activities for children, the hotel's intent is to target the parents who are attracted to the resort's adult appeal but who won't come without the kids.

By broadening their target market, some hotels may miss the mark on both customers—kids and parents. The Greenbrier in West Virginia is an upscale, five-diamond hotel with traditional standards. In the main dining room, the strict dress code requires no jeans at dinner, and males over the age of 10 must wear a coat and tie. Everyone is expected to dress up, no matter what their age. This kind of formal atmosphere may not be conducive to a fun time for children, even though The Greenbrier reportedly spent $260,000 renovating its Adventure Zone for kids.

Additionally, hotels that handle large conferences may find it difficult to please families and conference attendees at the same time. Finding a way to deal with difficult children may tax the hotel staff and budget, because the ratio of staff to children can be an important safety feature that parents will want to consider. Pleasing both adults and children may be a tough way to attract additional customers.

The Theme of It All

A theme park is an amusement park that has a specific motif or subject for its rides and attractions. Amusement parks measure their financial performance based on key indicators such as operating expenses, annual attendance, costs of capital or major equipment, cost of wages and salaries, and other expenses. Theme parks can have high costs and must continuously attract a large number of visitors to become and remain profitable.

Theme parks have copied new strategies from ski resorts to attract the mass affluent by offering premium tickets that provide special privileges. Premium ticket holders may skip long lines for rides or have special seating at shows. Most theme parks have a cap on the number of premium tickets they sell each day.

Stopover How is a tour different than a package?

_____

_____

Understand Marketing Concepts

Circle the best answer for each of the following questions.

1. Cross-selling means
    a. encouraging customers to purchase additional related products.
    b. using angry-sounding sales pitches.
    c. selling religious souvenirs.
    d. none of the above.

2. The guest cycle
    a. is found in the fitness center.
    b. is included in a package tour.
    c. is a discount room and meals.
    d. starts when a reservation is made.

Think Critically

Answer the following questions as completely as possible. If necessary, use a separate sheet of paper.

3. In what ways do hotel stays of the leisure traveler differ from those of the business traveler? Why is there a difference?

    _____

    _____

    _____

    _____

    _____

    _____

    _____

4. **Communication** You are a travel agent. A new travel customer wants to travel to Europe on a two-week trip. List products you might offer to the customer. Include an explanation of why you would offer each product.

    _____

    _____

    _____

    _____

    _____

    _____

    _____

    _____

    _____

Food and Hospitality

Goals

- Describe careers in food production.
- Discuss hospitality product/service life cycles.

All Aboard

Diners must plan two months in advance to obtain reservations for dinner at the French Laundry, located in the Napa Valley in Yountville, California. Even at two months in advance, a patron must begin calling at 10:00 A.M. Competition for the 17 tables is fierce, and all spaces are taken within an hour.

Once an actual laundry, the French Laundry is located in a 1900s stone building that is surrounded by a garden. *Mobil Travel Guide* ranks the restaurant as a five-star dining pleasure. Additionally, the restaurant has been recognized by two French hospitality associations and has received awards for international culinary excellence. The restaurant is known for its romantic ambience and luscious food.

Work with a group. List reasons why the French Laundry remains so successful. Discuss why ultra-premium customers will make restaurant reservations two months in advance.

TIME TO EAT

A major factor in how well people rate the enjoyment of a trip is the quality of the food they eat at their destination. People who are adventurous eaters with sophisticated tastes like to try new foods and seek out the best restaurants a location has to offer. Many restaurants that are off the beaten path serve the best local food at reasonable prices.

Photodisc

Culinary Arts

Just as with other travel and tourism businesses, restaurants must establish a target market. To remain profitable, they must continually please repeat customers while also attracting new customers. Restaurants need to have a steady local group of clients as well as visiting business or leisure travelers. The location of a restaurant in or near a convention center or tourist area can attract many one-time customers. The talents of the culinary artists keep the customers returning again and again. The **culinary arts** are the practice of selecting, combining, preparing, cooking, serving, and storing food and beverages.

Now We're Cooking

To become an *executive chef* in a well-known restaurant or hotel requires extensive training. The executive chef is responsible for the kitchen staff, menu planning, and all food purchasing, handling, production, and presentation. Deciding what to offer and having it available in the right quantity, at the right temperature, at the right time, and at the right place require vast amounts of planning.

Working directly under the executive chef, the *sous* (French for *under*) *chefs* assist in operating the kitchen. Depending on the size of the restaurant, there are generally additional levels of chefs who are in charge of specific types of food preparation. From creating a menu that will delight customers to placing the food on the serving dishes, chefs are in control of the success of any food-service operation.

Time Out

Local, county, or state departments of health perform periodic spot checks on food-service establishments to enforce the standards that prevent food-borne illnesses. More than 76 million people in the United States contract food-borne illnesses each year.

Describe the job of an executive chef.

_____

_____

Stopover

BEING HOSPITABLE

The hospitality industry, which includes hotels, restaurants, theme parks, and entertainment complexes, is impacted by the dynamic forces of an ever-changing marketplace. Global competition, technology, customer expectations, and consumer interests continually change. Just as with fashions, travel and tourism products and services fall in and out of favor. Customers may become bored with the same old vacation year after year and want to try something new.

Products and services have a life cycle. A **life cycle** begins at the time a product or service is introduced and lasts until it is no longer purchased. A life cycle generally progresses through four stages—introduction, growth, maturity, and decline.

1. **Introduction** When a new travel product or service is first introduced, many sellers create an excitement around the product or service to generate interest in it. For example, a new resort may give journalists and celebrities free air travel, rooms, and meals to attract them to the site and draw the attention of travelers to the glamour of the location. If the journalists and celebrities enjoy the resort and positive publicity is generated by their visits, the location may become the "in" place to be for those who follow trends.

2. **Growth** As the resort becomes known and larger numbers of people choose to vacation there, the business grows. If a resort is in a new area that is not fully developed and it becomes successful, other companies will want to open similar businesses in the same area. As competition picks up, the resort will need to add services and amenities to stay ahead of the competition. It may make a golf course available to guests or offer the services of a spa, based on the wants of the targeted customers. Promotion of the resort will be intense. Profits are generally at a peak during the growth period, if expenses are kept in line with the incoming revenue.

3. **Maturity** At some point, the growth of the resort peaks and the business is considered mature. Surrounding areas are built up with similar resorts offering the most popular features, and targeted customers are aware of the area. At this mature stage, competition becomes especially strong. Because all of the resorts are similar, price becomes the major competing factor.

4. **Decline** When consumers lose interest in the resort area, the final stage of the life cycle begins. Resorts fall into decline when income will not cover needed repairs and improvements, and some finally close.

Stopover Describe the maturity stage of the product life cycle.

_____

_____

Five-Star Traveler

PAM NICHOLSON

Pam Nicholson started behind the rental counter for Enterprise Rent-A-Car shortly after graduating from the University of Missouri. Soon she started to move up in management. Under her leadership, Enterprise grew from six offices on the West Coast to more than 300 locations throughout the United States.

Her success in California was rewarded with a promotion to corporate vice president, overseeing ten operating groups. Nicholson helped forge the first preferred-provider rental agreements with automakers, and Enterprise opened offices at automobile dealerships across the United States.

After 15 years with Enterprise, Nicholson is now executive vice president and chief operating officer, overseeing more than 45,000 employees and 500,000 rental cars in 4,500 locations. She believes the company will continue to succeed because Enterprise treats customers right.

THINK CRITICALLY

How has Pam Nicholson helped Enterprise Rent-A-Car become successful? What has she done to keep her career on track and moving toward upper management?

Understand Marketing Concepts

Circle the best answer for each of the following questions.

1. A sous chef
   a. is a French fry cook.
   b. is an assistant to the executive chef.
   c. waits on tables.
   d. is none of the above.

2. The four stages of the product life cycle are
   a. five star, four star, three star, and two star.
   b. hotels, resorts, spas, and theme parks.
   c. introduction, growth, maturity, and decline.
   d. planning, distribution, price, and advertising.

Think Critically

Answer the following questions as completely as possible. If necessary, use a separate sheet of paper.

3. Assume you are the owner/manager of a new restaurant. What steps would you take to ensure its success?

   _____

   _____

   _____

   _____

   _____

   _____

   _____

4. Why do people lose interest in a travel product or service over time? What can be done to slow or prevent a decline in customer interest?

   _____

   _____

   _____

   _____

   _____

   _____

   _____

Review Marketing Concepts

Write the letter of the term that matches each definition. Some terms will not be used.

_____ 1. Part ownership of a property, with access to it for a period of time each year based on the percentage of ownership

_____ 2. The process of gathering and using information about potential customers

_____ 3. The degree to which the service meets the needs and expectations of the customer

_____ 4. The percentage of business received compared to the total market

_____ 5. Begins at the time a product or service is introduced and lasts until it is no longer purchased

_____ 6. The variety of products and services offered

_____ 7. Offering additional related products to the customer

_____ 8. In the lodging industry, the places of contact with customers

_____ 9. The way a service is paid for

a. back of the house
b. cross-selling
c. culinary arts
d. exchange model
e. fractional ownership model
f. front of the house
g. guest cycle
h. life cycle
i. market share
j. marketing research
k. package
l. product mix
m. product/service planning
n. service marketing
o. service quality
p. tour

Circle the best answer.

10. A package may include all *except*
    a. transportation.
    b. a hotel room.
    c. access to local attractions.
    d. a tour guide.

11. Which of the following is *not* an activity performed at the "back of the house"?
    a. hiring employees
    b. keeping the property and guests safe
    c. transporting luggage
    d. maintaining heating and cooling systems

12. All the events that occur between the time a guest initially makes a reservation and finally checks out of the property make up
    a. the life cycle.
    b. the guest cycle.
    c. the front of the house.
    d. none of these.

Think Critically

13. Your mid-level-priced hotel wants to attract multiple generations of leisure travelers and is willing to add amenities to do so. You currently attract mostly business travelers. What would you add to your current product mix? Why?

_____

_____

_____

_____

14. You want to make sure your restaurant is providing the level of service quality stated in your written standards. How would you go about measuring the quality of service?

_____

_____

_____

_____

15. Why would cruise lines consider landlocked Las Vegas as competition? What can they do to attract customers away from Las Vegas?

_____

_____

_____

_____

_____

16. Your hotel wants to serve business conferences as well as families on vacation. The two groups do not mix well. Make a list of how to accommodate both groups.

_____

_____

_____

_____

17. Your hotel must cut costs in order to lower room prices, but it does not want to lose service quality. Make a list of cost-cutting alternatives. From the list, choose one as the best way to cut costs and explain why it is the best.

_____

_____

_____

_____

Make Connections

18. **Research** You are the manager of a budget hotel that is used by business travelers. You want to add quality amenities while keeping room rates low. Design a survey for your guests that you can use to determine what additional amenities they would find appealing.

_____

_____

_____

19. **Geography** You are a travel agent with a new client who wants to see exotic animals in their natural settings. The customer wants to feel safe in a location that has a pleasant climate. Use the Internet to find and describe the location you would recommend.

_____

_____

_____

_____

20. **Communication** Your cruise line's target customers are adults, ages 21 to 35. List five amenities you would offer to this age group, and give the reasons for your selections. Describe features of a web site that you would use to promote the selected amenities.

_____

_____

_____

_____

21. **Marketing Math** Your airline is examining the cost of all amenities in the product mix offered. A package of peanuts costs your airline $.03 per package. Each day, 365 days per year, 250,000 passengers are given one bag of peanuts, and 23,000 ask for a second bag. What is the yearly cost of the peanuts?

_____

_____

_____

_____

22. Research Develop a few questions to ask people who are over age 35 about the services they want from an airline. How much extra are they willing to pay for each service? Survey five people and compile the results on a spreadsheet.

_____

_____

_____

_____

_____

23. History What economic events took place in the 1920s and 1930s that impacted the economy? Use the Internet and research that era's economic climate. Write one page about how these events might have impacted travel and tourism.

_____

_____

_____

_____

_____

_____

_____

_____

EXTENDED STAY

Project Review the All Aboard feature about Soap Lake at the beginning of Lesson 6.1.

Work with a group and complete the following activities.

1. Search the Internet for the Soap Lake Chamber of Commerce. Review the information available on the web site. Read about the giant lava lamp project.

2. Work with your team to develop a list of products and services that would enhance Soap Lake as a tourist attraction. Describe your target market for the products and services.

3. List economical promotions you would use to make the target market aware of Soap Lake.

4. Create a brochure for your target market that you would send to travel suppliers to share with potential customers.

ORLANDO THEME PARKS COMPETE FOR TOURIST DOLLARS

Orlando, Florida, is well known for conventions and tourism. Disney and Universal Orlando Resort offer multiple theme parks for visitors to enjoy. Families flock to Orlando to enjoy the theme parks, while adding millions of dollars to the area's economy. Theme parks must consider competition, the latest themes, and special events in order to maximize ticket sales. They must also plan for "shoulder periods"—transitional times between peak and off-peak periods in the tourist calendar.

Disney and Universal both realize that rides and attractions must be updated to current movie themes and technology to hold consumer interest. An increasing attitude of "been there, done that" prevails as more families take their children to theme parks at young ages.

Disney World has celebrated a history of innovation to entertain individuals of all ages. The Magic Kingdom, MGM Studios, and Epcot offer something for everyone. Disney realizes that it is not the only game in town with competition from nearby Universal Orlando Resort as well as Sea World.

Theme parks must advertise heavily to attract their target customers. Disney's commercial following the Super Bowl asked the most valuable player what he was going to do now, and he replied, "I'm going to Disney World!" Disney has decided to no longer continue this advertisement because it did not reap the desired results.

Universal Orlando Resort differentiates its theme parks as being more attractive for adults. Universal prefers to use edgier themes for its attractions and commercials. Recent Universal commercials highlight how corporate America enjoys employees who do not fully use their vacation days. A funeral director in one of the commercials compliments workers who do not relax and take vacations.

Prices for theme parks have steadily increased. Families must make a sizable budget commitment to pay $60 for a one-day park pass. To encourage family attendance, special deals are offered to multiple ticket purchasers, such as buy four two-day passes and get one free.

To attract local residents, theme parks have developed annual ticket packages, discounts for low seasons, and unique activities for special occasions such as Halloween, Mardi Gras, and high school senior trips.

THINK CRITICALLY

1. Why must theme parks constantly add new attractions and remove older attractions?
2. Which resort is more attractive for adults—Disney or Universal? Why?
3. What is a *shoulder period*?
4. Why do theme parks offer special family deals and annual ticket packages?

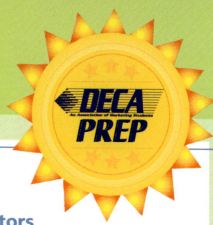

TRAVEL AND TOURISM MARKETING MANAGEMENT TEAM DECISION MAKING

During the period between the week of the New Year's holiday and the spring break season, Universal Orlando Resort has a shoulder period of moderate park attendance. In order to attract more people to the parks, Universal's marketing executives would like to introduce special-event weekends. They would also like to create some attractive packages that would encourage visitors to spend several days, rather than just one or two days, at the resort. The longer visitors are within the resort, the more they spend on food, drinks, and souvenirs. The special events and packages will need unique promotion.

You and a partner have been hired by Universal Orlando Resort to devise ideas for special-event weekends and packages during the shoulder period. The events should correspond with special occasions such as President's Day, Valentine's Day, Mardi Gras, and the Daytona 500. Packages should attract adults, families, and schools.

You and your partner must describe the target market, present suggestions for the special-event weekends, develop package deals, and describe effective marketing and advertising strategies.

You will have 30 minutes to develop your proposal, ten minutes to present it to Universal's marketing executives (the judges), and five minutes to field questions.

Performance Indicators Evaluated

- Identify the target market for Universal Orlando Resort.
- Describe the special weekend events for January and February.
- Demonstrate an understanding of packaging ticket prices for longer periods of time.
- Develop a marketing strategy for shoulder-period weekends at Universal Orlando Resort.
- Describe the advertising campaign for Universal Orlando Resort.

Go to the DECA web site for more detailed information.

THINK CRITICALLY

1. Why must theme parks such as Universal Orlando Resort develop special weekend events and packages during shoulder periods?
2. Describe the target markets for these special events and packages.
3. Would it be effective to advertise to schools for Universal's special-event weekends? Why or why not?
4. Could an educational conference be combined with fun at a theme park? Explain your answer.

www.deca.org

Travel Marketing Research

Photodisc

CHAPTER 7 · CHAPTER 7 · CHAPTER 7 · CHAPTER 7

7

Point Your Browser

▶ ▶ ▶ ▶   **travel.swlearning.com**

Winning Strategies

D.K. Shifflet & Associates Ltd.

Before investors are willing to risk large sums of money to start a travel and tourism business, they want to know that it has an excellent chance of succeeding. The investors want to know that a market exists for the products or services that will be offered. They want to know who the competitors are and what they have to offer. All of this information is provided by marketing research firms like D.K. Shifflet & Associates Ltd. (DKS&A).

DKS&A is a leading provider of travel and tourism market information to both public and private organizations. The U.S. Bureau of Economic Analysis and the Commerce Department use data from DKS&A, as do many of the industry's professional associations, such as the American Hotel & Lodging Association. Name-brand hotels, theme parks, investment bankers, and car rental companies use marketing research firms like DKS&A as well.

DKS&A provides information about market trends and current and projected data on travelers' behavior, which helps investors determine the potential for a return on their investment. In addition, DKS&A helps its clients use the information to make data-driven decisions by providing interpretations of the data.

THINK CRITICALLY

1. How could information from DKS&A help people who are considering starting a new travel and tourism business?

2. Why is it important to know what your competitors are doing?

Analyzing the Market

Goals

Describe the marketing research process.

Explain targeting of market segments and niche markets.

All Aboard

While many major, full-service airlines were cutting services, Primaris Airlines was just starting up. It ordered 40 new Boeing aircraft—20 737-800 jets and 20 7E7 Dreamliners. It planned to offer only business-class service between New York and other major U.S. cities. Primaris was basing its new business model on marketing data that indicated a specific need in a niche market. Primaris is building its airline around budget-conscious business travelers. It has researched what the business traveler really wants and intends to provide it on every flight. Primaris has selected its target customers, researched their needs and wants, and designed its products and services around those customers.

All of Primaris's seats are in "professional class." All seats have outlets for computers and high-speed Internet connections. Prices run below those of economy seats on other airlines. Travelers are able to bring unlimited carry-on luggage aboard, preselect a meal, and decide when they want it to be served. Primaris also offers repeat customers a loyalty-reward program.

Work with a group. Research the current status of Primaris Airlines. Is it able to actually fulfill all of its promises? How will Primaris know if customers are pleased with its service?

RESEARCHING THE MARKET

MARKETING–INFORMATION MANAGEMENT

It is too costly to create a tourism product that customers don't want. It is even more costly to alienate customers because the company does not know they are unhappy or why they are not buying. Marketing research involves staying tuned in to customers by setting standards, measuring if the standards are being met, and asking how to improve.

The Process

Marketing research is a process used to determine what customers want and to benchmark performance within the industry. **Benchmarks** are standards that define the desired performance. Businesses and convention and visitors bureaus (CVBs) are held accountable for reaching the benchmarks set for them. The owners, investors, or, in the case of CVBs, the public want to know that the organization is being run effectively and is providing the greatest return on investment possible.

The marketing research process involves collecting, organizing, and analyzing data and using the data to make decisions. For example, an airline might want to know if meals aboard long flights are demanded enough that customers are willing to pay extra for them. The customers can be surveyed and the results used to make the decision to offer or not offer meals.

Measuring Performance

Marketing research can be used to measure performance against benchmarks established by the International Association of Convention and Visitors Bureaus' Performance Measurement Team. During the development of the CVB benchmarks, two important marketing research questions were repeatedly asked.

- Are we measuring the right things?

- Are we measuring things right?

The CVB benchmarks were established to standardize the definitions of industry terms and performance measurement so that CVBs could be compared to one another. The standard data were needed to provide credibility to information given to CVB boards and the communities about the success of the publicly funded CVBs.

The mission of CVBs focuses on two areas—convention sales and travel trade sales. The convention sales mission is "to generate visitors, visitor spending, and economic impact" through events and conventions. *Economic impact* is the total of both direct spending by the visitors and indirect spending that results from the convention, such as food purchased by restaurants to feed the visitors. The travel trade sales mission is "to increase leisure visitor volume, visitor spending, and economic impact through promotion and distribution of the destination's travel products to the travel trade." **Travel trade** refers to any individual or company that creates and/or markets tours and/or independent packages. It includes tour operators, travel agents, individual travel planners, and online travel companies.

The two target groups, convention visitors and leisure visitors, are measured separately with different performance measures. **Performance measures** are references that define and quantify the results of the CVB activity. For example, a performance measure could be the number of confirmed conventions booked in the city's convention center due to the efforts of the CVB. Other performance measures that CVBs could use are

- the estimated and actual number of hotel rooms booked for each convention

- the estimated and actual number of attendees at a convention

- the number of conventions that were bid

- the number of conventions bid but lost

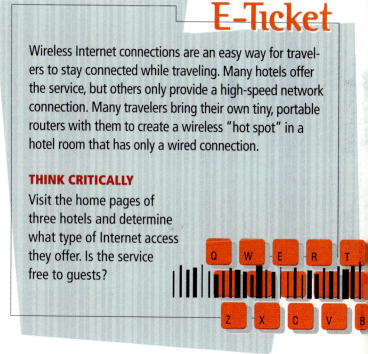

E-Ticket

Wireless Internet connections are an easy way for travelers to stay connected while traveling. Many hotels offer the service, but others only provide a high-speed network connection. Many travelers bring their own tiny, portable routers with them to create a wireless "hot spot" in a hotel room that has only a wired connection.

THINK CRITICALLY

Visit the home pages of three hotels and determine what type of Internet access they offer. Is the service free to guests?

A **bid** is a written proposal submitted to a convention planner that includes dates, costs, and blocks of hotel rooms. Keeping data on the conventions that were bid but lost to another city is critical to improving performance, the objective of performance measures.

Stopover What is a performance measure?

_____

_____

MARKET SEGMENTS

PRODUCT/SERVICE MANAGEMENT

Within the mass markets, there are market segments of people grouped by demographics and other characteristics. Specific travel businesses choose a market segment as a target. Travel products are created for the market segment once research has been conducted to determine what consumers within the segment want and need.

On Target

According to the Association of Travel Market Executives, there are three major marketing categories of leisure travelers—getaway/family travelers, adventurous/educational travelers, and gamblers/fun travelers.

©Getty Images/PhotoDisc

Getaway/Family Travelers tend to visit locations that are child-friendly, places where friends and family live, and laid-back areas known for rest, relaxation, and scenic views. They look for popular destinations with clean air, no congestion, and a variety of accommodations and restaurants.

Adventurous/Educational Travelers want to experience historical sites, museums, theaters, and cultural activities. Most will visit well-known places with excellent dining opportunities and a variety of hotels and amenities.

Gamblers/Fun Travelers want to vacation in areas with lots of nightlife, gambling, recreation, or outdoor activities. They are often budget-conscious travelers.

Focusing on one of these groups allows travel suppliers to create products and/or services that please the targeted customer. Each of these three major marketing groups may be further divided based on characteristics such as income, religion, or location of residence. For example, gamblers/fun travelers who live in Las Vegas would probably vacation somewhere else.

Focusing on a Niche

Groups of travelers can be further identified by their tastes and lifestyles. A small, specific group is often referred to as a **niche market**. Niche travel can be separated by category, such as travel for couples, honeymoon travel, or heritage travel. Niche markets can also be based on age and income. For example, Generation Xers—the 60 million people in the United States between the ages of 25 and 40—are a group of great interest to the travel industry. Information from travel research firm D.K. Shifflet & Associates shows that Xers are rapidly increasing the amount they spend on vacations. This group is smaller than the baby boomers but is likely to spend more per trip. Xers are less likely to call a travel agent, less likely to plan in advance, and more likely to add on extras. An extra such as an expedition to a mountaintop or desert can add about $300 to the original trip.

Destinations are designed to address a major mass market group or a niche market group. A boutique hotel is designed for a niche market and is generally small, with fewer than 150 rooms. A boutique hotel usually has distinct architecture, first-class service, and affluent customers. By focusing on a specific customer group, a hotel can provide the level of service customers want for the price they expect to pay.

Time Out

The United States is the second most visited destination for travelers from Chile. Chileans like the United States because of its excellent tourism infrastructure, entertainment, shopping, and recreational activities.

Stopover

What is a niche market?

_____

_____

Photodisc

Understand Marketing Concepts

Circle the best answer for each of the following questions.

1. The economic impact of convention travel is
   a. not an important factor.
   b. the total of direct and indirect spending by visitors.
   c. focused on the environment.
   d. none of the above.

2. Benchmarks are
   a. used in setting up parks.
   b. created to promote travel.
   c. standards that define desired performance.
   d. goals that are impossible for a business to meet.

Think Critically

Answer the following questions as completely as possible. If necessary, use a separate sheet of paper.

3. Review the CVB mission for travel trade sales. Why is it important to collect data on visitor volume and economic impact?

_____

_____

_____

_____

_____

_____

4. **Communication** Write three paragraphs—one each—to describe (a) getaway/family travelers, (b) adventurous/educational travelers, and (c) gamblers/fun travelers.

_____

_____

_____

_____

_____

_____

_____

_____

_____

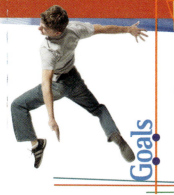

Collecting Data with Technology

Goals

- Describe data collection processes.
- Explain the need for data protection.

All Aboard

smartFocus Intelligent Marketing offers its clients the ability to gain a greater knowledge and understanding of their customers. smartFocus provides daily updates about how customers are reacting to up-selling and cross-selling campaigns.

smartFocus software promotes the acquisition of new customers, the retention of existing customers, and the growth of more profitable relationships with customers, which in turn provides more return on marketing expenditures. The software helps turn information into insight on what influences customers and helps predict consumer behavior. The software provides a full view of the consumer through the sales cycle, from potential customer to repeat customer.

Work in a group. Discuss the collection of data to enhance customer service. How can data help businesses better serve customers?

UNDERSTANDING TRAVELERS

MARKETING-INFORMATION MANAGEMENT

The rapid growth of travel and tourism and the need for accurate information on travelers' habits have prompted the industry to enhance and improve research methods. One focus of research is customer behavior. Focusing marketing efforts toward the right consumers requires knowing all about them. Collecting data about travelers has become a precise study of every detail of their experience.

Big Business Is Watching

A traveler driving through a major city may observe an electronic sign on the highway indicating that at 8:05 A.M. the travel time to the next major highway interchange is about 15 minutes. That information

Photodisc

is collected from data transmitted from cars with automatic toll-road passes. The passes are electronic transmitters that mount on the windshield of a car. Drivers purchase the toll-road passes to provide prepaid automated toll payments, allowing fast passage through toll collection points. The devices also transmit a signal that is collected at points along highways (both toll and non-toll), which is used to estimate the travel time posted on the electronic signs. Data are also collected about the number of vehicles using the roadways. The information is used for metropolitan traffic management and infrastructure decisions, such as when expansions are needed.

Air bag sensors, which were first installed in cars in the 1970s, collect information about seat belt usage and the speed and condition of the vehicle immediately before and after a crash. The collection of other data, like the location of the car, was an easy next step.

Land-based vehicles can also be tracked by a global positioning system (GPS). A GPS uses satellite-based technology to track vehicles' locations and speeds. GPS was originally intended for military applications, but in the 1980s the government made the system available for civilian use. A GPS works in any weather conditions, anywhere in the world, 24 hours a day. Car rental agencies and commercial transportation companies use GPSs to keep track of their vehicles. If the GPS indicates that a renter drove in excessive speeds or out of state when the driver shouldn't have, the rental company may charge the violator extra fees. A California law requires car dealers and car rental agencies to inform drivers when a GPS is being used on their rented vehicles. In New York, car rental agencies are restricted from using a GPS to track drivers and charge extra fees. In Connecticut, Acme Rent-A-Car was banned by court action from fining rental car users $150 for speeding. The charge had been automatically placed on customers' credit cards without prior notice.

Missing the Boat

The travel industry in the Caribbean island nation of Dominica has been accused of perpetuating a false story to encourage tourism. Dominica has a primarily undeveloped, pristine environment that reportedly contributes to the longevity of its people. The tourism industry reported that as many as 17 out of the 70,000 residents are over the age of 100. This would mean that Dominica has one of the highest concentrations of centenarians (people over the age of 100) per 1,000 people in the world.

At one point, a 128-year-old female resident of Dominica, named Elizabeth "Pampo" Israel, was thought to be the world's oldest living human being. The *Wall Street Journal* reported that, according to L. Stephen Coles, a co-founder of Gerontology Research Group, "Her ripe old age was 'a falsehood perpetrated by the tourism industry.'"

THINK CRITICALLY

1. What should be done to prevent the tourism industry from deceiving consumers? Who should protect tourists from false information and why?

2. Why would a country's travel industry want potential tourists to think its residents live to be centenarians? Discuss your opinion with others.

Keeping Track

Travel and tourism businesses electronically collect data about travelers and use the information to make decisions. Customers must provide personal information to travel suppliers when making travel arrangements. For example, travelers purchasing airline tickets through a travel agency may be asked to provide their name, address, phone number, and credit card number. The data are usually stored electronically and accessed the next time the customer transacts business with the agency. The agency may share the information with other suppliers in order to complete the requested travel arrangements. For example, the information may be transferred to a global distribution system. A **global distribution system (GDS)** is a computer reservation system jointly used by airlines and travel suppliers in many countries.

Collecting Cookies

When a travel consumer visits web sites or makes purchases online, a small piece of data from the visited web site, called a **cookie**, is stored on the consumer's computer. It is used to track the consumer's movements on the web site. The collected information is used for marketing purposes, such as tracking if the customer was referred to the site from another web site.

Temporary cookies terminate when the user closes the web browser, while others remain on the user's computer. The *permanent cookies* let the originating web site know that the user is a repeat visitor when the user visits the site again. They may also track a visitor's movement to other web sites. The cookies send data to the originator's site about customers' visits to help build user profiles. The collected information is usually general information that is not linked to a specific person.

Photodisc

Shopping the Competition

A long-used method of collecting data about competitors is to actually use the competitors' products and services and note the differences. It is a good way to find out whether competitors have matched or exceeded a business's offerings at a similar price.

In the lodging industry, a hotel employee, an individual hired to collect data, or a travel and tourism journalist may act as a business traveler and stay in competing hotels. In one such case, the traveler spent the first night in a recently renovated Omni Hotel. The second night was spent in a relatively new Marriott Hotel. Both were full-service hotels, and the traveler paid exactly the same price for a room at each hotel. The traveler noted differences in the features of the two mid-level, full-service hotels.

Satisfaction Factors	Omni	Marriott
Prompt, courteous staff	YES	YES
Reservation as requested	YES	YES
Upgraded mattress and bedding	YES	NO
Quiet, clean room	YES	YES
Linens folded in clever ways	YES	NO
Free in-room coffee service	One four-cup pot; additional cup $1.50	YES
Spacious tub/shower	YES	NO
Free Internet connection	YES	NO – $9.95
Newspaper delivered to room	YES	YES
After-stay satisfaction survey	YES, e-mailed	YES, slipped under door

Information such as this is valuable to both Omni and Marriott. Omni can use this information to advertise services that Marriott doesn't provide. Marriott can use this information to improve its level of services.

How Are We Doing?

PRODUCT/SERVICE MANAGEMENT

Hotels that are interested in continuous improvement can request feedback and collect data from guests through satisfaction surveys. The hotels can see what they are doing right and what needs improvement. An Omni survey sent by e-mail to recent guests included questions such as

- What was the purpose of the visit?

- Was the reservation accurate?

- Who made the reservation?

- How was the reservation made?

Additionally, the survey asked for ratings from "extremely satisfied to extremely not satisfied" on several quality factors such as cleanliness, shower pressure, temperature control, bath amenities, room smell, and work space. The survey asked customers to compare Omni to hotels where they had recently stayed. The survey assured customers that the information would be used toward the continuous improvement of services offered.

Why do travel and tourism businesses collect personal data from travelers?

_____

_____

RESPECTING PRIVACY

MARKETING – INFORMATION MANAGEMENT

Any data that can identify a specific individual is considered **personal data**. Protecting the personal data of consumers is a major concern. It has been a focus of worldwide efforts, prompting the passage of laws in many countries. In the United States, these laws are called *privacy laws*. In Europe, they are called *data protection laws*. The laws are intended to govern how businesses process personal data.

Data Protection

Collecting and converting data into usable information is referred to as **data processing**. The European Union has issued the *European Community Directive on Data Protection* that outlines how companies may collect, use, and transfer information that is identifiable to an individual. If customer data are not protected from unauthorized use, the damage to customers can be extremely detrimental, and it may take the business years to overcome the negative results.

Data protection includes creating backup files in the event that the original data files are lost as a result of viruses, hardware failure, or human error. It also includes preventing criminal access to the files. Travel retailers who sell products and services generally accept credit cards as payment. Both Visa and MasterCard have rigorous programs to ensure that their merchant clients take steps to protect retail customers from theft of personal data. Clients that do not comply lose the right to accept the credit cards from customers.

Bank of America discovered that tapes containing personal information on about 1.2 million customers were missing. The files included the personal data of 60 U.S. senators. As a result, there was a call for more oversight and laws regulating who can collect, store, and use personal information. There are already laws in California, Texas, and Vermont that allow consumers the ability to prevent access to their credit information without their permission. Additional states are considering the adoption of similar laws. The intent is to prevent identity thieves from using stolen information to open new credit card accounts or access current lines of credit. Further, the laws require companies to notify customers if unauthorized users have accessed their personal data. Interest in passing federal legislation that would standardize protection across the United States gained momentum after a series of data security breaches, including the Bank of America incident.

Time Out

Federal employees use the U.S. government's SmartPay card to pay for business travel. Benefits to the government include reduced administrative expenses, negotiated discount rates with travel suppliers, and an end to advance travel costs.

Marketing Myths

The U.S. government requires that employees of many of its departments, such as the Department of Defense, use a SmartPay card to pay for all business travel expenses. The card provides access to City Pairs, a program that offers reduced-price airline tickets. To be issued a SmartPay card, individuals must provide their social security number and other personal data, such as name and address. The cards are issued through banks, and the people receiving them are assured through advertising and sales presentations that their personal data are secure. The customers trust that the banks can keep their information secure.

In 2005, however, Bank of America admitted that tapes containing the personal information of about 1.2 million SmartPay customers were either lost or stolen. The loss of the tapes potentially exposed the personal data to misuse and identity theft.

THINK CRITICALLY

1. Should Bank of America customers trust the bank's promotional efforts in the future? Why or why not?

2. Is it a myth that all advertising is truthful? Discuss your opinion with others.

Consumer Protection

A number of U.S. and international laws are intended to protect individuals from misuse of their personal data. The laws in many countries impose criminal penalties, including fines and imprisonment, for failure to comply with privacy legislation.

U.S. companies with operations in Europe need to be familiar with European Union (EU) legislation that dictates how they must handle personal data from European customers. The European Commission developed wording to be included in contracts between EU and non-EU companies to ensure that data are protected when being transferred from one company to another. The EU pressured the United States to enact similar laws.

In order to improve U.S. compliance with EU privacy laws while minimizing the risk to U.S. businesses of penalties for violations, the United States entered into a Safe Harbor Agreement with the European Union. The wording required in contractual clauses was worked out between the EU and the U.S. Department of Commerce so that the clauses were acceptable to both groups. Participating U.S. businesses must register with the U.S. Department of Commerce and agree to comply with the Safe Harbor Codes. Compliance with the Safe Harbor Codes assures EU organizations that the businesses provide adequate privacy protection. The participating businesses are subject to enforcement actions only by U.S. regulators.

Stopover Why must travel and tourism businesses protect customer data?

_____

_____

Understand Marketing Concepts

Circle the best answer for each of the following questions.

1. Marketing information is collected
   a. by computer.
   b. through surveys.
   c. through web sites.
   d. by all of the above.

2. A cookie is a
   a. monster in a theme park.
   b. voice mail system.
   c. planning tool.
   d. small piece of data stored on a computer.

Think Critically

Answer the following questions as completely as possible. If necessary, use a separate sheet of paper.

3. How can hotels know how they are performing compared to their competition? What kinds of information should they seek? How can they use the information?

_____

_____

_____

_____

_____

_____

4. If you were the manager of the Marriott Hotel featured in the table on page 166, how would you use the information collected by the traveler? What changes would you make in your hotel if you were trying to improve its services?

_____

_____

_____

_____

_____

_____

Managing Marketing Information

Define marketing-information management.

Describe the uses of marketing information.

All Aboard

Blizzard Internet Marketing, Inc. is a firm that provides Internet marketing services to the hospitality industry. It uses technology to track the effectiveness of online marketing campaigns. The tracking is performed through the client hotel's web site, as well as through web sites with booking search engines that refer customers.

The information obtained by tracking customers can be converted into reports and analyzed. The data can indicate if a visitor started at a banner ad, an e-mail campaign, or a search engine. If at a search engine, then the search terms used to bring up the hotel's listing are indicated. The resulting reservation can be tied back to the visitor's starting point. This information is collected and reported to determine the effectiveness of each specific type of promotional campaign.

Work with a group. Discuss why a hotel would want to know the path a visitor used to get to its web site. What kinds of decisions might the hotel make using this information?

INFORMATION SYSTEMS

After data are collected, they must be stored and analyzed for use in decision making about the direction of the business. Many activities must be

Digital Vision

coordinated. Connecting all of the data functions—collecting, storing, reporting, analyzing, and using—forms a system of managing the marketing information. An effective marketing-information management system will provide information about the needs and wants of customers or business performance measures in a user-friendly way that is accurate, rapid, inexpensive, and useful in making decisions.

Reporting Data

Most data today are collected and stored electronically. The data are organized and reformulated into reports that are usable by decision makers. Because data are quickly out of date, electronic technology is used to sort and configure reports expediently to the specification of the reader. If an airline wants to compare the total on-line ticket sales made directly to consumers to the total ticket sales made through travel agencies over the last three months, a report of this data can be quickly configured so that the information is precisely as the user wants it. If a second report is needed based on ticket prices or outbound city of origin, technology can be used to pull information from the original set of sales data, re-sort it, and print the new report.

By reporting information using graphics, such as bar charts, pie charts, and line graphs, the data relationships can instantly become clear to the reader. For example, a hotel may report actual bookings and forecast bookings as shown in the bar chart below. Note that actual bookings in January, February, and April exceeded forecast bookings, whereas actual bookings in March fell short of goal. Providing information about actual results compared to the goals of the business can help decision makers know if new action plans are needed.

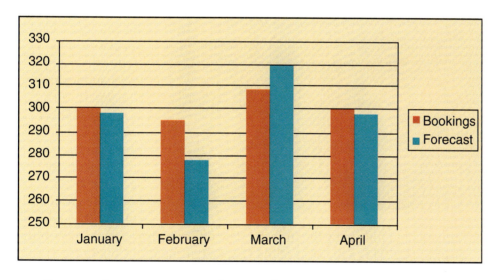

One popular way to present data is referred to as a *dashboard,* because graphs are presented in a row or group resembling the gauges and dials of an automobile. The goals of the business, such as the percentage of occupancy in a hotel, can be represented on a dial like a speedometer and the daily or monthly actual occupancy shown by the arrow point. The graphs are created from data pulled through the information system and may be updated daily or even hourly for managers to review—as often as new information is entered into the system. Whatever the format for the reporting of information, it must be meaningful to the people who use it to make decisions.

Analyzing Data

Describing, summarizing, and comparing data in a systematic way is referred to as **data analysis**. By converting the collected data into usable information, patterns of traveler behavior emerge and can be used to predict trends, including growth areas for the travel industry. More than two-thirds of adults say they have traveled in the last year. Forty percent of those who book travel through web sites say they make all of their own travel arrangements online. These statistics indicate growth in a worldwide industry and, together with other statistics, may drive the decision for a travel business to have a greater presence on the Web. Using information like this to make decisions about the business means making *data-driven decisions*.

Measuring Travel

Travel and tourism has a major impact on the U.S. economy, being the largest industry in 29 states. Approximately seven million people in the United States are employed in travel and tourism industry jobs. Travel and tourism jobs are positions in businesses that have direct contact with

Photodisc

travel and tourism consumers. An estimated additional ten million people are employed in businesses indirectly affected by travel and tourism consumers, such as airline caterers, aircraft and cruise ship manufacturers, and government agencies.

Many groups collect travel and tourism data for use by the industry. The Office of Travel and Tourism Industries (OTTI) is a division of the U.S. Department of Commerce. It collects and maintains information based on inbound and outbound travelers. **Inbound travelers** are nonresident visitors arriving in a region or country. **Outbound travelers** are residents traveling outside the region or country.

Measuring the growth of the travel industry requires information about travelers and travel and tourism businesses that can be compared from year to year. Measures of growth are based on the number and types of travelers, the number of people employed in related businesses, and the amount of money travelers spend.

Growth in the industry is also measured by how much money visitors spend on services, such as transportation, meals, lodging, and entertainment. The expenditures are categorized by the type of visitor, such as spending by inbound travelers, outbound travelers, and business travelers.

Time Out

In 2003, residents of the United Kingdom made 151 million overnight trips within the UK and spent more than £26.4 billion (approximately $50 billion).

Name three categories of information used to measure growth in the travel and tourism industry.

_____

_____

USING DATA

By knowing about their customers' wants and needs, businesses can more effectively satisfy their customers. If reliable data have been collected and reported, data-driven decisions can be made.

Effectively Managing with Data

PRICING

As consumers increasingly use the Internet to reserve travel services, travel and tourism suppliers have a greater need to maintain accurate and timely information. Hotels connected to online booking sites must keep an ever-changing inventory of available rooms. Additionally, changes in room rates must be managed, because the laws of supply and demand drive the rates charged for rooms. The **law of supply** indicates that when the price of a product or service increases, more will be produced. When the price decreases, less will be produced. When hotels are staying fully occupied at high prices, more hotels will be built in the area. When hotels are sitting empty and rooms are inexpensive, no additional hotels will be built. The **law of demand** indicates that when the price of a product increases, there will be less demand for the product. Inversely, when the price decreases, there will be more demand. As a hotel becomes more fully occupied, the room rates are raised, and the demand for rooms will slow.

Effectively managing the availability of rooms and prices in real time requires instant access to data and reports. Hotel managers must know how many rooms are booked and the price for each booked room. They also need information about what is going on in the surrounding area and what happened in past years, for comparison over time.

Data-Driven Decisions

MARKETING-INFORMATION MANAGEMENT

Basing decisions on data can help determine the success of a business. Use of the data can be as simple as checking the number of room reservations at a hotel for the upcoming weeks and using that information to schedule employees. If the hotel does not have many reservations, the part-time staff can be scheduled for fewer hours. If the hotel is fully booked, the hotel needs to be fully staffed to offer the expected level of service. The hotel's restaurant also needs the information to estimate the amount of food supplies to order.

More complex decisions can be based on data from a number of sources. Deciding to start a new airline or build an additional hotel is a highly complex decision requiring information about existing businesses, the economy in general, predictions for growth, and the costs of actually implementing the new business. Gathering all of the required information may involve spending a great deal of money.

Understanding relationships of data, interpreting the meaning of data, and using the data to forecast consumer behavior and improve desired products and services are the reasons for managing information. Providing the needed information to executives, managers, and other workers can help them make smart decisions and quickly respond to changing conditions.

Stopover

Provide an example of the laws of supply and demand.

_____

_____

Five-Star Traveler

JAFAR JAFARI

Jafar Jafari earned his bachelor's degree in Cornell University's well-respected hotel management program. Soon afterward, he realized that the day-to-day operation of a hotel was not the ideal career choice for him. He began seeking a broader field of travel and tourism and added international relations as a minor while completing a master's degree in hotel administration. The topic of his thesis for his graduate work was the role of tourism in developing countries.

Jafari soon joined the faculty at the University of Wisconsin–Stout and founded the _Annals of Tourism Research._ The quarterly publication provides a voice for the study of the socio-cultural and academic dimensions of tourism. The _Annals_ focus is on tourism as a subject of scientific research rather than on business applications. The journal was one of the original tourism research journals, which now number more than 50. In addition to being editor-in-chief of _Annals of Tourism Research_, Jafari is the founding president of the International Academy for the Study of Tourism.

THINK CRITICALLY

Why might the study of the social and cultural impacts of tourism be important to the industry? Why is tourism of concern to developing countries?

Understand Marketing Concepts

Circle the best answer for each of the following questions.

1. An effective marketing-information management system is
   a. inexpensive.
   b. accurate.
   c. user friendly.
   d. all of the above.

2. Data can often be more easily understood by
   a. using mathematical equations.
   b. using smaller words.
   c. depicting it graphically.
   d. repeating it.

Think Critically

Answer the following questions as completely as possible. If necessary, use a separate sheet of paper.

3. List five examples of data that might be needed to make a decision about building a new hotel. What information would you need to know about competitors' hotels in the area in which you plan to locate?

_____

_____

_____

_____

_____

_____

_____

4. How could information about the monthly occupancy rates of a hotel for the last two years be used to make decisions? What kinds of decisions might be based on this data?

_____

_____

_____

_____

_____

_____

_____

Review Marketing Concepts

Write the letter of the term that matches each definition. Some terms will not be used.

a.	benchmarks
b.	bid
c.	cookie
d.	data analysis
e.	data processing
f.	data protection
g.	global distribution system (GDS)
h.	inbound travelers
i.	law of demand
j.	law of supply
k.	niche market
l.	outbound travelers
m.	performance measures
n.	personal data
o.	travel trade

_____ 1. A written proposal submitted to a convention planner that includes dates, costs, and blocks of hotel rooms

_____ 2. Standards that define the desired performance

_____ 3. A small, specific group of travelers identified by tastes and lifestyles or separated by category

_____ 4. References that define and quantify the results of an activity

_____ 5. A computer reservation system jointly used by airlines and travel suppliers in many countries

_____ 6. Refers to any individual or company that creates and/or markets tours and/or independent packages

_____ 7. Nonresident visitors arriving in a region or country

_____ 8. Describing, summarizing, and comparing data in a systematic way

_____ 9. A small piece of data stored on a consumer's computer from the visited web site and used to track the consumer's movements

_____ 10. When the price of a product increases, there will be less demand for the product

Circle the best answer.

11. A marketing-information management system includes
    a. collecting data.
    b. storing data.
    c. analyzing and using data.
    d. all of the above.

12. Data are collected on automobile travel via
    a. air bag sensors.
    b. automatic toll-road passes.
    c. global positioning systems.
    d. all of the above.

Think Critically

13. In marketing research, what is the objective of performance measures? How are performance measures used in travel and tourism? Provide an example of a performance measure.

_____

_____

_____

_____

14. You are a travel supplier of package tours and want to please your customers. What do you need to know about your customers' likes and dislikes? Additionally, make a list of personal data you need to collect from customers.

_____

_____

_____

_____

_____

15. Why is it essential to protect the data that customers provide? What ideas do you have for protecting data?

_____

_____

_____

_____

16. Your cruise line is considering increasing its presence on the Web to attract a higher percentage of Internet bookings. What do you need to know to ensure that this is the right strategy? Make a list of the data you might need. How could you use the information?

_____

_____

_____

_____

17. Conduct an Internet search using the keywords "hospitality dashboards." Look at the software available to create dashboards for the hospitality industry. Write a descriptive paragraph of what you find.

_____

_____

_____

Make Connections

18. **Marketing Math** There are 5,354 hotel rooms available in your city. Last year the average occupancy rates by month were 87% in January, 89% in February, and 78% in March. As director of your city's CVB, you have been asked to increase the rates by 2% for January, 5% for February, and 6% for March. How many additional rooms will need to be occupied to meet each month's goal?

_____

_____

_____

_____

_____

_____

19. **Geography** You are considering investing in a niche tourism-related business in Tamil Nadu in southeast India. Use the Internet to search for information about the climate, existing tourist facilities, and local attractions that would be of interest to visitors. Select a target niche customer, and write a page about why a business in Tamil Nadu would be a good investment for attracting that customer.

_____

_____

_____

_____

_____

_____

20. **Technology** Use the Internet to conduct research about "cookies." Determine how they are used in marketing. Are they considered a threat to the security of personal computers or a harmless marketing tool? Write a paragraph about what you find.

_____

_____

_____

_____

_____

_____

_____

21. **Marketing Math** Create a graphic depiction of the following information. Last year, Property A had 395 rooms and a 91% occupancy rate. This year, Property A expanded to 490 rooms and had 86% occupancy. Last year, Property B had 1,100 rooms and an 89% occupancy rate. This year, Property B had 1,100 rooms and 92% occupancy. Draw at least one conclusion from the information.

_____

_____

_____

22. **Marketing** Think about the information you would need to make decisions about the product/service planning marketing function for a new theme park. Choose a target customer. Make a list of the kinds of data you would need, where you might find the data, and why you would need that data.

_____

_____

_____

23. **Communication** Conduct research on the Internet about ways to protect the personal data of customers. What is being done on the state and national levels? Write one page about this topic.

_____

_____

_____

_____

EXTENDED STAY

Project You are considering opening a new boutique hotel. You are trying to decide where to open the hotel and who your target customer will be.

Work with a group and complete the following activities.

1. Use the Internet to conduct research for information about possible locations and potential target customers.
2. What kind of data would you need in order to make a decision about a location that could support your business?
3. Who would be your customer?
4. What amenities would you offer?
5. Write a one-page summary of information about your findings. Include a graphic of data on a separate page. The graphic should support your plan.

SUCCESS RESULTS FROM KNOWING YOUR TARGET MARKET

Successful businesses constantly strive to improve the products and services they offer. New home builders add home features demanded by buyers, automobile manufacturers constantly update style and safety features on their vehicles, and hotels survey customers to improve the service and amenities they provide.

State travel and tourism departments must also conduct research to learn what customers in the target market want and to determine the possibilities for expanding the target market.

Hawaii, Florida, and California have mild climates and numerous attractions for tourism, but it takes more than such attractions to generate revenue from tourists. Each state's department of travel and tourism must determine its top tourist attractions and define its target markets.

Every state produces television commercials to attract tourists from other states. Thirty-second commercials can cost from $200,000 to $2.5 million, depending on the broadcasting channel and the time they are aired. Departments of travel and tourism must determine the effectiveness of commercials through consumer research.

A state's department of travel and tourism may prepare a state travel guide that is sent to people who respond to its commercials.

The number of travel guide requests from each state may be one measure of the success of advertising in that state. Any coupons printed in or accompanying the travel guide may be coded to track the source and can provide a measure of the success of promotional campaigns.

Surveys must be developed to learn what tourists like about the state and what can be done to attract repeat tourism business. Surveys are only as effective as the response rates. Most individuals prefer answering short surveys and will not take the time to fill out one that appears long. State tourism departments must determine the best time and place to conduct a survey. Some states have chosen rest stops or hotels to collect information from tourists. Results from surveys help states increase tourism dollars.

THINK CRITICALLY

1. Why is travel and tourism of interest to all states?
2. How can a state determine the effectiveness of its tourism commercials?
3. What would be the best place and time to survey state tourists?
4. Does the size of a survey affect the response rate? Why or why not?

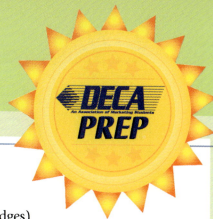

DECA PREP

HOSPITALITY AND RECREATION MARKETING RESEARCH EVENT

Travel and tourism depends heavily upon quality hotels offering top customer service. State departments of travel and tourism are interested in how well hotels take care of the state's tourists. You and a partner have been hired by your state's department of travel and tourism to conduct research on tourists' satisfaction with their hotel stays.

Choose a local hotel on which to conduct marketing research. Prepare a survey that focuses on the effectiveness of advertising, quality of customer service, and likelihood of the tourist returning for another stay. The survey should determine why the tourist came to the area (for example, for a family reunion, class reunion, vacation, or other reason) and why the visitor would/would not stay at the hotel again. Your survey should also include several questions to gain guests' perceptions of the state as a tourist destination. Work with the hotel to administer your survey to recent guests.

Analyze your marketing research results, and make recommendations to both the hotel and the state department of travel and tourism. The recommendations should be in the form of a business plan (limited to 30 pages) that describes the research methods used in the study, your findings from the study, and a proposed strategic plan for improvement.

You will have ten minutes to present your plan for improvement to the state tourism board (judges) and five minutes to respond to questions.

Performance Indicators Evaluated

- Select an actual hotel, and research the effectiveness of its advertising and customer service.
- Design a marketing research study.
- Conduct a marketing research study.
- Analyze the results of the research study, and prepare a strategic plan to enhance the hotel's current level of customer service.
- Present your findings and suggestions to key businesspeople.

Go to the DECA web site for more detailed information.

THINK CRITICALLY

1. Why must hotels and other tourism businesses conduct marketing research?
2. What is the best means for collecting information from hotel guests?
3. How can the response rates of surveys be increased?
4. Why might the state department of travel and tourism be concerned about customer satisfaction at hotels within its state?

www.deca.org

Travel and Tourism Technology

CHAPTER 8 · CHAPTER 8 · CHAPTER 8 · CHAPTER 8

8

Digital Vision

Point Your Browser

▶ ▶ ▶ ▶ travel.swlearning.com

Winning Strategies

CrewSolver

When weather disrupts the schedule of a major airline, revenue losses pile up. Included in the loss is the time it takes to reschedule the crew and equipment. Weather-grounded flights may leave a crew in Atlanta that was supposed to be ready to fly out of Boston. A crew can legally work only a specific number of hours per day, whether on the ground or in the air. The revised schedule must comply with the airline's business practices, federal regulations, and union agreements—and get passengers to their destination on time.

With more than 2,000 flights per day, Continental Airline's flight crew schedule requires massive coordination. Electronic Data Systems (EDS) Corporation is an information technology firm that provides products and services to the air transportation industry as well as many other industries. Working with crew scheduling experts from Continental and operations research experts from the University of Texas, staff from EDS developed CrewSolver, a crew-optimizing software program. Rescheduling after major weather disruptions used to take days, but thanks to CrewSolver, it can now be done in hours or sometimes minutes.

CrewSolver uses precomputed scenarios and powerful search capabilities to compile thousands of possible solutions in a matter of minutes. The solutions show the possible combinations of crew reassignments to available aircraft. With CrewSolver, crews can be quickly reassigned and rescheduled, returning planes to the air in a timely manner.

THINK CRITICALLY

1. Why would the speed of rescheduling airline crews be important?

2. In what ways is technology involved in rescheduling weather-grounded flights?

Electronic Systems

Goals

Define a GDS, and describe its purpose.

List and describe the four major automated GDSs.

All Aboard

Cisco Systems is a worldwide provider of technology networking equipment. Cisco has 38,000 employees worldwide and spends about $30 million a year on employee travel. It books about 75 percent of its travel needs through Sabre's GetThere online corporate travel system. The Sabre GetThere system has allowed Cisco to automate the routine processes of booking corporate travel and consequently reduce transaction costs.

Because Cisco has employees around the world, the GetThere system had to be customized to provide information for multiple countries, in multiple languages, and using multiple currencies. Travel data are tracked per country for Cisco to use in analyzing its employee travel needs. The GetThere system also ensures that employees are following corporate travel policies.

Work with a partner. Brainstorm challenges a large corporation might face in trying to manage travel throughout the world. What kind of help would it need?

CONNECTING THE SYSTEMS

Having worldwide reservation systems that interact with each other requires coordination and cooperation. The International Air Transportation Association (IATA) provides the forum for that cooperation.

Databases

MARKETING- INFORMATION MANAGEMENT

An airline generally has a database of its fares and reservations hosted through a global distribution system (GDS). The GDS is an online system that manages the information received from *intermediaries*, such as travel agents. The GDS is like a technology hub that connects travel agents, travel suppliers, and corporate travel departments. Information about passengers and their airline reservations is entered through intermediaries and kept in the technology systems on records referred to as **passenger name records (PNRs)**. A PNR can contain a great deal of personal information about an individual traveler. For example, if a traveler makes reservations for an air flight, car rental, and hotel room, the data stored in the PNR will include the traveler's name, address, credit card used, flight number, type of hotel room, and other personal data. The information in the PNR is used by the Transportation Security Administration (TSA) to screen passengers.

RESCOM

IATA's Reservations Committee (RESCOM) is responsible for developing all of the rules and regulations that govern airline reservations, including the protocol standards for transmitting data between the reservation systems of airlines and other travel suppliers. It is critical that all reservation systems have standard procedures and functions so they can communicate with each other.

The Computerized Reservation Systems Harmonization Working Group reports to RESCOM. This group focuses on standardizing the current and future reservation systems' tools, procedures, and functions. The group works on communication among the airlines, GDSs, and government regulators to help improve the reservation system standards and procedures.

By connecting the worldwide systems, a ticket agent for British Airways can retrieve a PNR created in the United States and match the data to the documents of a passenger ready to board a flight from London to Berlin. The data will show the passenger's flight from the United States to London and any other flights recently made. If the individual is on the transnational crime watch list, this information will also be available to the agent, and the individual will not be allowed to board the plane.

Time Out

In London, underground rail riders can use radio-frequency debit cards, much like electronic toll passes in the United States. The debit cards generate data about the passengers' trips, which are kept on file for eight weeks.

What is the purpose of a GDS?

_____

_____

Stopover

AUTOMATED SYSTEMS

MARKETING–INFORMATION MANAGEMENT

A few of the discount airlines, such as Southwest and jetBlue, maintain their own databases, but most major airlines keep their PNRs in the database of one of the four major GDSs in the world. The big four are Galileo, Amadeus, Sabre, and Worldspan. These computerized systems connect travel suppliers to intermediaries and travel buyers around the world.

Galileo

Galileo is the best known of the global distribution systems. It provides automated reservations, Internet travel solutions, and other travel products that support travel suppliers, travel agents, and corporate customers. Galileo is headquartered in Parsippany,

Photodisc

New Jersey, and originated in 1971 as a way for United Airlines to auto- mate its reservation and booking system. After being owned by a num- ber of airlines in partnership, Galileo became a subsidiary of Cendant's Travel Distribution Service in 2001. According to its web site, Galileo serves 43,500 travel agency locations, 460 airlines, 23 car rental compa- nies, 58,000 hotel properties, 430 tour operators, and all major cruise lines throughout the world. Galileo is used to reserve and purchase airline tickets, car rentals, hotel accommodations, cruises, and vaca- tion packages. Galileo connects travel agents and online customers to hotels through online services and multiple web sites. More than 750,000 hotel bookings are created each day through Galileo technology.

Amadeus

Amadeus is an information technology company that provides solutions to travel and tourism businesses, including airlines, car rental companies, hotels, cruise lines, and tour operators. Amadeus Global Travel Distribu- tion has its world headquarters in Madrid, Spain. Its slogan states, "Now you can sell the world, sell faster, sell smarter, and sell more!" More than 500 airlines sell tickets through the Amadeus system. Amadeus serves more than 64,000 travel agents and 16,000 airline ticket offices. The versatile system may be used in many ways.

The Amadeus system shows all flights between paired cities and can confirm the flight back to the booking agent in real time. Amadeus Cars is a division that provides users with a list of all car rental companies with their rates shown from low to high. Information about terms, rules, and car rental conditions are linked to the rates, along with data about vehicle types and surcharges. The Amadeus cruise system provides cruise package information from many cruise lines, regarding hundreds of destinations around the world. Availability, pricing, and selling come directly from the cruise provider's system, and Amadeus keeps a passen- ger record for the travel agent making the reservations.

Amadeus users have access to group booking capabilities through a partnership with Group Travel Planet, a leisure hotel group booking system. This partnership allows Amadeus users to plan, book, and man- age group reservations without having to contact each hotel directly. The automated system allows for addition and subtraction of bookings as the group size changes.

Sabre

The Sabre (Semi-Automated Business Research Environment) global distribution system provides products and services to travel agents, travel suppliers, and corporate travel departments. Sabre is headquartered near Dallas, in Southlake, Texas, and has about 6,000 employees in 45 coun- tries. Sabre's system includes more than 400 airlines, approximately 60,000 hotels, 37 car rental companies, 9 cruise lines, 35 railroads, and 220 tour operators. Sabre provides online distribution of travel products for travel suppliers and helps travel agents find the lowest fares available in the system.

DISTRIBUTION

Sabre offers airlines cost savings through its distribution efforts. The savings are passed on to travel consumers. Sabre offers access to all participating airlines' published fares and promotions and delivers the lowest fares to the corporate travel director. Sabre's Direct Connect Availability ᔆᴹ allows a corporate travel director to compare costs directly from the travel supplier's system. In 2003, Sabre introduced Travelocity Business—a program that allows small- and medium-sized companies to manage their corporate travel, use preferred vendors, and receive usage reports.

Worldspan

Worldspan is headquartered in Atlanta, Georgia, serves about 70 countries, and has about 2,500 employees. It uses high-speed, flexible networks and computer technology to provide data services that link about 800 travel suppliers around the world to customers. Worldspan hosts data for Delta and Northwest Airlines. It processes about 65 percent of all online airline transactions made in the United States. Travel bookings on Orbitz.com and Expedia.com are completed through Worldspan's global distribution system.

Worldspan specializes in low-fare search capabilities through a product called e-Pricing. Based upon a traveler's preferred search parameters, e-Pricing searches, integrates, and sorts itineraries containing intricate combinations, multiple fare types, and additional selected components, and delivers the lowest prices available. Available in three subscription levels, e-Pricing allows users to retrieve 10, 32, or 100 itinerary options in a single search.

Missing the Boat

GDS firms generally have agreements with third-party companies who can also provide services to GDS customers. For example, Sabre has a Qualified Vendor Program through which it officially recognizes companies that may provide additional travel products and services to its clients.

Although customers must purchase the products directly from the vendor companies, Sabre's web site states, "Our team carefully evaluates each vendor on criteria specific to our industry and selects only the vendors whose products will enhance or add value to our own extensive product and service portfolio." At the bottom of the same web page, Sabre states, "Any testing done by Sabre is solely for Sabre's use, and customers are advised not to rely solely on Sabre testing or the lack thereof to make purchasing decisions."

THINK CRITICALLY

1. Are the two quoted statements contradictory? Why or why not?

2. Would you feel confident about buying from one of Sabre's "qualified vendors"? Discuss your opinion with others.

Stopover

What are the four major global distribution systems?

_____

_____

Understand Marketing Concepts

Circle the best answer for each of the following questions.

1. RESCOM is responsible for
   a. developing the rules and regulations that govern airline reservations.
   b. improving airline customer relations.
   c. airline advertising effectiveness.
   d. none of the above.

2. The best-known global distribution system is
   a. Sabre.
   b. Amadeus.
   c. Worldspan.
   d. Galileo.

Think Critically

Answer the following questions as completely as possible. If necessary, use a separate sheet of paper.

3. Briefly describe why global distribution systems should have standardized procedures and functions.

_____

_____

_____

_____

_____

_____

_____

4. **History** Describe what it might have been like to keep track of airline reservations on paper, before computer technology automated this process.

_____

_____

_____

_____

_____

_____

_____

E-Commerce

Describe the use and importance of e-commerce in travel and tourism marketing.

Explain search engine optimization and how to achieve it.

All Aboard

Mexicana Airlines was one of the first Latin American airlines to offer a web site that allowed passengers to make reservations online. The site attracted such a large volume of traffic that Mexicana had to upgrade it to handle the extra business.

Mexicana wanted to continue increasing sales at the lowest possible cost while improving customer service. It wanted to give customers a personal and enjoyable online experience based on information collected about visitors' habits and tastes. Working with a team of experts, Mexicana built a web site that generates more than $1.5 million in U.S. dollars per month.

Work with a partner. Describe what a personal and enjoyable online experience with an airline's web site might include. What factors would influence you to return to make additional online reservations?

ONLINE

The Internet allows communication around the world 24/7, at a speed unthought of 20 years ago. Technology savvy people assume that a travel and tourism business of any size will have a web site. They also assume that the web site will be user friendly and provide more than just information. The site must allow interaction with instant results and feedback regarding availabilities, reservations, and pricing.

Making Connections

The Internet is like a super highway, allowing access to destinations all over the world. The Internet opens businesses to a global community of customers. It has become a first stop for people searching for travel information. **E-commerce** is the exchange of goods, services, information, or other business through electronic means. Travel suppliers that successfully use e-commerce to sell their products understand the **protocols**, or rules, that govern business transactions over the Internet. The protocols of e-commerce require that transactions be processed reliably and that sensitive data be encrypted to prevent someone from accessing customers' personal information. Behind a web site is software that protects the site and its users, collects data about the customer and the transaction, controls product inventory, completes accounting records, and creates reports that are used to make business decisions. E-commerce is expected to continue to grow and evolve until it is used worldwide as frequently and as reliably as telephones are used today.

Photodisc

Business-to-Business (B2B) E-commerce can be used in business-to-business (B2B) transactions, such as a travel supplier using a GDS to assemble a package that includes airline tickets, hotel room, and car rental. GDS systems have dramatically changed the distribution of travel products and services. It used to take travel agents hours on the phone to collect information about travel product availability and costs. Now an agent has access to **real-time data**, meaning the data are available immediately, are current, and are updated as often as every 100 milliseconds.

Business-to-Consumer (B2C) E-commerce can also be used by businesses to connect directly with consumers (B2C). E-commerce web sites provide information about the products available for sale as well as accept payment in a secure manner. About 90 percent of online transactions are paid by credit card. Other payment options include online checks, digital cash, debit cards, and payments by person-to-person (P2P) e-mail. Paying by P2P e-mail is actually a transaction through a financial service's online account, in which the information from the payer is e-mailed to the recipient. With P2P, no account numbers are exchanged in the e-mail. Instead, the recipient business receives a web site address where it can log on and have the payment sent to its account.

Being Friendly

Whether B2B or B2C, an e-commerce web site must be user friendly to attract repeat business. While web sites should be up to date, they should not be built with technology that is so cutting edge that most customers' web browsers will not support the new features. Web pages that are very busy, with every inch covered, are sometimes confusing to customers and make them work too hard to find needed information. If pages take too long to load, visitors will quickly move on to other sites. Too many advertisements and pop-ups can be annoying.

The web page layout is critical to its success. The design must be clean and easy to navigate. Using either *frames* or *includes*, pages can be broken into sections that operate independently of each other. These sections allow an identification (id) bar and a navigation bar to remain fixed in place while the visitor is browsing through the various sections of the site. The **id bar** identifies the site. The **navigation bar** is a menu list that allows the user to access other sections of the site that are of interest. With the id and navigation bars always in view, visitors remain oriented to where they are within the site.

How has the Internet changed travel purchases?

_____

_____

SEARCHING FOR ANSWERS

The Internet opens businesses to customers from around the world. Connected consumers can use search engines to help find web sites and global companies. An Internet **search engine** is a program that indexes web pages and then attempts to match relevant pages to users' search requests. There are many web sites, such as Google, that specialize in Internet searches. Customers seeking information about a particular destination or travel supplier can go to a search site, enter words or phrases (called *keywords*) into its search engine, and receive a list of web site addresses that correspond to the keywords.

Clicking for Dollars

PROMOTION

An e-commerce company wants to achieve **search engine optimization**, in which its web address will be at or near the top of any list generated by a search engine when keywords related to its business are entered. Many search sites will sell the top spots on lists generated by specific keywords. In addition, a web business may pay search sites to display its ad whenever certain keywords are used. For example, entering "European

Photodisc

E-Ticket

David Kong is president and chief executive officer of Best Western International. Kong announced that in 2005 Best Western began booking through its web site an average of more than $1 million in revenues every two days. Online bookings equated to 50 percent of all Best Western reservations. The company's web site bookings had grown by 54 percent during the five preceding years.

All of Best Western's online information is available in English, French, German, and Spanish. In addition, information about many of its Asian, Australian, and New Zealand properties is available online in Chinese, Japanese, and Korean. The company plans to upgrade and improve its web site with additional enhancements, such as virtual tours of its properties.

THINK CRITICALLY

1. How important is web presence to a travel and tourism business?

2. Search for Best Western's web site and evaluate its pages. What is Best Western doing right? What would you improve?

airlines" into Google's search engine may bring up sponsored ads for booking sites such as LowestFare.com. The company buying the ad space pays the search site a fee every time a visitor clicks on the ad.

Search engines will also list web addresses based on the metatags used at a site's home page. **Metatags** are keywords hidden in the coding of a site's home page. For example, if a business wants its site to be on a list generated from the keywords "Seattle hotels," then it will use those words in the hidden metatags of its home page. Additionally, search engines will list web sites depending on the amount of traffic they receive. A popular site receiving a high amount of traffic will most likely rank higher on a search list than a site receiving less traffic.

The Bottom Offer

Many cost-conscious travelers will take the time necessary to search and find the least expensive airline tickets. Looking on the airlines' web sites and using well-known travel sites such as Orbitz and Travelocity, bargain hunters can shop multiple airlines. Additionally, search sites are now available that scan hundreds of travel sites and offer side-by-side comparisons of the prices offered directly by the airlines and through travel intermediaries.

Because some airlines and hotels do not allow reservations to be made for their services through a third-party web site, the search sites can help find bargains on the airlines' or hotels' own sites. The search sites usually don't charge the user a fee, but are paid instead by referral fees from the airline or hotel when users make a purchase after starting from the search site. Some of the travel search sites include FareChaser and Mobissimo. They serve both corporate and leisure travelers and may search both domestic and international sites looking for the best rates. Mobissimo presents a price comparison of online travel agents, airlines, and consolidators. **Consolidators** are companies that buy in bulk from travel suppliers and sell at a discount. Sites like Mobissimo that bring together information from many sources are called **aggregators** or **metasearch sites**, allowing customers to easily comparison shop.

Stopover How can a search site help a consumer find the least expensive airline ticket?

Understand Marketing Concepts

Circle the best answer for each of the following questions.

1. E-commerce refers to
   a. the exchange of goods, services, information, or other business through electronic means.
   b. a program that indexes web pages and then attempts to match relevant pages to users' search requests.
   c. rules that govern business transactions over the Internet.
   d. advertising on web pages.

2. The most common method for making online payments is by
   a. credit card.
   b. debit card.
   c. P2P e-mail.
   d. digital cash.

Think Critically

Answer the following questions as completely as possible. If necessary, use a separate sheet of paper.

3. **Technology** Why is security such a big concern for online business transactions?

   _____

   _____

   _____

   _____

   _____

   _____

   _____

4. **Communication** Write a paragraph that describes what constitutes a user-friendly web site.

   _____

   _____

   _____

   _____

   _____

   _____

   _____

   _____

   _____

Technology Trends

Goals

Describe the technology infrastructure needed in today's hotels.

Discuss trends in travel and tourism technology.

All Aboard

At BallOfDirt.com, travelers can post a travel journal, photos, and maps of their trip for friends and family to enjoy. The service is free, but users of the site must sign up as members. After experiencing a fantastic day cruising on the Nile River viewing ancient ruins, you can sit down in a cyber café and let everyone at home share the experience.

The service began as a hobby, but turned into a business for its three owner–employees. BallOfDirt.com makes money by selling users high-quality prints of their photos, providing access to booking reservations at hostels and hotels, selling travel insurance, and providing travel-related products through Amazon.com.

Work with a group. Perform an Internet search for BallOfDirt.com or other web sites that offer travel journal space to travelers. Discuss other products and services that travel blog sites like BallOfDirt.com could offer their users.

TECHNOLOGY INFRASTRUCTURE

PRODUCT/SERVICE MANAGEMENT

Today's hotel buildings must be equipped with complex technology, both to support the operations of the business and to provide the technology services that guests expect. The operations side of technology ranges from managing the business's web site to electronically

Brand X Pictures

monitoring and controlling the hotel's lighting, heating, and air-conditioning systems. Internal phone systems called *private branch exchanges (PBX)*, point-of-sale (POS) systems, and public-address systems are needed. On the services side, guests expect easy Internet access, security systems, and in-room entertainment options while staying at the property. Extensive infrastructure is required to support the technology needed and expected.

Behind the Walls

According to the American Hotel & Lodging Association's (AH&LA's) Technology Committee, today's hotel owners and operators seek three standards in the technology installed in new or renovated properties.

- It must support all of the hotel's systems without failures.

- It must be cost effective.

- It must be maintainable and upgradeable.

The equipment required to operate and connect all of the hotel's technology should be located in a telecommunications room (TR) in a central location within the hotel. The TR houses the main distribution frame, which is a cable rack that connects the external technology cabling, such as phone lines coming into the building, to the internal cabling. The TR also houses the internal telephone system, in-room entertainment system, and other technology equipment. Intermediate distribution frame rooms are then located on each floor or near guest rooms as needed.

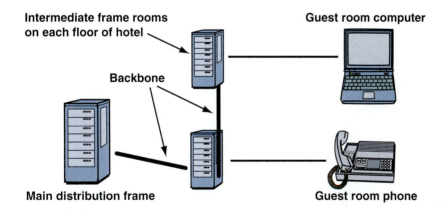

(Source: Adapted with permission of the American Hotel & Lodging Association, "Hotel Technology Infrastructure")

Getting Connected

The **backbone** is the cabling needed to connect the main distribution frame to the intermediate distribution frames. It is sometimes the difficult part of the infrastructure needed to bring existing hotels up to date. Even when offering guests wireless data communication, a structured cable system is still required. The backbone is needed to provide wireless communication in the places where guests want access. Wireless service is a convenient amenity to offer in special locations, such as around the swimming pool, on the golf course, or at special events areas.

Guests often have concerns about the security risks of wireless access. They are also concerned about the possible need to change the settings on their computers to use wireless services. Whether wireless or high-speed cable connections are offered, most hotels' Internet services are set up to accommodate common computer configurations, so no settings changes are needed. This is an important feature, because travelers do not want to make technical changes to their computers for the short time they are hotel guests.

Stopover

What are the three AH&LA standards for technology in hotels?

_____

_____

BUSINESS SOLUTIONS

All businesses are continuously looking for ways to cut costs and increase revenue. Travel-related technology can help do both.

Faster, Cheaper, Easier

DISTRIBUTION

Many large corporations have replaced their travel agent relationships with web-based software. The changeover has not always been easy. Employees have often been slow to use the new travel technology. Employees want a system that is fast and easy to use. Employers want a system that saves the company money.

Time Out

According to J.D. Power and Associates, half of U.S. air travelers wait in line for 19 minutes to check in, 18 percent check in at self-service kiosks, and 5 percent eliminate waits by printing boarding passes from airline web sites.

Photodisc

Changes in corporate travel web sites to make them more like typical e-commerce sites increase the likelihood that employees will successfully use them. For example, when a site allows employees to see all possible flights, they will generally choose the lowest possible fare and save the company money. Companies such as American Express have worked to improve their corporate travel sites by providing combined booking and expense-reporting software. The combination allows an employee to book travel and complete an expense report at the same time. Employers can see increases in employee use of sites that work well and are user friendly.

Gift Cards

Hotels and restaurants have moved from paper gift certificates to plastic gift cards. The new technology provides revenue to the businesses, as well as an electronic data stream. Not only is information obtained about the purchaser, but data are also obtained about the gift card user. Satisfied gift card users may become repeat customers, providing future business. Hotels may use gift cards as incentives for their loyalty programs or in cross-promotion with nearby restaurants.

Gift card programs are usually managed by a third-party gift card company. The cards are activated through a credit card terminal. Fees associated with offering the cards include a set-up/printing fee, a fee per card, monthly fees, and a cost per swipe, bringing the start-up costs to around $1,200. The value of having the "mini-billboards" in circulation makes them worth the cost. The number of gift cards sold that are never used averages from 5 to 10 percent for restaurants and from 10 to 20 percent for hotels. The unused cards become extra revenue for the restaurants and hotels.

What are some of the benefits for a business selling gift cards?

Marketing Myths

When you book a flight on an airline's web site, you may actually end up flying with a totally different airline. Many airlines sell seats on other airlines, but put their own code numbers on the flights and advertise them as if they were their own.

An airline may pair with as many as a dozen or more other airlines to "code share." The selling airline receives a portion of the fare. The airline actually providing the service gets extra passengers it might not have found without the partnership. Airlines say they are serving passengers by making it easier to coordinate connecting flights. Edward Hasbrouck, a travel agent and author, considers the practice misleading. If there are problems with the flight or luggage, the passenger may be shuffled between the two airlines, with neither taking responsibility.

THINK CRITICALLY

1. Do you think airlines should sell other airlines' flights as their own? Why or why not?

2. In the case of code sharing, whose responsibility is it if a passenger needs to change his or her ticket? Discuss your opinion with others.

©Getty Images/PhotoDisc

Five-Star Traveler

HELEN C. BROADUS

At a first-ever, historic joint meeting of the World Tourism Organization (WTO) and the Africa Travel Association (ATA), Helen C. Broadus received the Eighth Annual Inter-Continental Hotels Cote d'Ivoire Award. Broadus serves on the international board of directors for ATA. She was recognized for her major contributions to advancing tourism in Africa. Promoting travel and tourism opportunities for the continent of Africa has been Broadus's special focus for many years.

Helen Broadus trained as a sales associate with Marriott International, specializing in hotel and hospitality services. She is cofounder and current president of Venue International Professionals, Inc. (VIP). VIP is based in the Washington, D.C., area and is a full-service international travel and tourism consulting firm.

Broadus is an authority on travel destinations within Africa. She has frequently written articles covering African tourism for trade publications. A recent article in *Africa Travel* magazine detailed her participation in a familiarization tour to Nigeria, West Africa, as a member of Tourism Consortium International (TCI). The overall purpose of the trip was to experience the level of readi- ness of Nigeria's travel and tourism infrastructure, including its hotel accommodations, air and road transportation, hospitality amenities, and security services. Broadus found that although the tourism infrastructure in Nigeria is not as developed as in other places in Africa, Nigeria offers perhaps the best variety of tourist attractions and destinations in West Africa.

THINK CRITICALLY

How might technology improve tourism in Africa's developing nations? Why is tourism of concern to developing countries?

Understand Marketing Concepts

Circle the best answer for each of the following questions.

1. The costs associated with offering a gift card program generally include
   a. start-up costs of around $12,100.
   b. a percentage of the sale.
   c. the costs of redistributing unused portions.
   d. none of the above.

2. The backbone of a hotel technology system is the
   a. PBX system.
   b. cable system connecting the main and intermediate distribution frames.
   c. wireless connections.
   d. telecommunications room (TR).

Think Critically

Answer the following questions as completely as possible. If necessary, use a separate sheet of paper.

3. Why should a hotel's telecommunications room be centrally located? What is controlled through the TR?

   _____

   _____

   _____

   _____

   _____

   _____

   _____

4. **History** What has changed about the technology needs of a hotel over the last 20 years? Write a paragraph about the changing needs.

   _____

   _____

   _____

   _____

   _____

   _____

   _____

   _____

   _____

Review Marketing Concepts

Write the letter of the term that matches each definition. Some terms will not be used.

a.	aggregators
b.	backbone
c.	consolidators
d.	e-commerce
e.	id bar
f.	metasearch sites
g.	metatags
h.	navigation bar
i.	passenger name records (PNRs)
j.	protocols
k.	real-time data
l.	search engine
m.	search engine optimization

_____ 1. The exchange of goods, services, information, or other business through electronic means

_____ 2. Identifies the web site

_____ 3. A program that indexes web pages and then attempts to match relevant pages to users' search requests

_____ 4. Achieving top positions in search lists

_____ 5. Keywords hidden in the coding of a site's home page

_____ 6. Current data available immediately and updated as often as every 100 milliseconds

_____ 7. Companies that buy in bulk from travel suppliers and sell at a discount

_____ 8. Information about passengers and their airline reservations

_____ 9. Rules that govern business transactions over the Internet

_____ 10. A menu list on a web page that allows the user to access other sections of the site that are of interest

Circle the best answer.

11. The cost of an online ad is usually
    a. paid up front before running.
    b. a fee per click.
    c. paid by visitors to the site.
    d. free on search sites.

12. Information in a PNR
    a. may be entered by an intermediary.
    b. must be protected from misuse.
    c. is used by the TSA to screen passengers.
    d. is all of the above.

13. To ensure search engine optimization, a web business should
    a. pay search sites for top spots on generated search lists.
    b. use appropriate metatags in the coding of its home page.
    c. pay per click.
    d. do both a and b.

Think Critically

14. Discuss the big-four global distribution systems. How are they alike? How are they different? Where are they headquartered, and who are their major travel supplier customers?

_____

_____

_____

_____

_____

_____

15. Why is there concern for protecting the personal data contained in PNRs? Who has access? Who is responsible for preventing misuse?

_____

_____

_____

_____

16. Why are standards for airline reservation systems needed? What could result if the various GDS systems did not interact?

_____

_____

_____

_____

17. What features would a corporation want from a GDS travel information-management system? How can a GDS help manage travel costs?

_____

_____

_____

_____

18. Use the Internet to look up the cost of a flight from the closest airport to the capital of a nearby state on a specific date. Check the cost from an airline's web site, a travel consolidator like CheapTickets, an online ticket agency like Travelocity, and an aggregator like Mobissimo. Compare what you find, and write a statement about the results.

_____

_____

_____

_____

Make Connections

19. **Technology** Your customer lives in Memphis, Tennessee, and needs to get to Green Bay, Wisconsin, by the fastest and least expensive way possible. Use the Internet to explore options for flying, renting a car, riding a bus, taking a train, or using a combination of these modes of transportation. Using spreadsheet software, create a chart that includes the type of transportation, cost, number of hours in transit, any layovers, and major cities through which the customer will travel. Recommend the best way for the customer to travel.

_____

_____

_____

20. **Research** Conduct online research about PNR privacy concerns. Write one paragraph about why there are concerns and what is being done to protect the consumer.

_____

_____

_____

21. **History** Conduct online research about e-commerce. Write one page describing e-commerce and explaining how it has evolved over the last ten years.

_____

_____

_____

22. **Marketing Math** Your company's salesperson, Mateo, needs to be in another city at 8:00 A.M. tomorrow for important meetings. The meetings will last for two days. If Mateo leaves tonight, the airline ticket will cost $1,436. If Mateo waits and takes the 5:00 A.M. flight tomorrow, he can arrive on time, but the flight will cost $1,765. The hotel room is $135 per night, and meals are $60 per day. Which is the least expensive trip? What other factors may influence Mateo's decision?

_____

_____

_____

_____

23. Geography A client of your travel agency wants to spend two weeks visiting Greece and Italy and is considering a Mediterranean cruise. Conduct research and suggest at least four locations the person might want to visit. What are the special attractions of each location? Develop a trip itinerary for one day of the trip.

_____

_____

_____

_____

_____

24. Communication You are building a new, upscale hotel. Write a one-page description of the technology that you will make available to your guests.

_____

_____

_____

_____

_____

_____

EXTENDED STAY

Project A group of women are meeting in Durango, Colorado, from October 6–8. One woman is coming from Los Angeles, California; one from Houston, Texas; one from Pittsburgh, Pennsylvania; and one from Front Royal, Virginia. The women would like to arrive at approximately the same time and fly as inexpensively as possible. They are each willing to drive a maximum of four hours to get to Durango.

Work with a group and complete the following activities.

1. Use the Internet to research options for the women's trips.
2. For each traveler, look at a map and determine what cities are nearby that have commercial airline flights. Find airlines from these cities that fly into Durango or a nearby city. Locate a car rental, if necessary, to get from the airport to Durango.
3. Build a chart that shows the alternatives from each destination, including the costs.
4. Using presentation software, make a short presentation about your recommendations for the group.

FAKE WEB SITES CATCH DONORS OFF GUARD

Natural disasters, such as a hurricane, tend to bring out the best in people. Many individuals choose to donate money to well-known charities that will aid the disaster victims.

In December 2004, an undersea earthquake occurred in the Indian Ocean off the northwest coast of Sumatra. The quake measured 9.3 on the Richter scale and caused a tsunami, or tidal wave, that affected the coastal areas of Indonesia, Thailand, Sri Lanka, South India, and East Africa. Nearly 300,000 people were killed, and a million were left homeless. In all, citizens of 55 countries were affected, making it one of the worst world disasters in modern history.

President Bush appointed former presidents George Bush, Sr., and Bill Clinton to lead a relief effort for tsunami victims. Many Americans and others around the world chose to contribute to disaster relief by logging onto the web sites of well-known charities.

Cybercrooks use "phishing" and "spoofing" scam techniques, where they masquerade as someone trustworthy through official-looking e-mails and instant messages. The scammers go so far as to replicate web sites of charitable organizations. The higher-quality replicas use actual charities' logos and photos. After the tsunami, hundreds of thousands of people received spam e-mails with links to the charities. Donors who clicked on the links were directed to bogus web sites, where they gave their credit card numbers and other financial data to the con artists.

Similar phishing and spoofing schemes occurred in the aftermath of hurricanes Charlie, Frances, Ivan, and Jeanne in 2004 and Katrina and Rita in 2005. A record number of strong hurricanes battered the South, leaving thousands homeless and millions without power, adequate food supplies, and even drinkable water.

The Better Business Bureau received reports of questionable telephone solicitations, door-to-door cash collections, and Internet appeals. Online scams included get-rich-quick schemes and sales offers that claimed part of the proceeds would be donated to disaster relief efforts. Unfortunately, hurricane victims were not receiving assistance, while individuals with good intentions were becoming victims of scams.

THINK CRITICALLY

1. Why should individuals be cautious about the personal information they share over the Internet?

2. What advice would you give an individual who wants to donate money to disaster victims?

3. What is a cybercrook?

4. How can valid e-commerce businesses and online charities overcome the bad reputation caused by cybercrooks?

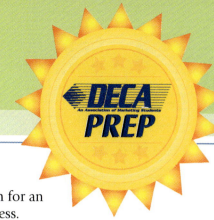

E-COMMERCE BUSINESS PLAN EVENT

Together with one or two of your classmates, design a plan for a travel-related business of your choice that will sell products and services to consumers over the Internet. Your written business plan must be limited to 30 numbered pages, including the appendix and excluding the title page and table of contents. Sections of the business plan must include

- Title Page
- Table of Contents
- Executive Summary
- Introduction
- Analysis of the Business Situation
- Planned Operation of the Proposed Business/Product/Service
- Planned Financing
- Conclusion
- Bibliography
- Appendix

You will be given ten minutes to present your business plan to potential investors (judges) and five minutes to respond to questions. No note cards are allowed for the presentation, but up to three posters may be used as visual aids.

Performance Indicators Evaluated

- Explain the increasing importance of e-commerce to the travel industry.

- Describe the competition for an e-commerce travel business.
- Explain the general operation and upkeep for an e-commerce travel business.
- Describe the business's web site and its features.
- Discuss the financial impact that e-commerce will have on the business.
- Explain why e-commerce is the best choice for the travel business.
- Present the business plan effectively, with equal participation from all team members.

Go to the DECA web site for more detailed information.

THINK CRITICALLY

1. Why are more consumers opting to buy goods and services online?
2. What concerns do many consumers have about purchasing online? How can an e-commerce travel business overcome those concerns?
3. What strategies can an e-commerce travel business use to overcome its competition?
4. What information should be included on the web site of an e-commerce travel business? Why is this information important?

Economic Impact of Travel and Tourism

9

Photodisc

Point Your
Browser

travel.swlearning.com

The Inn at Little Washington

"The problem with the Inn at Little Washington is this: At some point you're going to have to leave," stated Jane Wooldridge in an article she wrote for the *Miami Herald*. Washington, Virginia, known as "Little Washington," is located at the foothills of the Blue Ridge Mountains, 67 miles west of Washington, D.C. The restaurant and 15-room inn are the masterful creation of Patrick O'Connell and Reinhardt Lynch. They opened the inn in 1978 after saving about $5,000 and transforming a defunct garage/country store into a dining room and kitchen.

The fortunate first diners at the inn paid $8.95 for dinner. The next week, a restaurant reviewer from Washington, D.C., named the inn the best restaurant within a 150-mile radius, and it continues to hold this title year after year. The Inn at Little Washington was the first establishment ever to receive *Mobile Travel Guide*'s five-star rating for both its restaurant and lodging. It has been ranked by the *International Herald Tribune* as one of the top ten restaurants in the world.

Meals at the inn are priced *table d'hôte*, or one price for the entire meal. Patrons choose from multiple selections for each of five courses. Each course provides an extraordinary taste and a visual delight. Owner and chef Patrick O'Connell is considered one of America's greatest chefs. After experiencing dinner in the main dining room, the only way to top the experience is to have a luxurious meal at the chef's table in the elegant kitchen. This dining option starts at about $300 per person during the week and $450 per person on Saturday. The meal is served in O'Connell's dream kitchen, banked with a wall of windows, grandiose murals, and a 16-foot-long Vulcan range imported from France. Kitchen diners are entertained by watching 28 cooks, dressed in black tunics, skullcaps, and dalmatian-spotted trousers, prepare the inn's signature meals.

THINK CRITICALLY

1. Why is the Inn at Little Washington such a successful business?

2. Why would someone pay $300 for a meal?

Financial Analysis

Explain the role of financing in the travel and tourism industry.

Describe key financial business records.

All Aboard

Marriott International takes extra care to assure that all of its international managers receive the training needed to improve profitability, drive revenue, and develop leadership. To help develop management talent, Marriott managers attend a three-day training session that uses a computer-based hotel management simulation.

For their computer-based hotel, teams of managers make decisions about revenue and cost management, market positioning, sales, facility and service standards, and capital investment. The training simulation mimics real-life situations and prepares the managers to operate their own hotels more effectively and profitably.

Work with a partner. Discuss how a computer simulation of a hotel might help a manager understand the impact of financial decisions. What aspects of real-life hotel operations might be difficult to simulate?

MANAGING COSTS AND CASH FLOW

FINANCING

The costs of a travel and tourism business must be controlled and managed if the company is to stay in business. Decisions made about where and how to spend money impact the profitability of a business. **Financing** involves budgeting, finding ways to pay the costs of doing business,

Photodisc

keeping costs lower than revenue, and helping customers find ways to pay for the company's products or services.

Budgeting

Business budgets are plans for how a business will spend and make money. A budget is a road map for spending. It has a planned outcome—to control costs so they do not exceed the funds available. Budgets are usually prepared for one year and divided into monthly segments. The monthly costs of operation include costs of office space, equipment, utilities, computers and software, salaries, marketing, and taxes. Determining the costs requires experience. New businesses usually need help from financial advisors to make sure they have thought of all the costs, determined them correctly, and made allowances for unanticipated expenses. For example, if an airline budgets to pay for fuel and the price of fuel increases by 15 percent over what was budgeted, other expenses may need to be cut or sales prices increased to cover the extra cost of the fuel. Suppose the airline wins a large contract to be the main travel supplier of a major company. If the airline has to add flights to accommodate the increased business, the cost of the added flights, such as fuel and additional staffing, may need to be paid before the airline receives revenue from the new contract. A budget can help the business control how it will spend available funds.

Marketing Myths

In the *Wall Street Journal* article "Frequent Criers," Katherine Rosman tells about a couple celebrating their first wedding anniversary. They used 300,000 frequent-flyer miles to fly first class from London to Barbados on British Airways. They were expecting impeccable, adult-level service, but instead were asked to sit separately to accommodate some fidgety children. They also watched a nearby diaper change and had to listen to a baby cry during the entire flight.

After the trip, the couple wrote to British Airways and complained. The airline offered 30,000 frequent-flyer miles as compensation for their inconvenience.

THINK CRITICALLY

1. Should passengers with a first-class ticket expect better service? Why or why not?

2. Was the airline's compensation to the passengers adequate? Discuss your opinion.

Forecasting

Closely related to budgeting is **forecasting**, where a business predicts the expected income from potential sales and the expected expenditures and costs for a specified future period. *Fixed costs*, such as rent, are set costs and occur whether anything has been sold or not. *Variable costs*, such as shipping charges or the cost of fuel, change with the volume of business and are less easily predicted. Both fixed and variable costs are included in the forecast of expenditures.

The potential for income from sales is more difficult to predict. It should be predicted with caution, leaning toward a conservative estimate. Selling more than predicted can be better news than selling less than predicted and not having the expected revenue needed to cover costs. For an established business, expected future sales may be based on sales patterns during the previous year and adjusted for any changes in the economic environment.

The forecast is used to determine the flow of cash in and out of a business and to predict **cash flow gaps**, when there is not enough cash coming in to cover the cash being paid out. Not having enough accessible cash to pay bills, purchase new products to sell, or pay salaries can cause the business to fail. Forecasting and planning for ups and downs in the cash flow is an important part of business success.

Establishing Credit

Both large and small companies will set up a line of credit with a financial institution. A **line of credit** is an amount of money that a financial institution will loan the company for a short period of time to cover cash flow gaps. A line of credit should be set up well before the actual need exists. It can be arranged to allow the business to draw the money as needed.

A budget includes the sources of funds that will be used to pay all costs. Sources for financing the business may include personal savings or money borrowed from others, including loans from financial institutions or investors. Loans are made based on the creditworthiness of the business and its owners. To be creditworthy, an individual or business must have a history of paying bills on time, have a realistic budget and cash flow plan, and have *collateral*, or possessions that can be used to secure the loan. If the borrower can't pay back the loan, the lender becomes the owner of the collateral. Loans include *interest* stated as a percentage of the amount borrowed. Interest is paid to the lenders for the use of their money. Loan interest is another cost of doing business that must be included in the budget.

Stopover What is the purpose of a budget?

_____

_____

Digital Vision

FINANCIAL TOOLS

FINANCING

Keeping track of revenue and expenses is critical in determining the success of a company. The tools used to keep track of the financial performance of a business are **financial statements**. Two of the most important financial statements are the income statement and the balance sheet.

The Bottom Line

The **income statement** is the business's scorecard. It provides data that show whether the company has earned a profit or suffered a loss. It includes all of the revenue and expenses for the company *during a certain period of time*. Income statements are usually prepared yearly. Interim statements are prepared monthly to track how the business is doing throughout the year.

Tamika's Travel Company
Income Statement
For the Period Ending May 31, 20XX

Revenue		
Gross sales	$320,000	
Less refunds and rebates	3,045	
Net sales	$316,955	
Less cost of products	210,000	
Gross profit/margin		$106,955
Expenses		
Operating expenses:		
Salaries	$43,000	
Advertising	11,567	
Transportation	11,200	
Supplies	4,450	
Rent	3,000	
Insurance	2,500	
Interest expense	2,357	
Miscellaneous expense	500	
Total operating expenses		78,574
Net income before taxes		$ 28,381
Taxes		11,352
Net income		$ 17,029

Balancing Act

To determine if a business is financially stable, an investor or lender will want to see a **balance sheet** that shows the relationships among the assets, liabilities, and owners' equity. Unlike the income statement, the balance sheet represents a snapshot of the business *at a given time*, rather than covering a period of time.

Assets are the resources a company owns that will help it make a profit. Assets include cash, inventory, and equipment. *Liabilities* are the amounts of money or services owed by the company to others. The difference between total assets and total liabilities is *owners' equity*. Owners' equity is also known as *capital* and is the amount the owners have invested in the business. The term *balance sheet* is used because, as in the example below, the assets must balance with, or be equal to, the total liabilities and owners' equity. The balance sheet is an important tool that is used to monitor the financial health of the company and prompt changes before the company is too far in debt.

Ming's Travel and Tourism
Balance Sheet
May 31, 20XX

Assets

Cash	$88,000	
Accounts receivable	54,780	
Inventory	5,000	
Equipment/computers	14,000	
Total assets		**$161,780**

Liabilities

Accounts payable	$78,000	
Loans	23,500	
Taxes	11,352	
Total liabilities		$112,852

Owners' Equity

Capital invested	$30,000	
Retained earnings	18,928	
Total owners' equity		48,928
Total liabilities and owners' equity		**$161,780**

Stopover What are the differences between an income statement and a balance sheet?

Understand Marketing Concepts

Circle the best answer for each of the following questions.

1. Financing involves
   a. finding ways to pay the costs of doing business.
   b. helping customers find ways to pay for products or services.
   c. budgeting.
   d. all of the above.

2. A forecast is
   a. a way to please customers.
   b. the balance of assets and liabilities.
   c. a prediction.
   d. a slow period with little cash flowing in.

Think Critically

Answer the following questions as completely as possible. If necessary, use a separate sheet of paper.

3. Work with a partner. List several unanticipated expenses that might occur in a travel and tourism business.

_____

_____

_____

_____

_____

_____

_____

_____

4. Describe the difference between fixed costs and variable costs in operating a business. List examples of each.

_____

_____

_____

_____

_____

_____

_____

_____

_____

_____

Pricing

Describe pricing and yield management as related to travel and tourism.

Define taxes and fees, and understand how they affect travel suppliers and consumers.

All Aboard

Personal selling and customer service can be expensive as compared to providing these services over the Internet. A number of airlines now charge customers a $5 fee for booking their airline tickets over the phone and a $10 fee for buying tickets at the airport. The fees apply even if the tickets are purchased with assistance in an airline's airport club room, where travelers pay up to $250 per year to gain membership. Currently, no fees are charged for booking tickets online. Some airlines even offer bonus frequent-flyer miles for online ticket purchases.

Airlines have added fees in an attempt to drive more customers to the online distribution system, which is more cost effective to operate. In return, customers are demanding that the web sites become more user friendly. Some customers find ways around the fees by discussing travel options with airline representatives over the phone and then making their final purchases online.

Work with a partner. Discuss how the distribution system used to provide airline services can impact the provider's cost. Is there a balance to be reached between pleasing the customer and pricing of services? Do you believe airlines should charge fees for tickets that are not purchased online? Why or why not?

SUPPLY AND DEMAND

PRICING

Airline ticket prices are subject to change frequently, even hourly, as are hotel and car rental prices. An airline passenger may have paid hundreds of dollars more or less than the passenger sitting in the next seat. The reasons for the price variations are the shifts in supply and demand and the different passenger categories. One passenger may have booked a full-fare, refundable economy ticket at the last minute. Another passenger may have purchased a non-refundable ticket months in advance and received a discounted price.

Yield Management

Travel and tourism businesses seek to level out the number of travelers using their services at any one time and to maximize their **yield**, or revenue per person. To accomplish these goals, the businesses use a tool referred to as *yield management*. Yield management software tracks and analyzes demand patterns, cancellations, overbookings, traffic flow, and prices. The software offers solutions to help level out the demand for a business's products or services.

Because the travel and tourism industry has a fixed number of airline seats and hotel rooms available, more seats or rooms cannot be generated quickly or easily in response to an increase in demand. Travel products are also *perishable*, meaning that, for example, if a hotel room is not rented for a night, then the inventory cannot be stored. That night's rent is lost revenue that cannot be recovered. The standard for measuring revenue at hotels is **revenue per available room (REVPAR)**. It is determined by multiplying the average daily room rate by the occupancy rate. The **occupancy rate** is a percentage determined by dividing the total number of rooms sold by the total number of rooms available. REVPAR is improved with each additional room sale. The revenue from each additional sale helps cover the hotel's fixed costs, and each sale creates relatively few additional variable costs.

$$\text{REVPAR} = \text{Average daily room rate} \times \text{Occupancy rate}$$

$$\text{Occupancy rate} = \frac{\text{Total number of rooms sold}}{\text{Total number of rooms available}}$$

Airline tickets, hotel rooms, and car rentals are usually sold in advance, and their demand changes over time. Some customers are able to plan early and purchase their airline tickets months in advance. Others need tickets within a few days of departure. Yield management allows the seller to control inventory and maximize profits. The ideal solution is to find a balance between selling more seats in advance at a lower price and selling fewer seats immediately at a higher price. The forecasted demand helps determine the right price at the right time. Because an additional customer adds little to the variable cost of the existing service, maximizing volume and price can significantly improve yield.

Elasticity

A change in price can dramatically affect the demand for some travel products and services. The law of demand states that if price goes down, demand will increase. When a price change results in a change in demand, the demand is *elastic*. When a price change does not result in a change in demand, the demand is *inelastic*. If an airline flight's destination is an area that has an outbreak of a deadly disease, the demand for the flight will be inelastic. Lowering the price will not likely increase the number of tickets sold.

One of the factors impacting the elasticity of a product or service is the availability of alternatives. An area's only hotel can increase its price and have little impact on demand. If there are many competing hotels in the same area, the demand for any one of the hotels could be very elastic.

What is *yield management*, and how is it used?

Stopover

TAXES AND FEES

PRICING

Added to the price of travel products and services are taxes and fees. Both are paid by the consumer who purchases a product or service. A governmental body imposes taxes. It is sometimes difficult to determine who is imposing fees. Taxes and fees are stated separately from, and are in addition to, the base price.

Cost Add-Ons

Governments at the local, state, and/or national levels legally levy the taxes added to the cost of travel and tourism services. The taxes may be calculated as a percentage of the total retail cost or may be assessed as a flat amount. The product or service provider, such as a hotel, is required by law to collect the taxes and submit them to the taxing authorities.

Many states have taxes that are charged on hotel rooms, meals, and resort usage. Some states have additional taxes, such as convention or cultural center facility taxes. Salt Lake County in Utah has a tourism tax that adds 1 percent to the cost of all prepared foods and beverages and a room tax that adds 3.5 percent to the cost of all hotel rooms. The funds collected from such taxes are often used to promote tourism in the area and to provide public funding for tourism facilities.

The taxes and fees on airline travel have increased dramatically in recent years. For example, assume that a round-trip, direct flight from Houston to Orlando on Continental Airlines has a base fare of $202.80. The traveler will actually pay $232.40. The additional $29.60 comes from taxes and fees.

- Federal excise tax = $15.20. This 7.5 percent tax helps pay for the operation of the air traffic control system and airport infrastructure.

- Flight segment tax = $6.40. This flat-rate tax of $3.20 is charged for each flight segment (takeoff through landing) and is adjusted upward annually for inflation. The money pays for the Federal Aviation Administration (FAA) and airport activities.

- Security service fee = $5.00. This fee is used to pay for federally controlled security measures. The fee is $2.50 per passenger per "enplanement," meaning that it is charged each time a passenger boards a plane during a trip.

- Passenger facility charge = $3.00. The local airport assesses this fee for airport projects. The fee can be up to $4.50 per passenger.

Notice that the flight segment tax and security service fee would have doubled if the trip had included a layover and connecting flight.

Airlines feel the additional taxes and fees are hurting their business. Low-fare airlines, such as Southwest Airlines, feel that the flat-rate taxes and fees are particularly unfair to their customers. As a percentage, the airlines say that these taxes and fees shift a disproportionate burden to those customers who are trying to save costs with lower fares. As part of the base fare, airlines also include indirect charges for federal fuel excise taxes, federal and state income taxes, payroll taxes, and more.

Hidden Fees

Travel and tourism suppliers sometimes feel targeted by tax assessors, but the suppliers also have been known to sneak in some extra fees of their own. In the competitive, low- to mid-price range of the travel business, low advertised prices can make the difference in winning the business of the cost-conscious consumers. Winning loyal customers takes upfront honesty. Hidden fees are a sure way to alienate customers.

Hotel guests expect to have in-room telephones, even though most carry cell phones and never use the hotel phones. Usage of in-room phones was once a source of revenue for hotels. Some hotels now charge a flat fee for an in-room phone, whether it is used or not.

Some hotels "nickel and dime" their customers by adding fees to their final bills for items that consumers generally assume to be included in the room rate. *Consumer Reports'* readers complained about "sneaky" fees, such as a swimming pool fee assessed whether they used the pool or not, an early arrival fee of $50 for checking in before the regular check-in time, and a $50 fee for the front desk to receive a package delivery for a guest. Other fees may be added to cover housekeeper and bellhop gratuities, in-room coffee, local phone calls, and parking. *Consumer Reports* stated that hotels earned $1.3 billion in fees and surcharges in 2004. Hotels will continue to look for ways to increase revenue while remaining competitive with base prices.

Wingate Inns prides itself for not charging guests extra, unexpected fees. Wingate states on its web site that one of its goals is "to astonish you with one, all-inclusive rate that buys you lots of things other moderately priced and luxury hotel chains don't offer." Wingate also surveys customers to learn what additional amenities they would like to see offered. Wingate is winning loyal customers.

Missing the Boat

The cost of a cruise varies based on a number of factors, including the space per passenger, the number of crew members per passenger, the size and location of the booked cabin, the season, and the duration of the cruise. Most cruise lines offer discounts for advanced ticketing. Refund policies vary, and there are many complaints about denied refunds.

A party of four people had paid in full for a cruise. When one person in the party had to cancel, cruise line personnel told the remaining three that the price of their cruise had been quoted too low. Instead of giving a refund for the cancelled ticket, the cruise line representative applied the canceled person's payment to the new, higher cost for the remaining three travelers.

THINK CRITICALLY

1. Should a cruise line be able to increase the price once a trip has been paid in full? Why or why not?

2. Under what circumstances should a refund be given for cancelled trips? Explain your opinion.

How are taxes distinct from fees?

Stopover

Understand Marketing Concepts

Circle the best answer for each of the following questions.

1. To improve REVPAR, a hotel should
    a. increase salaries.
    b. sell additional hotel rooms.
    c. reduce costs.
    d. subtract expenses.

2. When a price change results in a change in demand, the demand is
    a. zero.
    b. elastic.
    c. inelastic.
    d. competitive.

Think Critically

Answer the following questions as completely as possible. If necessary, use a separate sheet of paper.

3. **Economics** Why would airlines and other travel suppliers be concerned about taxes that consumers must pay as part of buying the suppliers' products and services?

_____

_____

_____

_____

_____

_____

_____

4. **Communication** Explain in a written paragraph why vacant airline seats and hotel rooms are considered perishable products.

_____

_____

_____

_____

_____

_____

_____

_____

Economic Utility

Goals

Define economic utility and its four categories.

Describe how the marketing mix impacts economic utility.

All Aboard

The International Air Transport Association (IATA) sets guidelines on a wide range of matters, including ticket printing. The association currently has 270 airline carrier members. Until January 2005, the IATA members printed a code that showed where a ticket was purchased. The code allowed airlines to charge a price according to where a round trip originated.

A change in guidelines now allows passengers to save on fares for flights originating in low-fare markets. Previously, if passengers originated a round trip in a high-fare market, they paid the high fare for both segments. With the change, passengers can buy two one-way fares, booking the return flight from the low-fare market at the low-fare price. Passengers can buy the return ticket without physically being in the low-fare market area.

Work with a partner. Find a web site that sells airline tickets for international flights. Compare the difference in a round-trip ticket from London to Bangkok, first originating in London and then originating in Bangkok. Is there a difference in the price? Discuss your findings.

ECONOMICS

Economics is a social science that studies the production, distribution, trade, and consumption of goods and services. There are two main areas of economics. *Microeconomics* examines individual households and businesses. *Macroeconomics* focuses on the economy as a whole. Economics looks at the choices made based on constraints, such as limited money to spend on vacations and limited time off.

Photodisc

What a Concept!

The behavior of consumers is of great interest to economists and travel and tourism marketers. The **marketing concept** focuses on consumers' wants and needs during the planning, production, promotion, and distribution of travel products and services. Studying consumer behavior is one way to determine customers' satisfaction with products and services.

Maximum Satisfaction

Some economists believe that, given the opportunity, people will maximize their satisfaction, or **economic utility**, with products or services. Up to a point, more vacation time and more wealth will increase utility, but at a decreasing rate. Because most people have limited time and money to spend on vacations, they must make decisions on what will bring them the most satisfaction. For example, they can choose to buy a non-stop airline ticket that will allow them to arrive at their destination faster, but they may have to pay more for the flight.

Increasing the utility provided by products and services is a goal of travel and tourism marketers. Consumers are willing to pay more for a product that brings them more satisfaction. People expect to pay more for first-class service, but they are only satisfied if the service is truly better than the less-expensive alternatives. Utility improvements can take place in four categories—form, time, place, and possession.

Form Utility When the tangible parts of a product or service impact satisfaction, form utility occurs. If a hotel room is small, dark, and dirty, improving these physical characteristics will increase the utility for the hotel guest. Moving a passenger from a narrow seat in coach class to a wide, leather seat in first class will improve the passenger's form utility. Improving the tangible parts of the product or service can improve the customer's level of satisfaction.

Time Utility When the product or service is available when the customer wants it, time utility is achieved. A hotel room may be perfectly sized, decorated, clean, and well lit, but if it is not ready and available when the guest arrives at check-in time, the guest will not be satisfied.

Place Utility When the product or service is found at a desired location, place utility is ensured. A hotel's convenient location near an airport, freeway exit, or convention center may increase place utility for some customers. A location on the beach or near a tourist attraction will increase place utility for others. Conveniently locating a hotel for easy access may be expensive, but it increases place utility.

Possession Utility When the product or service is offered to customers at a price they can afford and with a convenient method of payment, possession utility is achieved. Arranging installment loans through local banks to help customers pay for large purchases is an example of improving possession utility. Allowing customers the convenience of purchasing with credit cards also increases possession utility.

THE MARKETING MIX

Using the marketing concept means keeping customer needs and wants in mind. It includes taking time to improve economic utility and to develop the right **marketing mix**—the right blend of products, pricing, promotion, and distribution. By improving economic utility through form, time, place, or possession, a marketer can improve customer satisfaction. Having the right product in the right place at the right price and letting customers know about it through promotion ensures higher utility.

Once a business has selected its target customers, it then begins to design its products and services around the customers' needs and wants. A target group may be selected based on demographics. One of the largest and fastest-growing groups in the United States is the Hispanic or Latino market. In the past 25 years, the number of Hispanics in the United States has increased from 10 million to over 25 million. As with any ethnic group, Hispanics cannot be characterized as all the same. Hispanics have a range of income and education levels that matches that of the general U.S. population. Many Hispanics prefer to be identified with the countries of their heritage, such as Mexican-American or Cuban-American. Knowing customers' preferences is a key to marketing.

Products, such as a vacation package, can be tailored to fit the known preferences of the target group. Including destinations known to appeal to the target group and then tweaking the specifics, such as optional side trips, can improve the product's utility.

Pricing a vacation package can take much time and thought. All of the features must be included and the pricing from the travel supplier understood, with no hidden fees. The final price must be within the range the target customer is able and willing to pay. Additionally, the

E-Ticket

Hotels and online booking agents have, in many cases, reached agreement on pricing. Hotel web sites and online travel agencies now offer the same price for rooms. While bargains were once available from the online agencies, many of the agencies have agreed not to undercut the prices that are on the hotels' web sites. Because the agency sites bring hundreds of bookings to hotels, the hotels wanted to continue using them. At the same time, the hotels wanted to bring customers back to their own, more profitable web sites. As a compromise, many hotels have agreed to pay online agencies as much as 20 percent of the cost of a room booked through the agencies' sites.

THINK CRITICALLY

Visit an online booking agency, and check the price of a hotel room. Then check the price on the hotel's own web site. Are they the same? Why would customers continue to use the online booking agencies?

travel agent putting the package together must include enough commission or other payment to make the time spent worth the effort.

Promotion efforts must be used to make the target customer aware of the product, especially when trying to attract new customers. The appropriate message must be crafted, and the right media must be selected, to get the message to those in the target group and cause them to act. Knowledge of advertising and the media most accessed by the target group is necessary to determine the right forms of promotion to include in the marketing mix.

Distribution of the product is the final element of the marketing mix. Delivering the product to the customer at the right time or offering the product to the customer at a convenient location can make the difference in customer satisfaction.

Finding the right combination of these four marketing elements creates the perfect marketing mix and leads to maximized utility for customers. Satisfied customers are repeat customers. They tell their friends about their wonderful vacation, leading to new potential customers.

Stopover

Why is it important to target a customer with the marketing mix?

_____

_____

Five-Star Traveler

XAVIER VILLALON

Bringing in top-name musical groups and special events to continually fill the 10,000 seats in the American Bank Center Arena in Corpus Christi, Texas, is a huge effort. The man in charge of making it happen is Xavier Villalon, director of marketing and sales for the American Bank Center and an employee of SMG. SMG is one of the largest convention, arena, and stadium management companies in the United States. It has more than 177 venues in the United States and Europe. SMG's customers are primarily large cities, and they are not always easy to please.

At age 31, Xavier Villalon came to SMG well prepared for the role of director. He graduated with a bachelor's degree in business administration with an emphasis in marketing. He began his career as a media coordinator for an advertising agency that pioneered targeting the Hispanic market. He then moved into national sales for Univision Communications, Inc., one of the leading Hispanic media networks in the United States. SMG sought out Villalon to help propel the American Bank Center Arena into a viable venue, to build a relationship with the community, and to build Corpus Christi into a center for entertainment and tourism.

THINK CRITICALLY

Look at the web site for the American Bank Center Arena. What is the next event? Name one way the web site works to improve utility for customers.

Understand Marketing Concepts

Circle the best answer for each of the following questions.

1. A category of economic utility is
   a. form.
   b. time.
   c. possession.
   d. all of the above.

2. The four elements of the marketing mix are
   a. purchasing, distribution, financing, and pricing.
   b. form, time, place, and possession.
   c. profit, loss, revenue, and yield.
   d. products, pricing, promotion, and distribution.

Think Critically

Answer the following questions as completely as possible. If necessary, use a separate sheet of paper.

3. **Communication** Describe an example of how a hotel could improve the possession utility for its guests.

_____

_____

_____

_____

_____

_____

4. Choose a specific travel product. List the elements of the marketing mix for that product. Who is the target customer? Does the marketing mix meet the needs of the customer? Why or why not?

_____

_____

_____

_____

_____

_____

_____

_____

Review Marketing Concepts

Write the letter of the term that matches each definition. Some terms will not be used.

_____ 1. Shows the relationships among the assets, liabilities, and owners' equity of a business

_____ 2. Satisfaction with products or services

_____ 3. Budgeting, finding ways to pay the costs of doing business, keeping costs lower than revenue, and helping customers find ways to pay for the company's products or services

_____ 4. The tools used to keep track of the financial performance of a business

_____ 5. The right blend of products, pricing, promotion, and distribution

_____ 6. Plans for how a business will spend and make money

_____ 7. The average daily room rate multiplied by the occupancy rate

_____ 8. When there is not enough cash coming in to cover the cash being paid out

_____ 9. Focuses on consumers' wants and needs during the planning, production, promotion, and distribution of travel products and services

_____ 10. Revenue per person

_____ 11. A business's scorecard that indicates whether the business has earned a profit or suffered a loss

a. balance sheet
b. business budgets
c. cash flow gaps
d. economic utility
e. financing
f. financial statements
g. forecasting
h. income statement
i. line of credit
j. marketing concept
k. marketing mix
l. occupancy rate
m. revenue per available room (REVPAR)
n. yield

Circle the best answer.

12. An example of a fixed cost is
    a. rent.
    b. profits.
    c. fuel.
    d. tickets.

13. Forecasting
    a. helps determine possible cash flow gaps.
    b. is closely related to budgeting.
    c. is predicting the expected income from potential sales and the expected expenditures and costs for a specified future period.
    d. can be all of the above.

Think Critically

14. How is a budget like a road map for spending? Explain this analogy.

_____

_____

_____

_____

15. What does it mean to be creditworthy? What does it take to reach that status? Why is creditworthiness based on an individual's past record and not on what the individual plans to do in the future?

_____

_____

_____

_____

_____

16. Provide an example, other than one given in the chapter, of improving each of the four categories of utility.

_____

_____

_____

_____

_____

17. Your target customer is a 25- to 40-year-old, well-educated business traveler. Choose a business, and describe the marketing mix you would develop to please your target customer. Explain why you chose each element of the mix.

_____

_____

_____

_____

18. Consider the students in your school. Write a paragraph about what would happen to the marketing mix if a travel supplier assumed that every student had the exact same preferences.

_____

_____

_____

_____

Make Connections

19. **Marketing Math** Your hotel averages occupancy of 120 rooms out of 150 available. Your average daily room rate is $128. What is your REVPAR? What happens to your REVPAR if you increase your occupancy to an average of 135 rooms?

_____

_____

_____

_____

20. **History** What is the oldest successful restaurant in your area? Research its history. Write a paragraph about what the restaurant has done in the past to create economic utility for its customers.

_____

_____

_____

_____

21. **Geography** Your client has an upcoming business trip to Athens, Greece, and plans to spend an extra three days there to sightsee. Her husband will take vacation time and go along on the trip. He is interested in learning about Greece and will have two days to explore on his own while his wife is in meetings. Use the Internet and/or other sources to make a list of sites for him to visit. Then, plan an itinerary for the couple for the remaining three days of their trip.

_____

_____

_____

_____

22. **Marketing Math** Use spreadsheet software to create an income statement for your travel agency based on the following information. What is your net income after taxes?

Gross sales, $150,000; refunds and rebates, $2,500; cost of products, $86,200; salaries expense, $10,000; advertising expense, $5,430; supplies expense, $1,500; rent expense, $800; interest expense, $500; taxes, $1,760

_____

_____

_____

_____

_____

23. Research The cost of fuel is a critical factor in travel. Use the Internet to research energy sources that are alternatives to petroleum-based fuel. Write a page about the alternatives, their current usage, and their expected future impacts on current modes of transportation.

_____

_____

_____

_____

_____

_____

24. Communication You want to be open and honest with your customers. You need to earn 20 percent above your costs to achieve a reasonable profit. Write a paragraph explaining your pricing policies.

_____

_____

_____

_____

_____

_____

_____

EXTENDED STAY

Project As the owner of a new travel and tourism business, you would like to establish a line of credit with a financial institution. The loan officer wants to see your personal balance sheet. Your assets and liabilities are as follows.

Assets: home, $230,000; car, $23,000; savings/investments, $23,000
Liabilities: home mortgage, $200,145; college loan, $12,000; car loan, $15,000

Work with a group and complete the following activities.
1. Develop a personal balance sheet using spreadsheet software.
2. If the lender is willing to offer you a business line of credit equal to your personal equity, determine how much you can borrow.
3. Make a list of things you can do to prove to the lender that you are creditworthy.

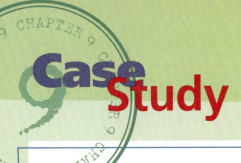
PAYING FOR TOURISM CAMPAIGNS

Competition among states for tourism dollars is fierce. Some of the best marketing campaigns include unique and memorable commercials, billboards, newspaper advertisements, web sites, and bulk mailings. Creative marketing campaigns cost large sums of money.

Many states have decided to collect extra taxes on lodging and car rentals to pay for the travel and tourism campaigns. Frequently, these special taxes are also used to pay for new entertainment venues directly related to travel and tourism. Voters must approve the taxes, and there is debate on both sides of the tax issue.

While the special lodging and car rental taxes provide an economic boost for effective state tourism marketing campaigns, these same taxes can actually stifle travel and tourism. The extra taxes can be as high as 10 percent of the total charges. Combined with regular sales taxes and other fees, the actual cost of a room can become excessive. A $150 hotel room can actually cost $170 per night, once all taxes are added to the bill. In one extreme example, taxes assessed at hotel checkout in Elko, Nevada, total 18 percent of the base room rate. Rental cars that cost $30 per day can actually cost $36 per day with the additional taxes. Multiply the extra charges by several days' stay, and the traveler ends up paying an additional $100 to $200 in taxes.

The additional charges on a hotel room or car rental can result in prices that are undesirable and burdensome to conference attendees and other travelers. When the costs end up exceeding travelers' budgets, they may think twice about returning, cut short future stays, or plan upcoming events in areas with lower tax rates.

Some people feel that special lodging and car rental taxes should be fully disclosed when prices are quoted. Out-of-state tourists wonder why they should pay the bill for another state's tourism campaigns.

THINK CRITICALLY

1. What is the purpose of special lodging and car rental taxes?
2. What additional goods or services could be taxed to help pay for state tourism promotions? Choose one alternative and defend it as the best source for additional funding. Should your source replace current tourism taxes? Why or why not?
3. Should hotels and car rental companies be required to quote their rates inclusive of all taxes and fees? Defend your opinion.
4. Should out-of-state tourists have to pay for the tourism marketing campaigns of the states they are visiting? Why or why not?
5. List an advantage and a disadvantage of special lodging and car rental taxes.

ADVERTISING CAMPAIGN EVENT

Travel and tourism is ranked in the top three financial industries for most states. Competition for tourism dollars becomes fierce, with unique television commercials and colorful, informative brochures. Successful advertising campaigns draw tourists to locations that they previously would not have considered visiting.

Together with one or two of your classmates, choose a state not well known for tourism. As a team, you will develop an effective advertising campaign to attract more tourists to the state. The advertising campaign should highlight activities and locations for tourists to visit.

You must prepare a written presentation, including outlined fact sheets, that describes your advertising campaign in detail. The body of the written document should be no more than ten pages, not including the title page and table of contents. You will then develop an oral presentation based on your written plan. You may use visual aids and/or a laptop computer to enhance your presentation.

You will be given a maximum of 15 minutes to present your campaign proposals to the state tourism board (judges) and five minutes to respond to questions.

Performance Indicators Evaluated

- Define the economic importance of travel and tourism for most states.
- Design an effective advertising campaign for the chosen state.
- Emphasize tourist attractions for the chosen state.
- Describe the forms of media to carry out the advertising campaign.
- Communicate the advertising campaign clearly to interested parties.

Go to the DECA web site for more detailed information.

THINK CRITICALLY

1. Why do states spend sizable amounts of money on travel and tourism advertisements?
2. How can a state that is not well known for tourism increase its market share of tourism dollars?
3. How does a state's tourism board select regional television audiences to target for its travel and tourism commercials?
4. List three marketing strategies a state can use to increase travel and tourism.

www.deca.org

Travel and Tourism Promotion and Sales

CHAPTER 10 • CHAPTER 10 • CHAPTER 10 • CHAPTER 10 • CHAPTER 10

10

Photodisc

10.1 Promotional Plans

10.2 Advertising and Public Relations

10.3 Sales Promotion and Selling

Point Your Browser

▶ ▶ ▶ ▶ ▶ ▶ **travel.swlearning.com**

Gulfood

Since 1987, the Gulf Food, Hotel & Equipment Exhibition (Gulfood) has helped exhibitors from the Middle East, Australia, South Africa, Russia, and other countries promote their goods. Gulfood is held in and around the Dubai World Trade Centre in Dubai, the capital of the United Arab Emirates. This four-day trade show for food, beverage, and food service technology, supplies, and equipment businesses attracts more than 29,000 people from 127 countries to view exhibits by more than 1,700 companies. It is the largest and most-attended event in the Middle East. Gulfood was held every two years until 2006, when it became an annual event.

Because Middle Eastern countries import the majority of their foods, the Gulfood trade exhibit is an important show for the food service and hospitality industries. Gulfood is seen as the ultimate opportunity to promote new products and equipment to an international audience and to make market comparisons with the competition. Visitors include buyers from supermarkets, bakeries, hotels, restaurants, hospitals, and governments. Attracting potential customers from North Africa, India, the Middle East, and Eastern Europe, Gulfood is considered the definitive promotional event for the region's food service industry.

THINK CRITICALLY

1. What geographic elements would cause Middle Eastern countries to import a large percentage of their foods?

2. What media would you use to promote Gulfood to potential exhibitors and visitors? State the reasons for your choices.

0
100
200
300
400

Promotional Plans

Goals

Describe the components of promotion.

List the steps involved in developing a promotional plan.

All Aboard

The original Disneyland in Anaheim, California, opened in 1955. Disney used its 50th anniversary in 2005 to launch an 18-month promotion of all of the Disney parks. The promotion was intended to spark new interest, increase sagging park attendance with new attractions, and keep visitors at each park for a longer period of time.

The promotion was Disney's first global advertising campaign. The campaign utilized a mix of media, including television, print, and the Internet, to create excitement for Disney's parks. Simultaneous ads ran on several television networks. The ads and other sales promotions attempted to embed the theme of a "once in a lifetime event" into the minds of consumers.

Work with a partner. Discuss Disney's promotional campaign. Who was the intended customer? What information would you need in order to determine if the campaign was effective?

PROMOTIONAL COMPONENTS

PROMOTION

Having the right product at the right price in the right place is of no use if consumers are unaware of it. The business must also have the right mix of promotional components to make customers aware of the product.

Photodisc

Promotion is the marketing function that provides information to customers about the business and its products and encourages them to buy. When Disney marketers ran ads on several television networks at the same time, they were using a technique called a **roadblock** to saturate the market. They were hoping that few people would miss the major promotion.

The Right Promotion

If the product, price, and place are all wrong, promotion will generally not increase sales. But, if these three elements are right, promotion is the catalyst that can make sales happen. There are at least four distinct types of promotion—advertising, publicity, sales promotion, and personal selling.

Advertising is the paid communication of information about products and services. The one-way communication that takes place between the seller and potential customers is intended to increase sales. If a hotel's managers want to let people know about the hotel's new amenities or low price, they can use advertisements to communicate this information.

Publicity is communication to the public about a business that is not paid for or controlled by the company. The public image of a business is critical. It can be improved when the business participates in or sponsors community events, thereby creating good **public relations (PR)**, or positive and mutually beneficial relationships with the public. A business can try to generate positive publicity by hosting a special event that might attract media attention. For example, an airline might use public relations to generate publicity by flying the families of injured military personnel to visit them. A news story may be written about the event and mention the airline's generosity.

Sales promotion includes activities or materials that offer the customer an added reason to buy. The activities or materials are intended to support the efforts of the sales staff. Sales promotions include trade show booths, contests, coupons, free trials, catalogs, and special displays.

Photodisc

Personal selling is a one-on-one interaction with potential customers to inform them about products and services and persuade them to buy. Personal selling has many advantages. It provides customers with a chance to see or test a product firsthand. The salesperson has the opportunity to answer customers' questions. Additionally, the salesperson can form a positive relationship with customers that may bring them back as repeat buyers.

Mixing It Up

Promotion is one of the marketing mix components. The product and the customer will drive the choice of how to mix each of the distinct types of promotion—advertising, publicity, sales promotion, and personal selling. Maximizing the benefits of promotion and effectively planning the promotional mix require knowledge of the business's target customers.

Stopover How are advertising and publicity different?

_____

_____

PLANNING FOR PROMOTION

PROMOTION

A promotional plan is one component of a business's overall marketing plan. The promotional plan shapes the selected types of promotion into a coordinated effort that persuades the customer to buy. A promotional plan typically covers a full year.

A promotional plan can take many forms and includes the following steps.

1. **Decide on a purpose.** Promotion has at least three purposes—informing, reminding, and persuading. Whether you are providing information about travel and tourism services or reminding potential customers about the business's community involvement, the promotion needs to have a solid purpose based on measurable goals. A **measurable goal** is a statement of desired outcome for which data can be collected to affirm its accomplishment. For example, a goal to increase sales by three percent during the first six months of the year is specific enough to be measurable.

2. **Design the message.** Based on the purpose of the promotion, you must design a message that will communicate with the business's targeted audience. The message should appeal to the needs and interests of the targeted customers.

3. **Determine the promotional mix and the media to use.** The message can be conveyed through any of the four types of promotion. The types of promotion can be used individually or in various combinations. The audience, the purpose, the message, and the type of promotion will be the bases on which you will choose the type of media to use. The media can include billboards, newspapers, magazines, television, radio, direct mail, or the Internet.

4. **Develop a budget.** Before committing to the promotional ideas, you must determine the costs and create an overall budget for the promotion. Owners of a new business will probably spend as much as five percent of gross revenue on promotions. Once a customer base has been established, the amount spent on promotions may decrease, especially if the business is operating at or near maximum capacity. Even then, some promotional activities may be needed to help maintain sales.

Digital Vision

5. **Create the specific promotions and schedule them for the year.** Working with professionals is a smart move when creating the actual promotions. Each type of promotion and media used requires knowledge and skill to ensure the promotion has the intended impact and fulfills the intended purpose. Promotions can be timed to help level out any expected dips in sales.

6. **Measure the effectiveness of each promotion and improve the plan.** Based on the measurable goal for each promotion, data should be collected to assure that the promotion was worth the time, effort, and money spent. Feedback can be obtained from customers regarding the promotion. Did they choose your business as a result of the promotional efforts? Knowing if a promotion was effective or ineffective is important information as you plan future promotions.

Why is planning for promotion a necessary step for a business?

Stopover

_____

_____

Understand Marketing Concepts

Circle the best answer for each of the following questions.

1. Types of promotion in a promotional mix may include all of the following except
   a. advertising.
   b. publicity.
   c. personal selling.
   d. pricing.

2. A promotional plan includes
   a. purpose, message, promotional mix, media, budget, and schedule.
   b. exchanges, distribution, pricing, and sales.
   c. purchasing, planning, advertising, and distribution.
   d. financing, pricing, creating, and measuring.

Think Critically

Answer the following questions as completely as possible. If necessary, use a separate sheet of paper.

3. **Communication** Briefly describe how you would use each of the four major types of promotion to promote tourism for a destination in your region.

   _____

   _____

   _____

   _____

   _____

   _____

4. **Research** Find an example of a travel or tourism print ad. Write a paragraph about who you think the target customer is and why. Include in your paragraph the purpose of the ad and the type of print media used.

   _____

   _____

   _____

   _____

   _____

   _____

   _____

   _____

Advertising and Public Relations

Goals

- Explain the purpose and types of advertising.
- Describe ways to measure the effectiveness of advertising.
- Explain the value of positive publicity.

All Aboard

The annual Snowfest in Houston attracts about 23,000 people to view exhibits, as well as ski, snowboard, and tube on the indoor ski slopes. In return for a donation to the area food bank, attendees receive buckets of snow to use for snowball fights or building a snowman. Ski resorts, lodges, airlines, equipment rental companies, tourism bureaus, and newspapers sponsor the event.

Snowfest's promotional mix includes a tabloid-size newspaper supplement, a quarter-page newspaper ad, and radio and television commercials. Previous attendees are e-mailed about the event. Snowfest primarily attracts well-educated, above-average-income customers who are over 35 years old.

Work with a partner. Discuss how you would attempt to gain additional publicity for Snowfest.

AD IT UP

PROMOTION

People are bombarded with advertisements and often ignore much of the constant tirade, making many ads ineffective. Finding effective ways to get the message through to potential customers is a continuous challenge. Because advertising is paid, nonpersonal communication with existing and potential customers, it must be carefully designed to accomplish a specific goal so that advertising money is not wasted.

The Message and the Media

An advertisement must have a specific intended purpose, such as to inform, remind, or persuade. A hotel chain's managers may want to inform people that the company is opening a new location or persuade them to spend their vacations at one of the chain's various

Photodisc

About $248 billion are spent each year in the United States on advertising. A Yankelovich Partners poll showed that 54 percent of the people surveyed avoid buying products that overwhelm them with advertising.

properties. Generally, a theme for the entire promotional campaign is repeated in the advertisements, no matter what media are used. For example, an airline may advertise in travel magazines and on the Internet, but the theme will remain consistent.

Most media can be classified into one of four basic types—print, broadcast, electronic, and outdoor. Within each of those basic types are multiple options. In print media, for example, an advertisement can be run in a newspaper, a magazine, the Yellow Pages, a flyer, or a brochure. Each type of advertising media has pros and cons.

Advertising Media—Pros and Cons			
Type of Media	Example	Pros	Cons
Print	Newspaper	Large readership	Short time in front of customer
Broadcast	Television	Large audience, low cost per person reached	Expensive in total, requires large budget
Electronic	Internet	Easy to measure, often pay only for click-throughs	Limited audience
Outdoor	Billboard	Low cost	Increasingly restricted

The selection of the media is based on five factors.

1. Target customer

2. Cost of the media

3. **Reach**—the total number of people who will see the advertisement

4. **Frequency**—the total number of times the target audience will see or hear the advertisement

5. **Lead time**—the time needed to prepare the advertisement

The necessary lead time must be built into the promotional plan. A newspaper ad may be published just a few days after being prepared, but a TV commercial may take months to produce before airing.

Design

No matter what media are selected, the form of the advertisement requires knowledge of the basic principles of design. Each moment of a TV commercial must be planned just as carefully as the layout of a print media ad. Television and other visual broadcast advertisements begin with a script that puts into writing what will be said to catch the customers' attention. Three of the most effective words in advertisements are *new*, *easy*, and *results*. Next, a **storyboard** is created, where the action for each scene is outlined with rough drawings.

To counter the barrage of usual advertisements, newer forms of promotion have been created. Company blogs, infomercials, and product sponsorship and placement on TV programs are examples. On the TV game show *Wheel of Fortune*, contestants vie to win trips on airlines to destination hotels. Whether the contestants win or not, viewers are informed about the airlines and hotels.

Stopover

What is meant by an advertisement's "reach"?

_____

_____

ADVERTISING EFFECTIVENESS

MARKETING-INFORMATION MANAGEMENT

Advertising is a necessary expense for a successful business, and the business's managers need to know that its advertising dollars are being well spent. The effectiveness of advertising must be tracked, in order to determine if the right choices have been made in selecting the media and the message for the target customer.

Big-Ticket Items

When people choose a hotel for a business trip, they may make the decision quickly. Yet when people choose an expensive purchase, such as a one-month vacation to another country, it takes long-term planning and involves a number of steps. According to Chadwick Martin Bailey, a marketing research firm, consumers use a five-stage, decision-making process when considering whether to purchase an expensive item.

1. Awareness of the product or service

2. Favorable opinion of the product or service

3. Intent to purchase the product or service

4. Consideration of the cross-purchase of related items

5. Advocacy of the product or service to others

Marketing research can pinpoint the number of target customers in each of the five stages of the process. This information helps a company focus its advertising on the types of promotions that will drive additional sales of products and services based on the decision-making stages of its

Missing the Boat

An airline's managers decided to give airline tickets to a low-income family whose child needed medical attention in a distant city. An airline employee contacted the family and arranged for the flight at no cost. On the day of the flight, the family was met at the airport by a large number of journalists seeking photographs and more information about the child's medical needs. The airline's managers had contacted the news media, thinking this was an opportunity for positive publicity about the company.

THINK CRITICALLY

1. Do you think the airline's managers acted ethically? Why or why not?

2. Should an airline use a family's misfortune as an opportunity for publicity? Discuss your opinion with others.

customers. Advertisements can be designed to motivate the behavior of the customers, thereby increasing sales.

Built-In Evaluation

Some advertisements have built-in evaluation tools that provide information on the ads' effectiveness. A special phone number or a coded coupon on such an ad can provide information to the business about where the customer received the communication related to the product or service. The business can record the number of people who called the phone number or used the coupon and then purchased the product or service.

NuBoard Media is a company that has patented a non-residue adhesive used to attach plastic bags to the seat backs in sports venues. If an airline advertises a discounted fare on the seat-back bag and includes a special fare code or phone number, the response rate will easily determine the effectiveness of the promotion. The number of people in attendance at the sports event will also provide information on the reach of the ad. This knowledge will help the airline shape future advertising plans.

Clicks on a hotel's web site can be tied directly to individuals who actually make a reservation and check into the hotel. The keywords an individual uses to find the web site may be tracked and can help tie the effectiveness of the web site to specific customer behavior. The total number of visitors to the site can be compared to the actual online reservations made to help determine follow-through rates.

Stopover Why is it important to know the effectiveness of advertisements?

_____

_____

PUBLICITY

Positive publicity can help raise awareness of a product or service. A primary advantage of publicity is that it is free. The main disadvantage is that a business does not have control over the publicity it receives, and not all publicity is positive. To help keep the business's name in front of the public in a positive light, the company may issue news releases, volunteer in community work projects, and donate to worthy causes.

News Releases

Grabbing the attention of journalists through a news release of current happenings within the business may bring positive publicity. A **news release** is a short article sent to members of the media prior to a special event, in hopes that the event will be newsworthy enough to generate attention. The news release may be sent as part of a *press kit* that includes photos and other materials that may raise journalists' interest.

Assume you run a travel agency. You are aware of a deserving high-school student who has an opportunity to attend an International DECA Career Development Conference in another city. You have decided to sponsor this student with a free airline ticket to the event. A news release written from the proper angle may catch the attention of a journalist looking for a community-interest story. The readers or viewers of the story may be proud to learn of the deserving student who has worked hard representing the local school and earned the chance to attend the conference. The focus is on the student rather than on your travel agency, but the resulting positive publicity may be of benefit to both the school and your business.

A news release must contain the business's contact information, so that journalists can follow up to obtain the details of the story. Sometimes it is best to call journalists directly and provide them with enough information to see if they are interested in the story. If they want to know more, then additional information can be provided.

Public Relations

Maintaining a positive company image in the community requires continuous action. Making donations to local charities and volunteering to help with community events can keep the business in the public eye.

Public relations involves publicity, but it is a much broader type of communication intended to keep the business in a positive light with the public. Public relations can also include communication designed to provide "damage control" during times of crisis. Some large corporations' managers have been known to use questionable ethics to slant public opinion in their business's favor; they focus on one positive aspect of a situation but do not fully disclose all the facts. Other companies' managers have outright lied to the press. Unethical behavior and cover-ups generally catch up with a company and cause more harm than the original truth.

Companies that are good corporate citizens of the community can establish and maintain positive public relations. Businesses that are honest and upfront in their dealings, make donations, and volunteer in times of need acquire a positive image in the eyes of the community. In return, customers feel good about supporting the businesses.

What is the difference between public relations and publicity?

Stopover

Understand Marketing Concepts

Circle the best answer for each of the following questions.

1. The four basic types of media include
    a. planning, communication, questions, and concepts.
    b. purchases, correspondence, invoices, and packages.
    c. free, inexpensive, expensive, and luxury.
    d. print, broadcast, electronic, and outdoor.

2. The selection of advertising media is based on
    a. the cost.
    b. the reach and frequency.
    c. the target customer.
    d. all of the above.

Think Critically

Answer the following questions as completely as possible. If necessary, use a separate sheet of paper.

3. **Communication** Write a headline for a print ad promoting a vacation package. Use one of the three most effective words in advertisements—*easy*, *new*, or *results*—in the headline.

    _____

    _____

    _____

    _____

    _____

    _____

4. **Research** In at least two different media, find current advertisements (or past ads that ran concurrently) for Disney destinations. What is consistent about the ads? Is there a common theme?

    _____

    _____

    _____

    _____

    _____

    _____

    _____

Sales Promotion and Selling

Describe sales promotion through the techniques of incentives and touchpoints.

List and explain the steps of the sales process.

All Aboard

The Oasis Inn is more than a special retreat to the thousands of loyal customers who return again and again for the luxurious feeling of relaxation and comfort. Dorothy Kelly, the owner, personally focuses on making each person feel that he or she is the most special guest during each visit. Kelly also works with staff to assure they consistently create a comforting atmosphere.

People who lead hectic, stressful lives visit the Oasis Inn to relax and unwind. The guests look for the special attention to detail that only the Oasis Inn provides.

Dorothy Kelly frequently steps back to examine the business from a customer's point of view and improves the business based on her observations. As a result, the Oasis Inn stays fully sold out.

Work with a group. Discuss what is meant by the "customer's point of view." How can sales be focused on the customer's point of view?

PROMOTING THE SALE

Sales promotion is self-defining in that it is action oriented and intended to increase sales. It can involve a host of activities that go beyond advertising to provide the customer with motivations and incentives to take action and buy.

Incentives

Offering customers a loyalty program that rewards them for repeat business or providing them with a gift in the form of a travel gift certificate are examples of incentives that promote sales. A contest, where individuals enter to win an all-expenses-paid vacation at a resort, can be used to gather information about potential new customers as well as to keep existing customers interested in returning to the sponsoring business.

According to Theodore Levitt, a marketing professor at Harvard, the bonuses offered with a product are often more important than the product itself. Offering a customer an additional free day's rental and a U.S. atlas for renting a car for a week can make the difference in getting a prospect to choose one car rental agency over another.

Sales promotions can also include special financing opportunities that make it easier for the customer to buy. For example, the ability to

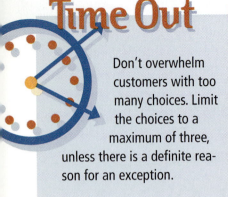

Time Out

Don't overwhelm customers with too many choices. Limit the choices to a maximum of three, unless there is a definite reason for an exception.

finance an expensive cruise at a low interest rate and pay for it over six months can make the decision to book the vacation a bit easier to make.

Touchpoints

At each point that a travel or tourism business makes contact with customers—whether it be over the Internet, by phone, or at hotel check-in—opportunity exists to increase sales for the business. Each of these opportunities is a **touchpoint** at which the relationship with the customer can be turned into increased revenue.

At each touchpoint, the customer must receive a consistently high standard of service. Mapping out the potential touchpoints and actually experiencing them as a customer would can help businesses obtain a customer's point of view. This experience can provide insight for offering additional products and services.

If a web site provides the ability to rent a car and reserve a hotel room while purchasing an airline ticket, additional revenue may be generated at this touchpoint. If, at the time of checkout, a hotel guest is invited to make reservations for the future, additional sales may be obtained. Each touchpoint is an opportunity for promoting additional sales.

Stopover   List two examples of incentives.

_____

_____

THE ART OF SELLING

Digital Vision

SELLING

The old saying "nothing happens until someone makes a sale" puts sales into perspective as a major function of marketing. Making a sale means using knowledge of the business's products and services to solve the customers' problems. Have you ever been approached by an employee in a retail store who asked, "May I help you?" Then, when you asked a question about the merchandise, did you find that the store representative couldn't answer? This employee was not a true salesperson. True salespeople know their products and services, and they take seriously their job of solving customers' problems.

Sharpening Your Skills

The most important skills for successful salespeople are the abilities to listen to the customers, read their emotional states, and help them without being aggressive. Using your eyes and ears, and not just your mouth, during a sales conversation can help you gain insight. Observe the customers' nonverbal communication for clues as to what they are thinking and feeling. Body language, such as folded arms or tapping feet, can indicate anger, disapproval, or nervousness. According to research, up to 90 percent of all communication is nonverbal. Learning to accurately read customers' nonverbal communication can put a salesperson ahead of the competition.

The Sales Process

People who have excellent sales skills are in high demand across the travel and tourism industry and are well paid for their abilities. Generally, effective selling can be organized into six steps.

1. **Pre-approach.** This is the time when you should be sure to learn everything possible about the products and services offered and when you should gather information about the target customer. You should also study the available marketing information and pre-pare for the first contact with the customer.

2. **Approach.** At the first contact with a customer, you need to listen to determine his or her needs and to begin to establish a relationship with the customer. You should have a plan for what to say when speaking with the customer, but it should be a flexible one.

3. **Demonstration.** At this point, you will present the product or service in a way that addresses the needs of the customer and shows enthusiasm. If all is going well, you may even ask the customer to buy at this point.

4. **Answering questions.** At this stage, a customer may voice objections to the product or service or have questions and concerns. The objections generally mean the customer is considering the purchase. Providing additional information to counter the objections may resolve the customer's concerns.

5. **Closing the sale.** Helping the customer make the final decision to buy may include offering a discount or an incentive gift for buying today. This is also the time to suggest additional items that will increase the amount of the sale. Customers like to receive suggestions

Marketing Myths

An old marketing myth states that if a salesperson is knowledgeable and has a good product or service, this is enough to be successful. Knowledge and a winning product, however, are not quite all that is needed to make a sale. The customer must be the winner in the sale, not the product or the salesperson. Helping customers see how they can win, or feel, or be better off by purchasing the product or service is the key to increased sales.

THINK CRITICALLY

1. What is meant by "the customer must be the winner"?

2. How can a salesperson help a customer win? Discuss your opinion with others.

for related products if the recommendations are valid. For a customer buying an airline ticket and booking a hotel, you might suggest that now is also a convenient time to purchase theme park tickets, rather than later when waiting in line at the park probably will be necessary.

6. **Follow-up.** After a sale, contact your customers to see if they are satisfied or have any concerns. Ask if you can be of any further service. If you sold a couple a vacation package, call them to see how the trip went and how they liked the hotel. The conversation may provide important feedback. Were their needs satisfied? Could you have handled something differently to achieve better results for these customers? Your expressions of concern may help you retain the couple as repeat customers, and the ideas generated may help you improve services for future customers.

Stopover   Why is listening so important to sales?

_____

_____

Five-Star Traveler

DONNA DEBERRY

Making diversity a key component of the corporate culture and the fabric of Wyndham International is the responsibility of Donna DeBerry, executive vice president of diversity and corporate affairs. Wyndham is a major hotel management company.

DeBerry is considered a national expert on diversity and is the highest-ranking African-American in the hotel industry. She was a featured speaker at the Women Who Are Shaping the World Leadership Summit, and she has been featured in both *Fortune* and *Essence* magazines.

DeBerry has launched a number of initiatives, including creating diversity committees at Wyndham. The following three committees support Wyndham's diversity initiatives and ensure the company is taking appropriate steps.

- Internal Diversity Steering Committee—made up of corporate executives who lead diversity efforts

- Diversity Field Input Committee—made up of employees from throughout the organization who provide guidance and feedback on diversity issues

- External Diversity Advisory Board—consists of outside experts who provide counsel on key diversity issues

Donna DeBerry was the director of national sales for emerging markets for Wyndham before moving into her current position. Previously, she worked for the National Football League and the U.S. Olympic Committee.

THINK CRITICALLY

How might a diversity committee help a company improve its sales? Why would a company need to be sensitive to diversity in its workforce and customer base?

Understand Marketing Concepts

Circle the best answer for each of the following questions.

1. Which of the following can be considered a customer touchpoint?
   a. hotel check-in
   b. web site visit
   c. telephone conversation
   d. all of the above

2. A salesperson listens to customers to determine their needs during the
   a. pre-approach.
   b. approach.
   c. demonstration.
   d. closing.

Think Critically

Answer the following questions as completely as possible. If necessary, use a separate sheet of paper.

3. **Communication** Write a statement you would make to open a conversation with an event planner if you were selling your city as a location for a convention.

   _____

   _____

   _____

   _____

   _____

   _____

   _____

4. With a partner, discuss why incentives offered with products or services are important. List five bonuses that might be offered to families to attract them to a vacation destination.

   _____

   _____

   _____

   _____

   _____

   _____

   _____

   _____

   _____

Review Marketing Concepts

Write the letter of the term that matches each definition. Some terms will not be used.

a.	advertising
b.	frequency
c.	lead time
d.	measurable goal
e.	news release
f.	personal selling
g.	public relations (PR)
h.	publicity
i.	reach
j.	roadblock
k.	sales promotion
l.	storyboard
m.	touchpoint

_____ 1. A statement of desired outcome for which data can be collected to affirm its accomplishment

_____ 2. A technique that involves running ads on several television networks (or other media) at roughly the same time in hopes that few people will miss the promotion

_____ 3. A contact with a customer that can be turned into increased revenue

_____ 4. A one-on-one interaction with potential customers to inform them about products and services and persuade them to buy

_____ 5. Creating and maintaining positive and mutually beneficial relationships with the public

_____ 6. Activities or materials that offer the customer an added reason to buy

_____ 7. The total number of times the target audience will see or hear the advertisement

_____ 8. The paid communication of information about products and services between the seller and potential customers

_____ 9. Communication to the public about a business that is not paid for or controlled by the company

_____ 10. The total number of people who will see the advertisement

_____ 11. The action of each scene in a broadcast advertisement, outlined in rough drawings

Circle the best answer.

12. Three purposes for advertising are
    a. to promote, publicize, and sell.
    b. to inform, remind, and persuade.
    c. to employ, profit, and explore.
    d. to approach, lead, and follow up.

13. An example of a sales promotion is
    a. running a television commercial.
    b. issuing a news release.
    c. offering a free hotel room upgrade.
    d. sponsoring a charitable community event.

Think Critically

14. Select a major destination, and find two or more examples of promotions for the location. What are the messages and the media used? How might the effectiveness of the promotions be measured?

_____

_____

_____

_____

15. Design a print ad for a resort in your state. Identify your target customer and the print media you would use to run the ad.

_____

_____

_____

_____

16. You are a salesperson for an airline. You want to sell a major corporation on using the airline as its preferred supplier for business travel. What do you need to know before you contact the customer?

_____

_____

_____

_____

17. You need to know the best media to reach students in your school. Develop ten questions to ask students that will help you design a promotional plan for increasing students' interest in visiting an area museum.

_____

_____

_____

_____

18. You are developing a new destination and want to attract people 25 to 40 years old. Develop a message that you would use to attract the attention of customers in this age group. What media would you use to reach this audience?

_____

_____

_____

_____

Make Connections

19. Communication Using the Internet to gather more information, write a one-page news release about the giant lava lamp project in Soap Lake, Washington, that was discussed in Chapter 6. Use a unique title for your news release that might catch the attention of the news media.

_____

_____

_____

_____

20. Management Develop two objectives for the promotional plan of an upscale resort. The objectives must be achievable through promotion, and they must be measurable.

_____

_____

_____

_____

21. Research Use the Internet and other resources to determine the cost of publishing the ad you designed in question 15. How is the cost determined for the media you selected?

_____

_____

_____

_____

22. Marketing Math You are selling a tour package for $5,000 per person. Your gross profit is $195 on each sale. On average, you sell about five customers out of each ten with whom you make contact. You are considering purchasing an ad that will cost $10,000. Your goal is to sell 120 tour packages. How many sales must the ad generate in order to cover its cost? How many potential customers must the ad generate in order for you to make enough sales to cover the ad's cost? How many potential customer contacts will you need to reach your sales goal?

_____

_____

_____

_____

_____

23. **History** Research a local attraction that is over 50 years old. Create a brochure that will promote the historical background of the location and attract additional visitors.

_____

_____

_____

_____

_____

_____

24. **Communication** You are employed by your favorite vacation destination as a blog writer. Write a one-page blog about the destination, with the intent of attracting new visitors.

_____

_____

_____

_____

_____

_____

_____

_____

EXTENDED STAY

Project The Travel Industry Association (TIA) of America sponsors a number of promotional activities that are described on its web site in the marketing section.

Work with a group and complete the following activities.

1. Use the Internet to find information about the TIA's promotional efforts. Write a paragraph describing these efforts, including the See America program.

2. Determine how a member travel destination might benefit from the TIA's efforts in promoting its location.

3. Develop a promotional plan for a travel destination that includes use of the TIA's special services and capabilities. Be sure to include measurable goals and indicate how data will be collected to evaluate the effectiveness of the plan.

4. Using presentation software, create a short presentation highlighting the features of the promotional plan.

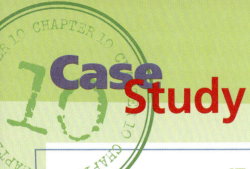

IT NEVER RAINS IN SOUTHERN CALIFORNIA . . . OR DOES IT?

Southern California is noted for a mild winter climate with limited rainfall. Average highs during the winter months are near 70 degrees, and there is plentiful sunshine. Travelers have traditionally flocked to Southern California in the winter to enjoy a break from the cold and clouds at home.

Although winter is actually the wettest time of the year in Southern California, the rain tends to come in only moderate amounts. The historical average rainfall for December is around 1.91 inches, and around 3.33 inches for January.

During the 1960s, a song proclaimed that "it never rains in Southern California." Mother Nature has recently proven the song to be false. In January 2001, heavy rains drenched Southern California, flooding major roads and triggering mudslides. Heavy rains in February 2003 did the same.

Pacific storms lashed the West Coast in December 2004 and January 2005, resulting in floods and giant mudslides that took out homes, businesses, and roads. Hundreds of residents and motorists were left stranded throughout Ventura County. Mid-January rainfall in downtown Los Angeles reached a record level of 21 inches. Higher elevations of California received record snowfalls, with 25 feet of snow falling in less than 15 days in the Lake Tahoe area. Storms in the Sierra Mountains dumped up to

5 feet of snow overnight. The 2004–2005 winter went down as the wettest on record.

Travel and tourism are important to California's economy. The tourism industry provides over one million jobs. Travel expenditures for the state totaled $78.2 billion in 2003, but were down three percent from the previous year. California had 309 million domestic travelers and 7 million international travelers in 2003. "California is the country's number one travel destination," said Caroline Beteta, executive director of the California Travel and Tourism Commission (CTTC), "but we cannot assume that people will continue to travel here." California travel and tourism businesses may need to redefine the mild climate they advertise for the winter months.

THINK CRITICALLY

1. How will the record rainfall and mudslides affect the travel and tourism industry in Southern California?

2. What could possibly be the cause of the dramatic weather changes in Southern California?

3. How can Southern California overcome bad publicity in media reports as a result of the bad weather?

4. What special promotions should Southern California use to attract more winter visitors?

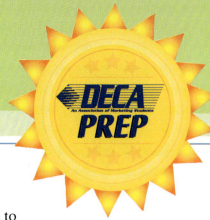

TRAVEL AND TOURISM MARKETING MANAGEMENT TEAM DECISION MAKING

Vail, Colorado, is well known for great snow skiing in the winter. Lodges, hotels, and condominiums command premium prices during the ski season. The Vail tourism commission has hired you and a partner to develop a marketing strategy to attract more tourists from April through October (the non-skiing season).

Art festivals, beautiful scenery, hiking, horseback riding, and outlet malls are tourist attractions offered by Vail during the summer. Spring and summer mountain scenery is awesome, with wildflowers blooming in abundance. Vail hosts some of the finest performing arts festivals during the summer, celebrating the best in music, dance, and theatre. While the rest of the country is sizzling from heat, Vail's climate is mild and pleasant.

Because the summer months are a shoulder period (between peak and off-peak seasons) for Vail lodges, hotels, and condominiums, reasonable prices are offered to tourists. Often, these prices are 50 percent less than the prices charged during the height of the ski season.

You and your partner must develop a marketing campaign to attract tourists to Vail during the summer months. You will have 30 minutes to develop your marketing strategy. You may use a laptop computer and presentation software to design and present your plan.

You will have ten minutes to present your ideas to members of the tourism commission (judges) and five minutes to answer their questions.

Performance Indicators Evaluated

- Develop a marketing campaign for Vail, Colorado.
- Design a marketing theme.
- Coordinate activities in the promotional mix.
- Write promotional messages that appeal to targeted markets.
- Highlight area tourist attractions.
- Design advertisements for travel magazines, major newspapers, and the Internet.
- Outline a television commercial for national syndication.

Go to the DECA web site for more detailed information.

THINK CRITICALLY

1. What characteristics about Vail should be highlighted to help increase summer tourism?
2. What major television audiences should be targeted with Vail tourism commercials?
3. What information should be included on a web site advertising summer tourism in Vail?
4. How will Vail overcome the reputation of being only a ski destination?

www.deca.org

Legal Issues in Travel and Tourism

CHAPTER 11 · CHAPTER 11 · CHAPTER 11 · CHAPTER 11 · CHAPTER 11

11

JUSTIN DART

Photodisc

Point Your Browser

▶ ▶ ▶ ▶ travel.swlearning.com

Final Flight

When the unthinkable happens and an airline goes out of business, travelers get stranded in the middle of a trip or left at the gate just before a flight. Consumer protection laws provide some assistance for travelers, but they offer even better protection for credit card companies.

Credit card companies have agreements with individual airlines to process transactions for ticket purchases. As a condition of doing business, most of the agreements include a provision that the airline must set aside a certain percentage of cash to protect the credit card company from massive refunds. If an airline goes out of business, passengers who used credit cards to purchase their tickets are able to apply for a refund of the ticket price from the credit card companies.

After intense lobbying from credit card companies, the U.S. Congress extended a law through November 2005 requiring that surviving airlines place passengers from a newly defunct airline on a standby basis, if space is available, at a cost not to exceed $50. This law, in effect, shifts the burden of assisting the failed airlines' passengers from the credit card companies to the surviving airlines. Under the law, passengers are expected to approach the other airlines to accept their tickets, rather than seek refunds from the credit card companies.

In the major hub of a defunct airline, extra seats on other airlines will be a rare commodity, and waiting on standby status for an open seat will be an inconvenient option. Passengers will likely be stuck paying full price for a new ticket. Some consumer advocates, however, believe the credit card companies are justified in refusing to grant refunds for a failed airline's tickets, saying the standby option is adequate for consumers.

THINK CRITICALLY

1. Should laws protect consumers from consequences resulting from failed travel businesses? Why or why not?

2. Should airlines have clear policies about how they will respond to a competitor's demise? Explain your answer.

Government Regulation

Describe the laws that impact travel and tourism marketing.

Explain the limits of consumer protection.

All Aboard

After smoldering in a first-floor deli, fire spread rapidly through the MGM Grand Hotel in Las Vegas, Nevada, in November 1980. Over 5,000 guests and employees were in the 26-floor, high-rise hotel shortly after 7:00 A.M. when the fire was first noticed. Exit doors locked behind people who entered smoky stairwells. Guests who tried to use elevators became trapped. By the time the fire was out, 85 people had died and about 650 were injured.

The MGM Grand opened in 1970 with very few fire safety features. A county building official had approved the hotel's construction with no sprinklers despite the protest of the fire marshals. The hotel saved $192,000 by not installing the sprinkler system, but the fire cost the hotel $223 million in legal settlements alone. Nevada now has one of the strictest fire sprinkler system laws in the United States.

Work with a partner. Discuss why fire, safety, and health laws are an important part of operating a successful travel-related business.

IT'S THE LAW

Feeling safe is important to travelers. Protection of people and property is generally the reason for a law. Businesses are subject to the laws of each country, state, and city within which they operate. U.S. federal travel laws became much stricter after the September 11, 2001, terrorist attacks.

Legal Implications

PRODUCT/SERVICE MANAGEMENT

When a business offers products or services to the public, it has an obligation to provide them in a way that protects consumers' health and safety. When guests sign a registration record upon checking into a hotel, they are entering into a legal agreement with the business. Guests are agreeing to pay the hotel for the rooms and other services received during their stay. The hotel, in turn, has an obligation to provide guests with a safe place to spend the night.

Hotels, restaurants, theme parks, and other travel-related businesses must comply with state and local laws governing fire, safety, and health standards. News reports of tragic deaths caused by the negligence of a tourism business can emphasize the importance of complying with safety laws. Fire codes and food handling laws are critical to the travel and tourism industry. Noncompliance can harm guests and employees and can even ruin a business.

Protecting Natural Resources

In 1996, the U.S. Congress passed the Recreational Fee Demonstration Program, which allows the National Park Service, the Fish and Wildlife Service, the Bureau of Land Management, and the Forest Service to retain part or all of the fees they collect from visitors to national parks. The fees are used at the site of collection to protect the park's natural resources and make park visits safe for guests. The program has been extended a number of times but may eventually expire if not reauthorized or replaced by new legislation.

Overprotection

Some laws are enacted to specifically protect a fledgling business or project. The Wright Amendment is such a law. Passed as a federal law in 1979, the Wright Amendment prohibits Southwest Airlines from providing direct flight service from Love Field in Dallas to any location outside the states that directly border Texas. The law was passed to protect American Airlines and other airlines that had moved their services from the old Love Field to the then-new Dallas/Fort Worth Airport.

Almost 30 years later, American Airlines is providing 82 percent of the flights out of D/FW, and its high fares show the lack of competition. In the meantime, Southwest Airlines has grown into a major discount carrier, but it is unable to provide a direct flight from New York or Chicago into its headquarters at Love Field due to the Wright Amendment. A study commissioned by Southwest Airlines shows that repeal of the Wright Amendment would add at least $4.2 billion to the local economies of North Texas and the seven-state perimeter. Interest is growing in the area to have the amendment repealed as a means to increase airline competition and, thereby, reduce airfares.

Marketing Myths

Some people believe that businesses that focus on profits over people are immoral. Others believe that all that really counts in a business is earning a profit, regardless of how it is achieved. Neither belief is on target.

A travel and tourism business is started with the goal of making a profit. Profits are the reward for the time and energy spent to effectively operate the business. Without profits, the business will not survive. Laws, ethical business practices, and competition from other companies guide the business on how to make a profit without violating others' rights or damaging property or the environment.

THINK CRITICALLY

1. How can laws help businesses make a profit without damaging the environment? Give specific examples.

2. How do you feel about businesses making a profit? Discuss your opinion with others.

Why is it important to enforce fire, safety, and health laws?

Stopover

PROTECTING CONSUMERS

PRODUCT/SERVICE MANAGEMENT

When customers enter a restaurant, they assume that the food they will be served will not cause them harm. When vacationers enter an amusement park, they do so believing that the rides there are safe. Consumers in the United States like to believe that someone is watching over them and protecting them from unscrupulous business practices that do not have consumers' best interests at heart. Many laws are in place and many nonprofit consumer protection groups work to keep consumers safe, but businesses must also continually look for ways to better protect their customers.

Photodisc

Ride Watch

One of the most visited locations in the United States is Orlando, Florida. According to the Orlando Convention and Visitors Bureau, 74 percent of Orlando's more than 20 million domestic leisure travelers visit a theme park. With such a large number of visitors, potential for accidents and injuries exists. Between 7,000 and 10,000 people are injured and an average of about three deaths occur each year at U.S. theme parks. However, federal law exempts fixed-site rides in theme parks from U.S. Consumer Product Safety Commission regulation. The **Consumer Product Safety Commission** is a federal agency charged with protecting consumers from dangerous products. Theme parks, therefore, are self-regulating when it comes to the safety measures taken to ensure their rides are maintained and operating properly.

Ship Shape

About 10 million passengers per year sail on cruise ships, and an estimated 76 percent of them are U.S. citizens, according to the International Council of Cruise Lines. Virtually all cruise ships that do business in the United States sail under foreign flags, called **flags of convenience**, because they are registered in other countries. Most cruise ships are registered in Panama, Liberia, or the Bahamas. Registry outside of the United States allows the cruise lines to pay lower taxes and to be free from tough U.S. legal requirements. Maritime law, which rules the sea, has always held that governments could not interfere with a foreign vessel; thus, cruise ships are not governed by U.S. law.

This exemption from U.S. law took a turn in 2005, when the U.S. Supreme Court ruled that cruise ships must loosely follow U.S. federal law banning discrimination against disabled people. The ruling stemmed from a 1999 lawsuit brought by three disabled people against the Norwegian Cruise Line, a subsidiary of a Malaysian company called Star Cruises. The cruise line was accused of charging higher prices for wheelchair-accessible rooms and not making public facilities, such as elevators, restaurants, and bathrooms, accessible. The ruling allows the disabled to sue for discrimination, but leaves unclear the extent to which the cruise lines must comply with the Americans with Disabilities Act (ADA).

Consumer Complaints

All U.S. airlines are required to submit monthly reports to the U.S. Department of Transportation's (DOT) Air Consumer Protection Division. The reports include information about flight delays, mishandled baggage, oversales, and other consumer complaints.

Over an eight-year period from 1987 to 2005, airlines averaged 78.7 percent of flights with on-time arrivals. A flight is considered to have an **on-time arrival** if the plane arrives at the gate within 15 minutes of the time scheduled.

Mishandled baggage, a continual problem for airlines, seems to increase when the airlines cut staff during periods of slow business. Most airlines average 4 or 5 pieces of mishandled luggage for every 1,000 passengers. Some airlines average up to 11 or 12 mishandled pieces per 1,000 passengers.

Oversales are caused when an airline overbooks a flight based on scheduling models that show a certain percentage of people will likely not show up for the flight. When a passenger who holds a confirmed reservation is denied boarding or is voluntarily "bumped" because the flight is oversold, the airline must report the incident to the DOT. The DOT publishes the information on a quarterly basis and divides it to show how many passengers voluntarily took a bump and how many were involuntarily denied boarding. About 1 in 10,000 passengers is involuntarily denied boarding. Both voluntarily and involuntarily bumped passengers generally receive some kind of compensation from the airline, including discounts on future tickets, free meals, and overnight accommodations.

Another section of the DOT quarterly report indicates the number of consumer complaints about misleading advertisements, rude employees, discrimination, poor treatment of animals traveling by plane, and more. All of the data are compiled and made available to the public on the DOT web site.

Time Out

Some countries do not have the sanitation facilities to properly purify drinking water. Tourists should learn about the quality of water in the areas they will be visiting and avoid drinking water of unknown purity. Locals have developed an immunity to the organisms in the water, but tourists introduced to the organisms will become ill. Raw, unpeeled fruits and vegetables may also be contaminated with the impure water.

Stopover

Name two agencies that protect U.S. consumers. What areas do the agencies oversee?

_____

_____

Understand Marketing Concepts

Circle the best answer for each of the following questions.

1. Safety laws are meant to protect
   a. consumers.
   b. property.
   c. businesses.
   d. all of the above.

2. The federal agency charged with regulating the safety of fixed-site theme park rides is
   a. the Consumer Product Safety Commission.
   b. the Department of Transportation.
   c. the Parks Department.
   d. none of the above. Fixed-site rides are exempt from federal law.

Think Critically

Answer the following questions as completely as possible. If necessary, use a separate sheet of paper.

3. Briefly describe the fire protection measures in your school. Compare them with the fire protection measures that might be found in a hotel. How are they alike and different?

   _____

   _____

   _____

   _____

   _____

   _____

4. **Communication** How should cruise ships modify their facilities to accommodate passengers in wheelchairs, and why should they go to the expense? Write two paragraphs expressing your opinion.

   _____

   _____

   _____

   _____

   _____

   _____

   _____

   _____

Ethical and Legal Practices

Explain the impact of unethical behavior on the travel industry.

Describe ethical issues of business conduct in travel and tourism.

All Aboard

When Lakisha Reins received a phone call stating that she had won a trip to Hawaii, she was thrilled. She had recently signed up for a chance to win the trip while she was attending a car show. The trip sounded too good to be true—seven days and six nights in a luxurious hotel on the beach. The airfare and meals were included, and all Reins had to pay for was the hotel room. The friendly person on the phone just needed Reins's credit card number to confirm her interest in taking the trip, and all the information would be mailed to her.

When Reins's credit card bill came the next month, she discovered a $1,500 charge for the hotel room, even though she had not yet scheduled the trip. After making several phone calls, she found the same trip could be purchased for $700, including airfare, hotel, and meals. Reins learned to never give out her credit card number to a stranger who originates a call.

Work with a partner. Find information about travel-fraud, including information from the Federal Trade Commission. List ideas to help tourists protect themselves from travel fraud.

TROUBLED TRAVEL

The Internet has contributed to the growth of fraudulent travel scams that offer vacations but only produce stress and misery. Unscrupulous web auctions, pop-up ads, and online travel agents offer hard-to-resist travel bargains that ultimately cost a fortune. According to the National Consumer League, people generally lose about $1,200 when they are tricked into a travel scam.

Digital Vision

Fighting Crime

Deceptive and illegal travel scams hurt legitimate, ethical travel providers. The scams make it difficult for customers to distinguish between the legitimate and deceptive travel providers, and customers eventually lose trust in all of them.

The American Society of Travel Agents (ASTA) hosted a conference on travel fraud and consumer protection to help identify problems, offer solutions, and confirm its commitment to ethical business behavior. Educating consumers about how to protect themselves was an important focus of the conference.

For more than 100 years, the National Consumer League (NCL) has been acting to protect both consumers and workers. Noelle Nachtsheim is the director of law enforcement services, National Fraud Information Center/Internet Fraud Watch for NCL. Speaking at the ASTA conference on travel fraud, she told the group that travel scams are among the top ten most frequent scams in the United States. She advised the group to help educate the traveling public about deceptive practices.

A number of governmental and private organizations focus on travel fraud. The Federal Trade Commission (FTC) offers tips on its web site for how to avoid being swindled, as well as a phone number to call for help. The FTC has targeted trip scammers who overpromise and underproduce on travel deals, tell consumers they have won "free" trips that aren't free, and hide fees in complete trip packages.

The Better Business Bureau (BBB) advises consumers to work only with travel providers who are members of professional organizations. Additional tips for avoiding travel fraud are offered on the BBB web site.

E-Ticket

Not all travel insurance is created equally, nor is it priced the same. Different policies and companies cover varying events and circumstances. Finding the right travel insurance may take some investigation on the part of the traveler seeking coverage.

Many online services provide a comparison of travel insurance coverage from a number of companies. The information helps educate the consumer on the coverage offered.

THINK CRITICALLY

Visit the Web and find insurance from three different companies to cover trip cancellation due to a medical emergency of a family member who is not traveling. Create a spreadsheet to compare the coverage offered by the three companies. Which policy would you choose? Why?

Insuring Travel

Trips may be cancelled, delayed, or interrupted for many reasons. Serious illness of the traveler or a family member is a frequent reason for changing travel plans. Other reasons might involve bad weather, a job change, or a problem with the travel provider. Just as smart consumers insure their homes, cars, and health, travelers can purchase **travel insurance** to provide coverage for a financial loss on an expensive trip.

About 25 percent of travelers purchase travel insurance. It is intended to pay the insured traveler for the costs incurred on a single trip if the trip is cancelled or interrupted, luggage is lost or mishandled, or injury or illness occurs. Insurance coverage for expensive trips is a sensible option to protect the consumer. Conditions for claims vary among insurance providers and are very specific. Only those conditions listed in the policy are covered.

Most travel insurance policies will cover the loss to the insured of costs associated with the financial default of a travel provider. A **financial default** occurs when a company stops providing services due to lack of funds to pay its financial obligations. The insurer will provide the customer with a list of all travel suppliers covered. Travel suppliers who are having financial problems or are on the verge of bankruptcy are not usually covered by travel insurance. In 2005, United Airlines was considering filing for bankruptcy and, consequently, was not listed as a covered travel supplier by many insurance companies.

Travel insurance companies sometimes are faced with unethical customers who submit false claims. Insurance companies are constantly on the lookout for claims that are fabricated or padded to increase the amount of the settlement. Insurance companies also exchange information with each other and with law enforcement agencies in order to detect suspicious patterns, suspected scammers, and the latest types of schemes. Fraudulent claims increase the costs for all insurance policyholders.

How do travel scammers hurt legitimate travel businesses?

_____

_____

_____

TRAVEL BUSINESS ETHICS

Ethics is a guide to action based on right versus wrong. Ethical people make the right decisions, even when the decision is not to their personal or professional benefit. People in travel and tourism businesses, as well as all people, frequently face ethical decisions.

Developing Ethics

Moral values are those values judged by a group to be right or wrong based upon principles. They are the basis for interaction among the members of the group. Morality is developed as one matures from childhood into an adult. If adult role models act on moral principles, then children are also likely to act as moral individuals.

Ethical behavior involves the actions and decisions based on the moral values of an individual. Ethics are not just for show. Mature, ethical adults act based upon principles, even when no one knows about their actions. Ethical people can be trusted to consistently act in a principled manner.

It can sometimes seem that the majority of people are unethical, because bad actions make the news much more frequently than everyday, ethical behavior. Some people think that unethical behavior is appropriate because everyone else is behaving that way. This is not true, and those who behave unethically risk their reputations, their careers, and even their businesses. Customers, employees, and suppliers quickly identify

Time Out

The World Tourism Organization (WTO) has a global code of ethics for tourism. The code recognizes the vulnerability of travelers and their need for protection.

Missing the Boat

Cruise lines frequently offer passengers two ways to book a cruise—a set price for a specific stateroom location or a lower, guaranteed price. Travel agents understand these options, but some inexperienced travelers can end up being unexpectedly bumped from their cruises.

For the somewhat lower cost, the cruise lines offer a guarantee that a customer will be provided a stateroom, but they provide no information about the precise location of the room. If all rooms in a lower-price category are filled, the customer receives an upgrade to a higher-quality room. Just as with airlines, cruise lines oversell their available rooms based on a formula that forecasts the number of expected cancellations. If fewer cancellations materialize, a customer may receive a phone call announcing that no rooms are available, making the "guaranteed" space a misnomer.

THINK CRITICALLY

1. Do you think cruise lines are being straightforward with customers? Why or why not?

2. How should cruise lines handle oversales? Discuss your opinion with others.

unethical people and lose trust in them. Customers and suppliers will likely discontinue doing business with those they cannot trust.

Code of Ethics

Most professional associations have **codes of ethics** that are used to guide the behavior and decisions of their members. Codes of ethics can help members make difficult decisions and help assure the traveling public that the members act in ethical ways.

The American Society of Travel Agent's (ASTA) code of ethics outlines the responsibilities of all members of the society. It includes principles that state that each member will be competent, will deal fairly and with integrity toward all customers, and will provide the consumer with the agreed-upon products or services.

The ASTA code of ethics specifies acting in favor of the customer when a conflict of interest arises. A conflict of interest is an instance in which the right decision for the customer may conflict with the gain, financial or otherwise, of the businessperson. A travel service provider may receive a higher commission from cruise line A, but may know that cruise line B offers higher-quality service. The ethical decision would be to recommend cruise line B to the customer.

The ASTA code of ethics also addresses the interaction of members of the society and their businesses. Complaints about members' violations of the code can be filed with the ASTA Consumer Affairs Department, although the department acts only as a mediator to resolve issues between the parties in dispute. The society cannot force a member to issue a refund. However, members may be censured, have membership rights suspended, or be expelled from ASTA for code violations.

Stopover Define ethical behavior.

_____

_____

Understand Marketing Concepts

Circle the best answer for each of the following questions.

1. Travel insurance can cover
   a. buses, trains, and automobiles.
   b. hotels, restaurants, and movie theaters.
   c. trip cancellation, trip interruption, lost luggage, and medical expenses.
   d. lost business for the travel agency.

2. A code of ethics is
   a. a law.
   b. a resource for travelers.
   c. a guide for professional behavior.
   d. a contract with customers.

Think Critically

Answer the following questions as completely as possible. If necessary, use a separate sheet of paper.

3. **Geography** Briefly describe the problems U.S. travelers might incur if their tour group goes out of business midtour in Pécs, Hungary. Additionally, state how the travelers might get home to the United States.

   _____

   _____

   _____

   _____

   _____

   _____

   _____

4. Describe the kind of person who can be trusted to treat all people fairly. Why would you want to do business with this person?

   _____

   _____

   _____

   _____

   _____

   _____

   _____

   _____

International Law

Goals

- Explain the impact of international law on travel and tourism.
- Describe the role of the travel industry in educating consumers about international travel.

All Aboard

Thirty years ago, Cancun was an unpopulated area near a sleepy fishing village on the east coast of Mexico. The construction of luxury hotels on its beautiful beaches has turned Cancun into a major tourist area. Thousands of U.S. tourists now visit there every week.

In April 2005, the U.S. Department of State issued a public announcement to U.S. citizens regarding the police in Cancun. The State Department had received a number of complaints from tourists who were driving rental cars and were forced to pay bogus fines directly to police officers or face imprisonment. No proof was shown of any infractions on the part of the tourists. The deterioration in local law enforcement ethics was blamed on a persistent shortage of municipal funds to pay for police personnel salaries and other public services.

In a group, discuss the obligation the State Department has to U.S. citizens. What obligations does the Mexican government have to its tourists?

KNOW BEFORE YOU GO

Travel and tourism businesses have two duties in relationship to the law. First, they must abide by laws themselves. Second, they must help their customers become aware of the laws governing their travel destinations and their return trips.

Photodisc

U.S. Citizens Traveling Internationally

When people in the U.S. travel industry are assisting customers with international travel, they must be aware of both U.S. and international laws that will impact the travelers. U.S. citizens who travel internationally are subject to many rules and regulations that are constantly changing in the post-9/11 environment.

The U.S. Customs and Border Protection (CBP) is an agency within the Department of Homeland Security. The CBP's primary purpose is to prevent terrorists and terrorist weapons from entering the United States. It also facilitates the flow of legitimate trade and travel across U.S. borders.

The CBP screens all people entering the United States and may inspect their luggage. The CBP requires that all returning U.S. travelers declare, on a form provided by the airline or cruise ship on which they are traveling, any item they are bringing into the United States that they did not have with them when first leaving the States. Some items will be duty free, while others will have a duty due on their value. A **duty** is a type of tax imposed on certain imported goods. Returning U.S. citizens are generally exempt from paying duty on up to $800 worth of items each 30 days.

In the past, U.S. citizens traveling within the Western Hemisphere, including to and from Mexico, Canada, the Caribbean, and Central and South America, were not required to show their passports in order to reenter the United States. In December 2006, a phase-in of the Western Hemisphere Travel Initiative (WHTI) was scheduled to begin. WHTI requires a valid passport or other accepted form of identification from citizens before they can reenter the United States. WHTI is considered a major loss of freedom for people in states that border Mexico and Canada who had been able to freely cross these international borders. Mexican and Canadian citizens, who could previously enter the United States without a passport, will not be able to do so after WHTI is fully implemented. However, Mexican citizens may be permitted to use a *laser visa*, or a border crossing card, to enter. A travel agent who stays up-to-date on international laws, passport, such as WHTI, and other changes taking place in destination countries will help smooth customers' travels.

Identification Documents

A passport is an internationally accepted document that verifies the identity and nationality of the bearer. Almost nine million passports were issued in 2004 alone. In the United States, passports are issued

Both parents must be present to obtain a passport for a child under age 14. If the second parent cannot appear, then the parent who is present must provide a notarized form of consent from the second parent or show documentation, such as a death certificate, indicating why the second parent cannot be present.

through the Department of State. A U.S. citizen who is seeking a passport for the first time must appear in person at one of over 7,000 passport service locations in the United States and must provide two photographs, a birth certificate or other proof of U.S. citizenship, and a valid form of photo identification, such as a driver's license.

U.S. citizens wishing to visit another country as tourists can obtain information about the exact documents required for the visit from the State Department's web site, under "Foreign Entry Requirements." The information is listed by country. Requirements often include not only a passport but also an additional photo of the traveler that the destination country will keep.

Welcome, Visitor

Most travelers from outside the United States must obtain a visa, an official authorization added to a passport, in order to travel within the United States. The process for obtaining a visa includes the following steps.

- Make an appointment to visit a U.S. embassy or consulate. An **embassy** is a diplomatic mission to a foreign country headed by an ambassador. A consulate houses the offices of a **consul**, an official appointed by a government to reside in a foreign country and represent his or her government's commercial interests and assist its citizens there.

- Bring a valid passport, a completed application for the visa, and proof of employment, along with money to pay the applicable fees.

- Submit the documents for review through a security database.

- Receive the visa, giving permission to travel to a U.S. port of entry.

The process for obtaining a visa can take from four to six weeks to complete. In some countries, access to a U.S. embassy or consulate may be limited, because only 216 U.S. embassies and consulates exist worldwide. The applicant must sometimes travel hundreds of miles to the U.S. embassy or consulate to apply for a visa. The U.S. Department of State defends the lengthy process as being necessary for reasons of national security.

When a visit to the United States is for 90 days or less, nationals of 27 countries are exempt from needing visas through the Visa Waiver Program (VWP). Countries qualify for the VWP by accepting U.S. citizens as visitors without needing visas, issuing machine-readable passports, and generally working with the United States to control fraudulent entry. Complete, up-to-date information on VWP can be obtained from the U.S. Department of State's web site. The U.S. government holds transportation companies, such as airlines, responsible for not allowing people from the 27 VWP countries to travel to the United States without a machine-readable passport and fines the transporters $3,300 per violation.

Some countries make it easy for visitors to travel to their areas. After a number of incidences that left a negative impact on tourism, Indonesia began a process of allowing citizens from 34 nations to visit Indonesia for 3 to 30 days using a system where visas are issued upon arrival. At the same time, Indonesia and many other countries consider overstaying a visa's expiration date a serious offense punishable by fine or imprisonment.

What documents are required for obtaining a U.S. passport?

_____

_____

Stopover

TRAVELERS, BEWARE

PRODUCT/SERVICE MANAGEMENT

When people travel to areas with which they are not familiar, they are exposing themselves to possible danger. Travelers who are not familiar with the way locals dress may stand out as tourists and be targeted for criminal activity. Good travel suppliers keep their customers informed of dangers and safe travel practices.

State Department News

The U.S. Department of State offers traveler information on its web site, including travel warnings, consular information sheets, and public announcements. A *travel warning* is issued when the State Department is recommending that U.S. citizens do not travel to a specific country. The warnings are usually issued when the United States is asking nonessential government employees and their families to leave a country due to a high level of danger resulting from such crises as civil unrest or the outbreak of war. *Consular information sheets* are filled with information about destination countries, including health conditions and crime statistics. *Public announcements* are made when the State Department wants to communicate quickly about a short-term travel risk that is in the best interest of U.S. citizens to avoid. In 2005, at least three public announcements were made concerning travel to various parts of Mexico.

American Services and Crisis Management

Even with the best of plans, U.S. citizens traveling outside the United States can find themselves in more trouble than they can handle. The U.S. Office of American Services and Crisis Management offers assistance to U.S. citizens in other countries. The agency works with U.S. embassies and consular offices to provide assistance in cases of crime victimization, arrest, missing persons, medical evacuation, and death.

Too Good to Be True

As with all types of businesses, fraudulent web sites exist that offer to help people obtain documents needed to enter the United States. The illegal businesses advertise that they can speed up the process or otherwise help customers obtain documents for a fee. To start the process, they ask customers for personal information needed to obtain the documents. Unfortunately, the documents never materialize. Customers are left having paid for something they never received, while providing criminals with their personal data that may be used for identity theft or other illegal purposes.

Trafficking

Slavery and human trafficking (the selling of people) are major problems, not just in developing countries with widespread poverty, corruption, and lack of education, but worldwide. Women and children are especially vulnerable and are often tricked into situations of involuntary slavery. Travelers may be offered assistance to find work in other countries only to find themselves trapped when the formerly helpful people take away their passports and other identification, withhold salaries, and demand payment for travel expenses.

Children are literally bought and sold in many areas of the world where human trafficking is tolerated. The United Nations International Children's Emergency Fund (UNICEF) estimates that 1.2 million children are trafficked each year. Travel professionals can help stop human trafficking by reporting suspicious activities to law enforcement agencies.

Stopover What does *human trafficking* mean?

_____

_____

_____

Five-Star Traveler

LAURA WRIGHT

Southwest Airlines is financially stable and accomplishing success, even while other airlines are struggling. Laura Wright receives a great deal of credit for Southwest's achievements. When asked about the airline's success, Wright stated, "We are successful because we have the lowest costs in the industry and the best customer service. Our service is no frills (that is, no meals, assigned seats, or in-flight entertainment), but is friendly, fun, reliable, and safe."

When Southwest Airlines promoted Laura Wright to the position of chief financial officer (CFO), she became the only female CFO among the top seven airlines. Wright, who became Southwest's CFO at age 44, had been the vice president of finance and treasurer for the airline. As the vice president of finance, she was responsible for the corporation's overall finance strategy, its capital market and aircraft financing activities, new and used aircraft acquisitions, corporate tax and insurance programs, cash management and investing functions, and stock-option programs.

Wright is a certified public accountant with a master's degree. She would like for high school students who are considering career options to know that the "airline industry is very tough—capital intensive, energy intensive, labor intensive, and cyclical. But, it is also very exciting, and airlines are a significant factor in the country's economic engine."

THINK CRITICALLY

Write a two-page report explaining the success of Southwest Airlines. Explain how someone in Laura Wright's position helps ensure that success. Also, discuss how ethical and legal practices impact the position of CFO for a large corporation like Southwest Airlines.

Understand Marketing Concepts

Circle the best answer for each of the following questions.

1. The Western Hemisphere Travel Initiative (WHTI)
    a. exempts U.S. citizens from showing passports.
    b. exempts U.S. citizens from paying duties on imported items.
    c. applies to U.S. citizens returning from Mexico, Canada, the Caribbean, Central America, and South America.
    d. both a and c.

2. The U.S. Department of State issues
    a. travel warnings advising avoidance of specific countries experiencing war or civil unrest.
    b. consular information sheets that list important information travelers should know about specific countries.
    c. public announcements about short-term travel risks.
    d. all of the above.

Think Critically

Answer the following questions as completely as possible. If necessary, use a separate sheet of paper.

3. **Research** Use the Internet to learn how the events of September 11, 2001, caused changes to travel documents needed by U.S. citizens. Write a paragraph of your findings.

    _____

    _____

    _____

    _____

4. **Communication** Look for the consular information sheet for Singapore on the U.S. Department of State's web site. Read the section on criminal penalties. What is the difference in laws regarding jaywalking, littering, and spitting between the United States and Singapore? Write a paragraph to help first-time visitors to Singapore avoid problems.

    _____

    _____

    _____

    _____

    _____

    _____

    _____

Review Marketing Concepts

Write the letter of the term that matches each definition. Some terms will not be used.

_____ 1. When a plane arrives at the gate within 15 minutes of the time scheduled

_____ 2. A diplomatic mission to a foreign country headed by an ambassador

_____ 3. A guide to action based on right versus wrong

_____ 4. Occurs when a company stops providing services due to lack of funds to pay its financial obligations

_____ 5. National flags of cruise ships legally registered in foreign countries in order to pay lower taxes and avoid tough U.S. legal requirements

_____ 6. When an airline overbooks a flight based on scheduling models that show a certain percentage of people will likely not show up for the flight

_____ 7. A federal agency charged with protecting consumers from dangerous products

_____ 8. Provides coverage for a financial loss on an expensive trip

_____ 9. A type of tax imposed on certain imported goods

_____ 10. Used to guide the behavior and decisions of professional associations' members

_____ 11. Those values judged by a group to be right or wrong based upon principles

a. codes of ethics
b. consul
c. Consumer Product Safety Commission
d. duty
e. embassy
f. ethics
g. financial default
h. flags of convenience
i. moral values
j. on-time arrival
k. oversales
l. travel insurance

Circle the best answer.

12. Each month, airlines must report
   a. flight delays.
   b. oversales.
   c. mishandled baggage.
   d. all of the above.

13. U.S. Customs and Border Protection (CBP) oversees
   a. U.S. tourists returning from foreign countries.
   b. people and products entering the United States.
   c. the U.S.–Mexican border.
   d. all of the above.

Think Critically

14. Spend five minutes discussing with a group how a business can balance its costs with the safety of its customers and employees. List three important points from your discussion.

_____

_____

_____

_____

15. Go to the U.S. Department of Transportation's web site and review recent Air Travel Consumer Reports. Select two airlines and create a spreadsheet that compares the results for their oversales and on-time arrivals.

_____

_____

_____

16. Assume you are the manager of a hotel. Two guests arrive with a prepaid receipt for a double room for two nights. You know the company that issued the receipt has not booked the room and has no intention of paying the hotel. Describe how you would handle the situation and what you would say to the guests.

_____

_____

_____

_____

_____

17. Some people will cheat others at any opportunity. How can you protect your travel business and customers from opportunists? Discuss the issue with another student and outline your ideas. Share with the class.

_____

_____

_____

_____

18. Use the Internet to make a list of countries that are currently on the U.S. Visa Waiver Program. How does a country get approved for the U.S. Visa Waiver Program?

_____

_____

_____

_____

Make Connections

19. **Marketing Math** You and a friend have paid $2,500 per person in advance for a hotel barge cruise on the Canal du Midi in France. Your airline tickets cost $700 per person. None of the costs are refundable. You can buy travel insurance that will pay if the travel provider cancels or financially defaults or if you or an immediate family member becomes ill. To provide coverage for a full refund, the insurance will cost 15 percent of the total cost of the trip. Coverage for a 50 percent refund will cost 5 percent of the total cost of the trip. How much will each type of coverage cost? Which coverage would you choose? Why?

_____

_____

_____

20. **History** Briefly research the history of the *R.M.S. Titanic*. When was it built, when did it sail, and when did it sink? How many people died? How have laws regarding safety on passenger ships changed since the *Titanic* sank?

_____

_____

_____

21. **Research** Use the Internet and other sources to determine if any agency in your state is in charge of consumer safety on fixed-site amusement park rides. If yes, what is the extent of the agency's responsibility? If no, do you believe a state agency should oversee amusement park rides? Why or why not?

_____

_____

_____

22. **Marketing Math** About 250,000 people per month fly on SkyView Airlines. On average per month, 12 bags are lost and never recovered for every 10,000 passengers. The airline pays passengers $750 for each lost bag. How much is the airline spending per year to cover lost luggage? If a baggage handler is paid $30,000 per year, how many additional baggage handlers could be hired with the money now being paid for lost luggage?

_____

_____

_____

_____

_____

23. Research What travel freedoms have U.S. citizens lost due to terrorism? Write two paragraphs about your findings.

_____

_____

_____

_____

_____

_____

24. Communication Your job is to convince food-handling employees that effective hand washing is critical to customer health and safety. How would you accomplish this job? How will you know you are successful?

_____

_____

_____

_____

_____

_____

_____

EXTENDED STAY

Project You are working with a client who wants to fly tourists to the United States from Olinda, Brazil. Your job is to gather information that will make the tourists' entry into the United States as smooth as possible. You want to present the information to your client in a concise and user-friendly format.

Work with a group and complete the following activities.

1. Find out as much as you can about Olinda, Brazil, so you understand the tourists' background and culture.

2. Use the Internet to find the most current U.S. government requirements for the entry of first-time visitors from Brazil.

3. Determine the U.S. embassy or consulate located closest to the tourists and find it on a map.

4. Determine what documents the tourists will need for entry into the United States and the timeline for securing these documents.

5. Using presentation software, develop a step-by-step process for your client.

HIGHER PRICES, MORE SECURITY, LESS PLEASURE

United Airlines' marketing tagline used to be "Fly the friendly skies." Flying was viewed as a pleasurable way to quickly get to a vacation or business destination. Providing friendly, efficient service was a major theme of the airline industry. Airline passengers looked forward to courteous airline attendants greeting them and accommodating staff serving them hot meals during their flights. The goal of the airline industry was to provide stress-free travel.

The terrorist attacks of 9/11 changed many things for the airline industry. The initial impact of the tragedy was a dramatic decrease in the number of air travelers. This decrease had a negative, spiraling financial impact on major airlines. Many airlines had to reorganize under a bankruptcy plan. Prices of airline tickets were raised to pay for increased security procedures. The number of flights to specific destinations was decreased, making schedules harder to coordinate and causing longer waits for connecting flights. Financially strapped airlines reduced meal service, did away with it completely, or began to charge an additional fee for a full meal and other services that were once considered standard with a ticket.

Passengers are now asked to arrive at airports two hours before their flights, where they often wait in long lines for security screenings.

The screenings may include head-to-toe X-rays, wanding, and probing of travelers. Many passengers are randomly pulled aside for additional screenings. Additionally, the compact seats installed in many airplanes as an economic measure can result in muscle cramps and, in severe cases, deadly blood clots on longer flights. The once pleasurable flying experience has become a major hassle to endure.

As the friendly skies have become less accommodating, many individuals have chosen alternative means of travel, vacation destinations closer to home, or simply not to travel as often. Airlines are finding it difficult to juggle customer service with financial and security pressures.

THINK CRITICALLY

1. Why have airlines cut services offered to passengers?
2. List two things that have made flying less desirable.
3. What can the airline industry do to regain and strengthen consumer confidence?
4. How can airports improve security while causing less inconvenience to airline passengers?
5. If you were managing a major airline, what would you do to improve customer relations while keeping costs down and maintaining security?

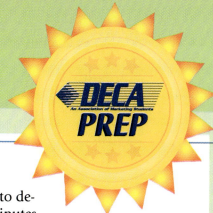

MARKETING MANAGEMENT ROLE-PLAY

Working for the airline industry is less enjoyable today than in the past due to tighter regulations, increased financial difficulties, rising fuel costs, and fewer employees. Passenger frustration levels have increased with the additional regulations, higher ticket prices, and reduced customer service. Some airlines charge an additional fee for tickets not booked online. Most airlines serve limited meals or no meals at all. Increased security means longer waits and somewhat humiliating screening procedures. The increased hassles of air travel have resulted in a greater number of unhappy customers who frequently take out their frustrations at the ticket counter.

Airline managers are challenged with selling tickets, following the latest regulations, and pleasing customers who feel they are receiving less for their money. Ticket sales agents book flights and check in passengers. Many times, passengers are not happy for a variety of reasons.

Your goal as an airline manager is to motivate ticket sales agents to provide outstanding customer service that will result in a more favorable image and repeat business. The role-play involves developing a strategy for ticket sales agents to follow. It should cover everything from greeting customers to handling situations where customers have missed their flights. It should also include security procedures.

You will have 30 minutes to develop your strategy and ten minutes to present it to the airline's executives (judges). The executives will then have five minutes to ask questions.

Performance Indicators Evaluated

- Define outstanding customer service and relate it to repeat business.
- Discuss the reasons for airline security procedures.
- Describe how body language and demeanor of ticket sales agents affect airline passengers.
- Outline airline strategies that will result in greater customer satisfaction and repeat business.

Go to the DECA web site for more detailed information.

THINK CRITICALLY

1. Why do fewer people today want to fly?
2. Why must airlines make a dedicated effort to maintain a positive image with customers?
3. Give two examples of a ticket sales agent's body language that may cause customers concern.
4. Describe a strategy for dealing with an irate airline passenger who has missed a connecting flight due to security delays.

www.deca.org

Creating a Travel and Tourism Business

CHAPTER 12

12.1 Developing a Business Plan

12.2 Risk Management

12.3 Memorable Marketing

Photodisc

Point Your Browser

▶ ▶ ▶ ▶ travel.swlearning.com

Winning Strategies

Boyne USA Resorts

Everett Kircher's love of skiing drove him to start one of the largest privately owned resort corporations in North America. The business began in 1947 when Kircher purchased 40 acres of land and a used chairlift to start Boyne Mountain Resort in Boyne Falls, Michigan. Boyne Mountain continues today as a year-round resort that offers 50 ski slopes, two championship golf courses, and a 250-room hotel.

Since its modest beginnings, the corporation known as Boyne USA Resorts has acquired additional resorts throughout Michigan, Washington, Utah, and Montana. The resorts' accomodations range from value-priced, limited service to four-star, luxury service. The family-owned business continues to grow under the leadership of Kircher's sons and daughters, who now operate the company.

From 2001 to 2011, Boyne USA Resorts will spend more than $400 million for improvements at Big Sky Ski Resort in Montana. Big Sky is a two-season resort offering breathtaking vistas and exciting winter and summer activities. From a used chairlift to a major resort corporation, Boyne USA Resorts has thrived under the caring attention of private ownership.

THINK CRITICALLY

1. List at least three elements that make Boyne USA Resorts' properties different from most resorts.

2. To what do you attribute the success of this family-owned business? Explain your answer.

Developing a Business Plan

Goals

Explain the contribution of small businesses to the economy.

Describe a business plan.

All Aboard

Many opportunities exist in the travel and tourism industry. You may join an existing company or start your own business. Travel and tourism businesses vary in size, complexity, and structure, ranging from a giant airline, such as American Airlines, to a small bed-and-breakfast, such as The Apple Farm.

The Apple Farm, started in 1984 in Philo, California, is family owned by Don and Sally Schmitt and their daughter and son-in-law, Karen and Tim Bates. The Apple Farm organically grows 80 varieties of apples. In addition, it houses a weekend cooking school and provides three cottages for overnight stays.

Work with a group. Compare working at a luxury hotel with working at The Apple Farm. List positives and negatives of each.

ENTREPRENEURSHIP

Nations with the weakest economies and the poorest people often erect many barriers to opening new businesses. However, new businesses create jobs and help economies grow. Governments that want a strong economy will find ways to encourage new travel and tourism businesses.

As existing products and services decline in popularity, economic growth depends upon entrepreneurs starting new businesses and introducing new products and services. An **entrepreneur** is an educated risk taker who pursues the rewards of owning a successful business.

Educated Risk

Some people think that owning a business is less risky than working for someone else. Entrepreneurs see establishing a business as a way of having control over their lives and their income. One of the risks of opening a business is the chance that the business will fail. But, when the business succeeds, the risk is rewarded with financial gain. An educated risk taker prepares and plans to limit the risk of failure.

Avoiding Common Pitfalls

In an interview for the *Wall Street Journal*, entrepreneur Bruce Judson discussed ways to avoid common mistakes when starting a business.

- Be honest with yourself about having the right personality and level of energy to work alone and build a new business.

- Test the idea for the new business on professionals with no connection to you. Family and friends are too close to the idea to be good judges. If people with no connection are interested in investing money in the idea, then it is worth pursuing.

- Do not quit your day job until the business is producing an income. This provides a chance to work out all the problems before depending on the business for an income. Many businesses are started at home with the owner working at night. It is important to follow any policies of your daytime employer that may require notification that you are starting a business outside of company time. Judson recommends never mentioning your business again after that initial notification. Your employer and co-workers need to know that you are focused on your day job.

- Focus on the work you do best. Keep the business small, and find a few freelance workers who can fill in the gaps of your expertise. A *freelance worker* is an independent contractor who is self-employed and is hired by a company to complete a specific job.

Entrepreneurs enjoy venturing into something exciting and new. They are usually found doing something they really enjoy and that they believe gives them control over their future.

Time Out

The Small Business Administration (SBA) is a service organization of the federal government that can provide a wealth of information to people starting their own businesses. The SBA has sample business plans on its web site.

Stopover

Why are new businesses important to the economies of all nations?

_____

_____

THE PLAN

Coming up with an idea for a new travel product or service is the creative part of entrepreneurship. Building an organization that functions as a business to market the new travel product or service requires a detailed plan.

Putting It Together

Becoming an educated risk taker involves learning everything you can about how to successfully operate a business and planning all aspects of the business so that the risks are limited. Most new businesses that fail do so because of poor planning and inadequate financial management. Research and planning will help you realize the extent of involvement needed for success.

Photodisc

Small Business

Before investors and lenders will fund a small business, they will want to see a complete business plan that includes financial statements. A **business plan** is a guide that is used to map out the decisions the owner must make and to help "sell" the business to potential investors and lenders. The Small Business Administration (SBA) recommends building a business plan in four sections—description of the business, promotion, finances, and management.

1. **Description of the business.** This section of the plan should include a clear description of the business, the products and services it will offer, its target customers, its location, and its hours of operation. The owner should also include goals and objectives and provide information that will help a lender make the decision to extend financial assistance. The description needs to show the owner's passion for creating the business and should interest the reader in investing in the company.

2. **Promotion.** The promotional plan should include advertising, publicity, sales promotion, and personal selling. The ratio of the promotional mix is important, and the emphasis on promotion at the start of the business should be heavy.

3. **Finances.** Because so many businesses fail due to poor financial management, extra care should be taken to plan for financial needs. This section of the business plan should include a budget for needed equipment and supplies, a projected balance sheet and income statement, a cash flow plan, an estimate of all startup costs, and the sources of the funds to cover the costs. Sources of funds might include personal investments, issuance of stock, and the desired amounts to be financed by loans.

4. **Management.** This section should include information about how the business will be managed, including the organization's structure, management team, other employee positions, and duties of each person.

E-Ticket

Internet domain addresses ending in ".travel" became available in late 2005. The travel domain was being held for hotels, casinos, and airlines, among other businesses. Industry groups like the Restaurant Association screen companies to help assure the public that legitimate travel businesses or groups are using the domain. According to travel journalist Edward Hasbrouck, the domain excludes the largest class of people. Individual travelers are not allowed to establish web sites using the travel domain.

THINK CRITICALLY

1. Discuss with a partner who you think should be allowed to establish a web site using the travel domain.

2. What kind of screening should be conducted on businesses or groups who want to use the travel domain? Explain your answer.

Stopover What is the purpose of a business plan?

_____

_____

Understand Marketing Concepts

Circle the best answer for each of the following questions.

1. One of the economic impacts of barriers to new businesses is
   a. a weak economy.
   b. fast growth.
   c. low sales.
   d. many jobs.

2. The SBA recommends that a business plan be divided into four sections of
   a. name, location, product/service offerings, and goals.
   b. description, promotion, finances, and management.
   c. products, services, employees, and managers.
   d. goals, objectives, questions, and answers.

Think Critically

Answer the following questions as completely as possible. If necessary, use a separate sheet of paper.

3. What is meant by the term "educated risk taker"? What kind of education does the entrepreneur need?

_____

_____

_____

_____

_____

_____

_____

4. **Communication** An entrepreneur who is starting a new bed-and-breakfast in your area has asked for your help in writing a descriptive paragraph for the business plan. Write the paragraph, including information that potential investors and lenders would want to know about the business.

_____

_____

_____

_____

_____

_____

_____

Risk Management

Goals

- List and describe organizational structures for travel and tourism businesses.
- Explain methods of managing risk.

All Aboard

Juan and Sherrie Silva opened The Red Hacienda bed-and-breakfast in a large family home they had inherited. The business quickly grew to the extent that they hired a bookkeeper, Carl Wong.

Wong had previously worked for a hotel in another city. He indicated that the Silvas would need to buy a computer for his use. Wong said he could save them the cost of accounting software since he had a copy from his former employer.

He installed the software on the business's computer, and all was well until the Silvas received a letter informing them that the Business Software Alliance was suing them for illegal use of the software. Because the Silvas were operating The Red Hacienda as a sole proprietorship with Juan as the owner, all of their personal savings and investments were at risk of being taken to settle the lawsuit.

Work with a group. Discuss how the situation could have been avoided. How might the Silvas have protected their personal finances from a business lawsuit?

THE STRUCTURE

FINANCING

Regardless of business size, owners of travel and tourism companies have a choice to make about the organizational structure of their businesses. The choice should be driven by the need to limit the owners' liability and risk and to make the most advantageous tax decisions. **Liability** is the legal responsibility for loss or damage. The structure chosen for a business can make a difference in the types of liability and the risk owners assume.

Sole Proprietorship

A **sole proprietorship** is a business that is owned and operated by one person. For a small business, such as a bed-and-breakfast, this can be the perfect organizational structure. A sole proprietorship is the simplest form of business to start. Profits are taxed as personal income to the owner.

A sole proprietorship has disadvantages, especially when it comes to liability. If the business fails or faces a large lawsuit, the owner's personal savings and property can be taken to pay creditors or settle the lawsuit. As the business grows, another structure might need to be chosen in order to limit the liability of the owner and to clearly separate business liability from personal liability.

Partnerships

Two heads are sometimes better than one when it comes to operating a business. A **partnership** is formed when a business is owned and operated by two or more people. Partnerships are similar to sole proprietorships in that they are easy to start. In a partnership, all profits are taxed as personal income based on the percentage of ownership of each partner. As with a sole proprietorship, a partnership does not limit the personal liability of the partners. The potential for personal liability and the income tax implications will often influence the partners of a travel and tourism business to consider forming a corporation.

Corporations

A **corporation** is a form of organizational structure that sets up the business as a separate, legal entity that can operate apart from its owners. A corporation limits the liability of the business's owners.

A corporation is the most complex of the business structures and requires that a charter be issued by the state in which it will operate. The **charter** is also called the *articles of incorporation*, and it defines the business's structure and management. The two most common forms of corporations are C corporations and S corporations.

C Corporations A C corporation has three groups of people involved in the business—shareholders, a board of directors, and officers. A **shareholder** is a person who has invested money in a corporation by purchasing shares of the company's stock. A **share of stock** is a unit of ownership issued to shareholders who control the company. The shareholders elect a **board of directors**, the people who make the major business decisions about the company. The board of directors appoints the officers of the company. A C corporation must have at least three officers—a president, a treasurer or chief financial officer, and a secretary. In a small corporation, one person can serve in all three jobs.

The earnings of the C corporation are taxed as profits of the corporation and are taxed again as personal income of the shareholders when the earnings are distributed as dividends. This double taxation requirement is considered a disadvantage of the C corporation form of structure.

S Corporation An S corporation requires only one shareholder and one officer. A board of directors is not needed. In an S corporation, the profits are taxed only as the personal income of the shareholders rather than also being taxed at the corporate rate.

Missing the Boat

Executives from Cendant—a major travel services company that owns Ramada, Howard Johnson, and Avis, among others—were found guilty of securities fraud. The Securities and Exchange Commission (SEC) filed the charges because of the company's accounting irregularities.

Accounting irregularities occur when fraudulent financial reporting makes a company falsely appear to have high earnings. In Cendant's case, high-level executives were accused of pressuring accountants to make the company's financial situation look good. Cendant's stock dropped to a quarter of its high value just prior to the fraud becoming public.

THINK CRITICALLY

1. Why would a firm falsely report its earnings?

2. Why is honest financial accounting critical to businesses? Discuss your opinion with others.

Stopover Name three types of organizational structures.

_____

_____

HANDLING RISK

In addition to limiting the liability risk of the business's owners and investors through the selection of the right organizational structure, the risks of the business's customers and property must also be managed. Opening a travel and tourism business involves a certain level of risk. The risks can include the possibility of a disaster, such as a fire or flood, or financial mismanagement resulting in the loss of the business. **Risk management** is the process of addressing potential risks in order to prevent them or to lessen their negative impacts. Risk management is accomplished through risk avoidance, risk transfer, risk insurance, and risk retention.

Risk Avoidance

Avoiding risky business situations takes thought and preventive actions on the part of the owners and managers. Locating the business in a relatively crime-free area can be a starting point. Added measures, such as security guards, video surveillance, controlled access to public and private areas, and security training for all staff members, may be needed. Taking the necessary steps to prevent or reduce risks is called **risk avoidance**.

Hotels are responsible for guest safety. Guests can be vulnerable to criminal activity when they are not familiar with their surroundings. They may be distracted while removing their luggage from their cars and may not notice suspicious people in the facilities' parking lots. About one-third of hotel crimes are committed in the parking lots. Most hotels maintain surveillance cameras in vulnerable areas in an effort to avoid the risk of guests being robbed. Guests should be reminded to take safety precautions while they are on the property of a hotel or resort. Locking doors, not admitting strangers, and maintaining control of their room keys are helpful safety tips for guests.

Risk Transfer

FINANCING

When a company's owners do not want to deal with a risk, they may transfer the risk to another company. They may hire another company to complete a risky activity—one in which the other company is an expert. For example, rather than the business extending credit and dealing with the risk of customers not paying their bills, the business may instead accept bank credit cards. The risk of nonpayment is then managed by the financial institutions issuing the credit cards. When starting a new business, the owners may not want to bear the entire financial risk alone. Instead, the owners may want to transfer some of the risk to others who will invest their money in the new company. Through **risk transfer**, business owners allow others to assume some or all of a risk.

Risk Insurance

Businesses contract with insurance companies to cover the risks of possible financial losses. **Risk insurance** pays for financial losses that are *predictable*. For example, fire losses are predictable in the sense that insurance companies maintain statistics on their past occurrences at similar businesses. Based on these statistics, the insurance companies can predict the likelihood of future losses. Businesses pay the costs of risk insurance in the form of *premiums*. The premiums from many businesses are pooled and used to pay for the losses that a few businesses will experience. Because not all risks are insurable, risk management requires smart planning to avoid or transfer risks whenever possible.

Photodisc

Risk Retention

When a travel business assumes the cost of a risk, this is referred to as **risk retention**. Owners of a travel business understand that they may not sell as many vacation packages as planned due to uncontrollable circumstances. If an economic downturn keeps travelers from buying, the company may suffer a loss on the product. The business must retain the risk associated with the loss of sales.

Risk retention also occurs when a business decides to self-insure instead of purchasing risk insurance from an insurance company. A self-insured company must maintain a certain level of cash to pay for accidents, thefts, fire destruction, or other liabilities that are normally paid by risk insurance. Small companies with low cash reserves usually cannot afford to self-insure.

Stopover

How can a business manage its risks?

_____

_____

Understand Marketing Concepts

Circle the best answer for each of the following questions.

1. The owner of a sole proprietorship
   a. has limited liability.
   b. has unlimited liability.
   c. shares ownership with one other person.
   d. does all of the above.

2. Ways to manage risk include
   a. avoidance.
   b. transfer.
   c. insurance.
   d. all of the above.

Think Critically

Answer the following questions as completely as possible. If necessary, use a separate sheet of paper.

3. Why would a small business owner want to choose incorporation as the structure for the business? What are the advantages and disadvantages of the corporate structure?

_____

_____

_____

_____

_____

_____

4. Why might a small business owner want to buy risk insurance? What are two events that could be covered by risk insurance?

_____

_____

_____

_____

_____

_____

_____

_____

Memorable Marketing

Goals

- Define customer obsession.
- Explain how to transform disgruntled customers into raving fans.

All Aboard

Nataline Kardoush was disgusted with the lack of cleanliness in her hotel room, the level of noise outside the room, and the lumpy bed, but she didn't tell anyone at the hotel. Instead, she left the hotel, thinking she would never return. Later, she completed a customer satisfaction survey from the hotel, giving the details of her disappointing stay.

The hotel's managers acted upon her satisfaction survey. A vice president of the hotel called Kardoush and offered an apology, a complete refund of the cost of the room, and a free future stay. The hotel's managers had made a successful attempt to retain Kardoush as a customer by showing her they appreciated her opinion and her business. On her return visit, she was thrilled to find a sparkling room and an upgraded mattress.

Work with a group. Discuss why a hotel would want to transform a disgruntled customer into a satisfied, repeat customer.

CUSTOMER OBSESSION

PRODUCT/SERVICE MANAGEMENT

When all of the planning is complete, the financing available, the ads placed, and the doors of the business ready to open, all attention must turn to the customer. Advertising excellent products and low prices may initially attract customers. In the long run, however, the customers' level of satisfaction is the final determinant that will differentiate the business from its competitors and establish a repeat-customer base.

Beyond Good

Good customer service is the minimum level required to stay in business, according to Rick Sidorowicz, editor and publisher of *The CEO Refresher*, but good services is not enough. In a series of articles for the newsletter, Sidorowicz introduced

Photodisc

Marketing Myths

During exceptionally busy periods, business owners may sometimes convince themselves that business is so good that they do not need to spend time or money on promotions. They are highly focused on their current customers and projects and don't look toward the future.

A marketing plan that includes ongoing promotion can help keep business steady, rather than alternating between busy and slow periods. It is best to plan and prepare promotions well in advance. When a resort is in the midst of accommodating tourists during peak season, a promotional activity that was previously prepared can be whisked off to the media with little time and effort. The promotion may bring in new customers before business has a chance to slow down after peak season.

THINK CRITICALLY

1. How can planning promotions in advance help smooth out a business's busy and slow cycles?

2. How can promotions exhibit a business's customer obsession? Give examples.

the concept of "customer obsession." Customer obsession goes beyond just talking about being customer focused and realizing the importance of customers to the success of the business. **Customer obsession** means every employee provides memorable service to every customer every time. Through customer obsession, the company gains a distinct competitive advantage.

Customer obsession is not a program that can be implemented and then forgotten, but is instead a value and an ethic. It must permeate every level of the business, and every employee must be empowered to "wow" customers. Providing customers with exceptional service that is beyond what they expect creates raving fans out of ordinary customers.

Obsessive Behavior

Sidorowicz cites many examples of businesses where a few of the employees provide exceptional service but customer obsession is not a part of the culture. Unless all employees consistently apply customer obsession, the business will lose customers. Sidorowicz believes Delta Hotels, a Canadian hotel chain, is an example of a company with customer obsession. Delta Hotels' corporate commitment to both employees and customers shows in its low employee turnover and its numerous awards as one of "The 50 Best Places to Work in Canada." Part of Delta Hotels' mission statement reads, "A great place to work where a culture exists that recognizes 'the way we deal with our employees will be reflected in the manner that they interact with our guests.'" Delta Hotels also guarantees that guests will find their rooms in perfect order when they check in or their first night at the hotel will be free. As a result of its customer obsession, Delta Hotels has incredibly loyal customers, as well as dedicated employees.

Stopover

Describe what is meant by customer obsession.

_____

_____

SERVICE RECOVERY

PRODUCT/SERVICE MANAGEMENT

Customer obsession provides memorable marketing that leaves customers telling everyone about their great experiences. Occasionally, though, even a customer-obsessed travel business makes a customer unhappy. A major difference between a customer-obsessed company and other companies lies in what happens next.

Adding the Wow Factor

Many customers leave a business less than satisfied with the product or service they received and will simply never return. Others speak up about the poor product or service and are made even more unhappy when they receive no response from the business. Imagine a blank look on the face of an employee who is listening to a customer's complaint. A slight shrug of the employee's shoulders is the final indication of a lack of concern. One more customer is lost for good.

It is much less expensive to retain loyal customers than to attract new ones. **Service recovery** is a way to manage disgruntled customers and turn them into raving fans. Service recovery empowers every employee with the ability to not only respond to a customer's dissatisfaction, but to "wow" the customer. This requires a corporate culture of customer obsession. Service recovery consists of three steps for the employee.

1. Sincerely apologize and take accountability for the problem.

2. Ask the customer what it will take to correct the situation. Then, listen to what the customer says and act upon it.

3. Add the "wow" factor by providing something beyond just correcting the problem.

If a customer-obsessed travel agent promises to have tickets and the itinerary for a cruise vacation ready by 11:00 A.M. today, the agent will work hard to make it happen. Sometimes there are unavoidable delays, such as those caused by a computer system going down, that result in the vacation package not being ready when the customer arrives to pick it up. The agent in a customer-obsessed travel agency would apologize, accept blame for the problem, and do everything possible to remedy the situation immediately. Adding the "wow" factor could include delivering the package to the customer's home or office and providing a $50 gift card to spend in the cruise ship's gift shop.

Time Out

British Columbia's tourism industry has established an organization called go2 that helps attract and provide training to employees. Tourism is one of the Canadian province's largest industries.

Photodisc

Cost and Benefits

The cost to a business of adding the "wow" factor can be much less than the cost of advertising to attract a new customer. John Tschohl, author of *Loyal for Life*, states that advertising is for the masses, while service recovery is for the individual. Service recovery is an attitude, not a response that can be outlined by management. Hampton Inn's service recovery program is estimated to cost the company about $9.2 million each year. The estimated revenue from retaining customers is $49 million per year, which brings Hampton Inn a $5 return on each $1 invested in service recovery, according to *USA Today*.

The benefits of customer obsession and service recovery to a business include loyal employees who are empowered to solve customers' problems, happy customers who are raving fans, and a loyal customer base that provides continued business. Marketing is, after all, a series of activities that creates an exchange that satisfies the individual customer as well as the travel and tourism business.

Stopover List the three steps of service recovery.

_____

_____

Five-Star Traveler

W. RICHARD WEST

W. Richard West, Jr., is the founding director of the National Museum of the American Indian (NMAI). NMAI is one of the nation's most important and prominent cultural accomplishments. The museum is part of the Smithsonian Institution's cultural resources and exhibition of national collections. The museum opened its third phase in 2004 as part of the National Mall in Washington, D.C. West has worked to ensure that all three phases of the museum are premier cultural tourist attractions.

Rick West is a Southern Cheyenne who grew up in Muskogee, Oklahoma. He is the son of American Indian master artist, Walter Richard West, and musician, Maribelle McCrea West. West received a bachelor's degree in American history, a master's from Harvard, and his doctor of jurisprudence from Stanford, where he served as editor of the *Stanford Law Review*. West practiced law for a number of years and represented Indian tribes before the U.S. Supreme Court. West also served as a volunteer board member of Indian cultural organizations before moving to establish the NMAI museums. West's job includes empowering his staff to provide what it takes to have visitors who rave about the museum and return for additional visits.

THINK CRITICALLY

Look at the web site for the National Museum of the American Indian and find examples of marketing strategies that are used to encourage repeat visitors. In a group, brainstorm a customer-obsession strategy that the museum is not currently using.

Understand Marketing Concepts

Circle the best answer for each of the following questions.

1. Customer obsession includes
   a. creating raving fans.
   b. wowing customers.
   c. providing memorable service.
   d. all of the above.

2. Service recovery is
   a. a way to attract new customers.
   b. providing Internet access.
   c. providing clean hotel rooms.
   d. none of the above.

Think Critically

Answer the following questions as completely as possible. If necessary, use a separate sheet of paper.

3. Describe the difference between a customer-focused travel supplier and a customer-obsessed travel supplier.

_____

_____

_____

_____

_____

_____

_____

4. Describe a service recovery situation that might take place in a luxury hotel.

_____

_____

_____

_____

_____

_____

_____

_____

Review Marketing Concepts

Write the letter of the term that matches each definition. Some terms will not be used.

_____ 1. A business that is owned and operated by one person

_____ 2. The legal responsibility for loss or damage

_____ 3. An educated risk taker who pursues the rewards of owning a successful business

_____ 4. When business owners allow others to assume some or all of a risk

_____ 5. A guide that is used to map out the decisions the owner must make and to help "sell" the business to potential investors and lenders

_____ 6. A way to manage disgruntled customers and turn them into raving fans

_____ 7. When every employee provides memorable service to every customer every time

_____ 8. The process of addressing potential risks in order to prevent them or to lessen their negative impacts

_____ 9. Issued by the state in which a corporation will operate and defines the business's structure and management

_____ 10. A person who has invested money in a corporation by purchasing shares of the company's stock

a. board of directors
b. business plan
c. charter
d. corporation
e. customer obsession
f. entrepreneur
g. liability
h. partnership
i. risk avoidance
j. risk insurance
k. risk management
l. risk retention
m. risk transfer
n. service recovery
o. shareholder
p. share of stock
q. sole proprietorship

Circle the best answer.

11. A freelance worker
    a. is an independent contractor.
    b. is a paid employee.
    c. works for a single employer but with a flexible schedule.
    d. all of the above.

12. Providing safety training for all employees is a means of
    a. risk transfer.
    b. risk avoidance.
    c. risk retention.
    d. risk insurance.

Think Critically

13. Why do travel and tourism entrepreneurs take the risk of opening new businesses? How can they limit the risks of starting new businesses?

_____

_____

_____

_____

14. Think about a travel and tourism business you would like to own. Write a paragraph that enthusiastically describes the business.

_____

_____

_____

_____

15. Interview an owner or a manager of a travel and tourism business to determine what the business does to avoid, transfer, insure, or retain risks.

_____

_____

_____

_____

16. Describe what customer obsession would be like in a moderately priced hotel that has business professionals of all ages as its target customers. How might customer obsession be different if the target customers were young professionals, ages 18 to 25?

_____

_____

_____

_____

17. Assume you are the president of the hotel described in the All Aboard feature in Lesson 12.3. You are unhappy that the hotel did not find out about Nataline's dissatisfaction until after her stay. What measures would you put in place to obtain customer feedback sooner?

_____

_____

_____

_____

Make Connections

18. **Research** Using the business you described in question 14, list the necessary steps to open the business as a corporation in your state. Conduct your research using the Internet or other sources.

_____

_____

_____

_____

19. **Geography** Select a country that has a weak economy and a large percentage of population living in poverty. Write at least two paragraphs about how you could involve the local people in a travel and tourism business. Describe the country's specific cultural and geographic features that might be of interest to tourists.

_____

_____

_____

_____

20. **Technology** Use the Internet to research effective web page design. Design the home page of a web site for the business you described in question 14. Include some links to other web sites that would be of interest to your target customers.

_____

_____

_____

_____

21. **Marketing Math** Armando Mercado is purchasing fire insurance for his hotel. It would cost $5,987,000 to replace the hotel building if it were destroyed and another $3,500,000 to replace the furnishings. The insurance will pay for 95 percent of the replacement costs. How much cash will Armando need to pay out of his pocket to restore the hotel and furnishings should they be completely destroyed by fire?

_____

_____

_____

_____

22. **Marketing** Assume you are the manager of a hotel who wants to empower your employees with the ability to "wow" customers who are not happy with the hotel. Provide guidelines for extra perks and incentives that employees may offer to guests to make up for their bad experiences and turn them into repeat customers. The guidelines should be flexible, allowing for discretion and creativity on the part of each employee.

_____

_____

_____

_____

23. **Communication** Conduct research on the Internet or in travel magazines. Find two examples of hotel or resort advertisements. From the ads and other information available, determine the organizational structure of the businesses. Decide which business would be the better employer, and explain your reasoning.

_____

_____

_____

_____

_____

_____

EXTENDED STAY

Project You have decided to open a travel and tourism business and need to develop a business plan.

Work with a group and complete the following activities.

1. Use the Internet to conduct research for information about business planning. Visit the Small Business Administration's web site as part of your research.
2. Select the type of business you will open and give it a name.
3. Create a business plan. Divide the plan into four sections as outlined in Lesson 12.1.
4. Include a description of your target customers and how you will meet their needs.
5. Determine and list the additional education and work experience you will need before you are an "educated risk taker" who is ready to open this business.

TRAVEL AGENCIES FACE STIFF COMPETITION FROM INTERNET INTERMEDIARIES

Travel agencies organize travel packages for both business and leisure travelers, with business travel being the largest source of revenue. The agencies are paid commissions on all travel business they generate, receiving a percentage of the prices of airline, hotel, and cruise bookings.

Business travel made up 35 percent of the travel market prior to 9/11. Inbound international travel made up another 15 percent. Both of these segments traveled significantly less in the months after 9/11. Even as the post-9/11 economy recovers, businesses are not loosening their travel budgets. Additionally, domestic leisure travelers are spending more of their travel dollars closer to home.

Financially strapped airlines have reduced or eliminated the amount of commissions they pay to travel agencies. They now encourage consumers to book online instead. Most major airlines offer better ticket prices to individuals who book their flights using the Internet. Web intermediaries, such as Expedia, Priceline, and the web sites of major airlines and hotel chains, have taken business away from traditional travel agencies. More travelers are making their own reservations online and being rewarded with lower prices.

Business travelers like the reliability and convenience of travel agents planning the itineraries for their business trips. A large percentage of business travelers have remained loyal to travel agencies. However, many companies have realized the cost savings from booking travel plans online.

Many travel agencies have downsized or consolidated with other agencies to achieve economies of scale. Others have gone out of business due to lost revenues. Surviving travel agencies are faced with developing new strategies, such as customer obsession, to stay in business. Travel agents can no longer see themselves as primarily airline ticket sellers. Their future lies in adding value across a range of various travel products and services.

THINK CRITICALLY

1. Why have travel agencies lost business?
2. Why have many business travelers remained loyal to travel agencies?
3. Why have some businesses changed from using travel agencies to booking their own travel arrangements online?
4. Why do airlines reward customers who book their reservations online?
5. Name ways that travel agencies can add more value than online booking sites.

ENTREPRENEURSHIP PARTICIPATING EVENT

Target market, product, and location are key factors to consider when proposing a new business. Serious consideration must be given to demand and competition.

Banks and other financial institutions require a business plan when deciding whether to finance a new business. Research must be conducted to write a realistic, effective business plan. Defending a proposal for a new business is much easier when reference is made to information found through research.

Together with one or two of your classmates, design a business plan for a travel-related business of your choice. The business plan will be limited to ten pages and must include the following sections.

- Executive Summary
- Description
- Analysis of the Business Situation
- Proposed Marketing/Promotional Mix
- Proposed Financing
- Conclusion
- Bibliography
- Appendix

You will have 15 minutes to convince the bank loan officers (judges) to finance your new business. The judges will then have five minutes to ask questions about your business plan.

Performance Indicators Evaluated

- Explain the need for your travel business.
- Describe the target market for your business.
- Describe the competition for your business and how you will overcome your competitors.
- Identify the promotional mix for your business.
- Present a realistic, three-year projection of revenues and expenses.
- Use visual aids to reinforce the need for your business.
- Present your information in a clear, confident manner, answering any questions asked by the judges.

Go to the DECA web site for more detailed information.

THINK CRITICALLY

1. What type of travel and tourism business is demanded today?
2. What level of service do customers expect from a travel and tourism business?
3. Why does a bank require a three-year financial projection?
4. Should a travel and tourism business collect feedback from its customers? Why or why not? How could the business use the feedback?

www.deca.org

Glossary

A

Activities age a measure of one's cognitive age related to the age a person identifies with while enjoying travel activities (p. 84)

Adventure travelers travelers who push themselves through physical activity and take risks without doing harm to others or the environment (p. 121)

Adventurous/educational travelers travelers who want to experience museums, theaters, and cultural activities (p. 160)

Advertising the paid communication of information about products and services; the one-way communication that takes place between the seller and potential customers intended to increase sales (p. 233)

Aggregators web sites that bring together information from many sources and allow customers to easily comparison shop (p. 192)

Application a data-collection form an employer provides to a potential employee (p. 68)

B

Back of the house areas out of the view of customers that include the engineering/facilities staff who take care of the building and equipment (p. 142)

Backbone the cabling needed to connect the main distribution frame of a communications network to the intermediate distribution frames (p. 195)

Balance sheet shows the relationships among the assets, liabilities, and owners equity; represents a snapshot of the business at a given time (p. 211)

Benchmarks standards that define the desired performance (p. 158)

Bid a written proposal submitted to a seller in which a buyer offers to pay a certain price for a good or service (p. 160)

Biometrics systems that measure biological features, such as the iris of the eye, fingerprints, or face (p. 31)

Board of directors people elected by the shareholders who make the major business decisions about the company (p. 285)

Brand an established identity or image for a product or service based on its target market (p. 90)

Business budgets plans for how a business will spend and make money which have a planned outcome to control costs so they do not exceed the funds available (p. 209)

Business conferences events that bring together people employed in the same industry to learn, share, and socialize (p. 16)

Business plan a guide that is used to map out the decisions the owner must make and to help "sell" the business to potential investors and lenders (p. 282)

Business-management risks risks that are speculative and uninsurable because the results are not predictable (p. 43)

C

CAD/CAM an acronym for Computer-Aided Design/Computer-Aided Manufacturing (p. 58)

Cash flow gaps occur when there is not enough cash coming in to cover the cash being paid out (p. 210)

Certified meeting professional (CMP) person who demonstrates the standard of knowledge and skills needed in the convention industry (p. 109)

Charter defines the corporation's structure and management; also called the articles of incorporation (p. 285)

Closed Shop when management makes an agreement with the union that only members can be hired (p. 62)

Codes of ethics guidelines most professional associations have that are used to guide the behavior and decisions of their members (p. 264)

Cognitive age age with which a person most closely identifies (p. 84)

Collective bargaining the right of the union to be the sole negotiator for all employees (p. 62)

Consolidators companies that buy in bulk from travel suppliers and sell at a discount (p. 192)

Consul an official appointed by a government to reside in a foreign country and represent his or her government's commercial interests and assist its citizens there (p. 268)

Consular information sheets contain information about destination countries, including health conditions and crime statistics (p. 269)

Consumer Product Safety Commission a federal agency charged with protecting consumers from dangerous products (p. 258)

Continuous improvement process consists of the four functions of management; each cycle begins when a control review shows the plan needs to be revised (p. 61)

Controllable risk when loss can be prevented or the frequency of loss can be reduced (p. 42)

Convention and meeting professionals people who effectively plan, organize, budget, publicize, and manage for group events of any size (p. 109)

Cookie a small piece of data from a visited web site (p. 165)

Corporation form of organizational structure that sets up the business as a separate, legal entity that can operate apart from its owners (p. 285)

Cover letter letter sent along with a resume to explain more fully or provide additional information (p. 68)

Cross-selling offering additional products of a package to a customer who may have called to purchase only one element, such as a plane ticket (p. 143)

Culinary arts the practice of selecting, combining, preparing, cooking, serving, and storing food and beverages (p. 147)

Cultural tourism tourism focused on the culture of the region, including its heritage, art, food, clothing, geographic points of interest, historic sites, and museums (p. 88)

Culture predominant attitudes and behavior of a group of people including their language, religion, ethnicity, food, clothing, and politics (p. 87)

Customer obsession means every employee provides memorable service to every customer every time (p. 290)

D

Data analysis describing, summarizing, and comparing data in a systematic way (p. 172)

Data processing collecting and converting data into usable information (p. 167)

Data protection creating backup files in the event that the original data files are lost as a result of viruses, hardware failure, or human error, and preventing criminal access to the files (p. 167)

Demographics characteristics of a target market, such as age, gender, ethnic group, income, physical or mental disability, and level of education (p. 82)

Destination major stops or attractions for travelers (p. 16)

Disabled legal definition of a person who has a physical or mental impairment that substantially limits one or more major life activities (p. 82)

Discount airlines airlines that make frequent stops and do not offer food or reserved seating, making boarding first-come, first-serve (p. 108)

Distribution moving products and services from producer to consumer by the best means possible (p. 6)

Distributors the businesses that sell products and services directly to the consumer (p. 15)

Diverse distinguished from others by a unique set of physical, mental, and cultural qualities (p. 81)

Duty a type of tax imposed on certain imported goods (p. 267)

E

E-commerce the exchange of goods, services, information, or other business through electronic means (p. 189)

Economic utility the concept that customers will maximize their satisfaction with products or services (p. 220)

Ecotourism responsible travel to natural areas that conserves the environment and sustains the well-being of the local people (p. 117)

Embassy a diplomatic mission to a foreign country headed by an ambassador (p. 268)

Entrepreneur an educated risk taker who pursues the rewards of owning a successful business (p. 280)

Environmental risks usually pure risks that are preventable, predictable, and generally insurable (p. 43)

Ethics a guide to action based on right versus wrong (p. 263)

Event coordinator full-time staff person who works with the group sponsoring an event; his or her responsibilities may include concept development, marketing, project management, and post-event analysis (p. 58)

Exchange model the way a service is paid for (p. 134)

Exhibit manager person who manages the budget for the trade show portion of the annual association conference; must be knowledgeable about current trends and technologies in the meeting and exhibition industry (p. 58)

Export assistance service provided in the form of gathered market-analysis data that may be used to attract more international travelers (p. 33)

F

Financial default occurs when a travel provider stops providing services due to lack of funds to pay its financial obligations (p. 263)

Financial statements tools used to keep track of the financial performance of a business (p. 211)

Financing includes budgeting, finding investors, record keeping, funding the business operations, and helping customers find ways to afford the products and services (p. 208)

Fixed costs portions of a business's budget that include items, such as rent, that are set costs and occur whether anything has been sold or not (p. 209)

Flags of convenience foreign flags under which virtually all cruise ships that do business in the United States sail (p. 258)

Forecasting the process by which a business predicts the expected income from potential sales and the expected expenditures and costs for a specified future period (p. 209)

Form utility when the tangible parts of a product or service impact satisfaction (p. 220)

Fractional ownership model occurs when a customer has part ownership of a property, with access to it for a period of time each year based on the percentage of ownership (p. 134)

Freelance worker an independent contractor who is self-employed and is hired by a company to complete a specific job (p. 281)

Freelance writers writers who submit articles to various publications and are paid for each article that is used (p. 57)

Frequency the total number of times the target audience will see or hear the advertisement (p. 238)

Frequent-user programs programs designed to reward customers for repeat business; programs generally award points based on use of the service and grant free services after a number of points are collected (p. 111)

Front of the house all areas of a hospitality business to which the public has access, such as the lobby, guest rooms, fitness center, meeting rooms, restaurants, and gift shop (p. 142)

G

Gamblers/fun travelers travelers who want to vacation in areas with lots of nightlife, gambling, or recreation and outdoor activities (p. 160)

Genealogical trips include visits to find legal documents, such as birth and death records, or to discover long-lost relatives (p. 12)

Getaway/family travelers travelers who tend to visit locations that are child-friendly, places where friends and family live, and laid-back areas known for rest, relaxation, and scenic views (p. 160)

Global distribution system (GDS) a computer reservation system jointly used by airlines and travel suppliers in many countries (p. 165)

Guest cycle all the events that occur between the time a guest initially makes a reservation and finally checks out of the property (p. 142)

H

Heritage tours trips that are based on providing historical information about a location and its most prominent historical sites (p. 12)

Hostel an inn that provides the budget tourist a minimal sheltered place to sleep for a minimal price (p. 116)

I

ID bar section of a web page that identifies the site (p. 191)

Inbound travelers nonresident visitors arriving in a region or country (p. 172)

Income statement provides financial data that show whether the company has earned a profit or suffered a loss; includes all of the revenue and expenses for the company during a certain period of time (p. 211)

Infrastructure the supporting structure beneath an industry (p. 35)

Insurable risks pure risks for which the chances of a loss occurring are predictable (p. 42)

Internships work-based experiences usually connected to a high school or college course; the work is often unpaid but is rewarded with the valuable, firsthand experience in the desired career field (p. 56)

L

Large-scale events major event such as the Super Bowl or a NASCAR race (p. 16)

Law of demand indicates that when the price of a product increases, there will be less demand for the product; when the price decreases, there will be more demand (p. 173)

Law of supply indicates that when the price of a product or service increases, more will be produced; when the price decreases, less will be produced (p. 173)

Lead time the time needed to prepare the advertisement (p. 238)

Liability the legal responsibility for loss or damage (p. 284)

Life cycle begins at the time a product or service is introduced and lasts until it is no longer purchased; generally progresses through four stages—introduction, growth, maturity, and decline (p. 147)

Line of credit an amount of money that a financial institution will loan the company for a short period of time to cover cash flow gaps (p. 210)

M

Managers creative problem solvers who plan, organize, lead, and control business activities (p. 60)

Market segments subgroups based on demographics or psychographics (p. 90)

Market share percentage of business received compared to the total market (p. 135)

Marketing concept focuses on consumers' wants and needs during the planning, production, promotion, and distribution of travel products and services (p. 219)

Marketing mix the right blend of products, pricing, promotion, and distribution (p. 221)

Marketing research process of gathering and using information about potential customers to determine what customers want and expect from travel service providers (p. 133)

Marketing-information management collecting and using data to make decisions for a business; information must include data about what potential customers want and how much they are willing to pay to obtain the products and services (p. 7)

Mass affluent the number of people earning between the average and top incomes, creating a center level of people (p. 115)

Measurable goal a statement of desired outcome for which data can be collected to affirm its accomplishment; for example, a goal to increase sales by three percent during the first six months of the year is specific enough to be measurable (p. 234)

Merger when two companies are integrated into one company (p. 15)

Metasearch sites web sites that bring together information from many sources and allow customers to comparison shop easily (p. 192)

Metatags keywords hidden in the coding of a website's home page (p. 192)

Moral values those values judged by a group to be right or wrong based upon principles (p. 263)

Multinational corporations travel companies with operations in many countries (p. 37)

N

Navigation bar menu list that allows the web site user to access other sections of the site that are of interest (p. 191)

News release a short article sent to members of the media prior to a special event, in hopes that the event will be newsworthy enough to generate attention (p. 240)

Niche market a small, specific group (p. 161)

O

Occupancy rate percentage determined by dividing the total number of rooms sold by the total number of rooms available (p. 215)

On-time arrival the plane arrives at the gate within 15 minutes of the time scheduled (p. 259)

Outbound travelers residents traveling outside the region or country (p. 172)

Override when a contracted number is met, a company may receive an incentive payment from the preferred vendor (p. 108)

Oversales situation caused by an airline overbooking a flight based on scheduling models that show a certain percentage of people will likely not show up for the flight (p. 259)

P

Package usually an unescorted travel product that bundles several elements, such as transportation, hotel room, sightseeing, admission to local attractions, and possibly meals (p. 143)

Partnership business formed when it is owned and operated by two or more people (p. 285)

Passenger name records (PNRs) information about passengers and their airline reservations; entered into computers through intermediaries and kept in the technology systems; if a traveler makes reservations for an air flight, car rental, and hotel room, the data stored in the PNR will include the traveler's name, address, credit card used, flight number, type of hotel room, and other personal data (p. 184)

Passport an internationally accepted document that verifies the identity and nationality of the bearer (p. 31)

Performance measures references that define and quantify the results of an activity (p. 159)

Perk an added benefit that may be used as a means to attract and keep good employees or customers (p. 107)

Personal data any data that can identify a specific individual (p. 167)

Personal selling a one-on-one interaction with potential customers to inform them about products and services and persuade them to buy (p. 233)

Pilgrimage travel undertaken for a religious purpose (p. 89)

Place utility when the product or service is found at a desired location (p. 220)

Possession utility when the product or service is offered to customers at a price they can afford and with a convenient method of payment (p. 220)

Preferred vendor vendor with which there is a negotiated agreement for discount prices based on volume (p. 108)

Premiums payments businesses make to cover the costs of risk insurance; premiums from many businesses are pooled and used to pay for the losses that a few businesses will experience (p. 287)

Press kit package sent to journalists that includes news release, photos, and other materials that may raise their interest in a product or service (p. 240)

Price points represent the range between the top price and the bottom price customers are willing to pay (p. 115)

Pricing establishing the price of the products and services (p. 7)

Product mix the variety of products and services offered by a company or business (p. 132)

Product/service management combines the right mix of products and services to match customer wants and needs (p. 7)

Product/service planning determining the combination of product or service classifications and price points within a company's product or service mix (p. 133)

Professional organizations groups of people who meet for professional growth and to network with people employed in related businesses (p. 17)

Profit the amount of money, from sales and services, remaining after all costs have been paid (p. 6)

Promotion communicating to potential customers about travel and tourism products and services through various avenues, including advertising, publicity, public relations, sales promotions, and personal selling (p. 7)

Protocols rules that govern business transactions over the Internet (p. 189)

Psychographics ideologies, values, attitudes, and interests that a group has in common (p. 90)

Public announcements made when the State Department wants to communicate quickly about a short-term travel risk that is in the best interest of U.S. citizens to avoid (p. 269)

Public relations (PR) means by which a business can improve its public image; for example, it can participate in or sponsor community events, thereby creating good or positive and mutually beneficial relationships with the public (p. 233)

Public-sector organizations agencies set up by governments to promote travel and tourism in their areas (p. 16)

Public/private ventures when the Travel Business Roundtable, Chamber of Commerce, and other private trade organizations work with government to jointly improve travel and tourism (p. 31)

Publicity communication to the public about a business not paid for or controlled by the company (p. 233)

Pure risk there is no chance to gain from the event and loss of income occurs when a business is no longer able to operate because of a catastrophe, such as a flood that closes a golf resort for weeks (p. 42)

R

Reach the total number of people who will see an advertisement (p. 238)

Real-time data current data that are available immediately and updated as often as every 100 milliseconds (p. 190)

Regulatory agencies governmental entities with the legal authority to issue rules and regulations that impact travel and tourism businesses (p. 16)

Restricted domestic flights flights begun and completed within the continental United States that are available only on certain dates and at certain times (p. 111)

Resume a written summary of a person's education, accomplishments, and work experience, including unpaid or volunteer work (p. 67)

Revenue per available room (REVPAR) standard for measuring revenue at hotels determined by multiplying the average daily room rate by the occupancy rate (p. 215)

Risk avoidance taking the necessary steps to prevent or reduce risks (p. 286)

Risk insurance pays for financial losses that are predictable (p. 287)

Risk management the process of addressing potential risks in order to prevent them or to lessen their negative impacts (p. 286)

Risk retention a travel business assumes the cost of a risk (p. 287)

Risk transfer business owners allow others to assume some or all of a risk (p. 287)

Risks hazards, or exposures to possible loss or injury (p. 41)

Roadblock technique marketers use to saturate a market, such as running ads on several television networks at the same time so few people would miss the major promotion (p. 232)

S

Sales promotion includes activities or materials that offer the customer an added reason to buy (p. 233)

Search engine an Internet program that indexes web pages and then attempts to match relevant pages to users' search requests (p. 191)

Search engine optimization an e-commerce company pays search engine sites to make certain its web address will be at or near the top of any list generated by a search or to display its ad whenever certain keywords are used (p. 191)

Selling communicating directly with customers to determine, and then satisfy, their wants and needs with appropriate products and services (p. 7)

Service marketing selling work or acts without physical attributes to customers (p. 134)

Service quality the degree to which the service meets the needs and expectations of the customer (p. 135)

Service recovery a way to manage disgruntled customers and turn them into repeat business raving fans (p. 291)

Share of stock a unit of ownership issued to shareholders who control the company (p. 285)

Shareholder a person who has invested money in a corporation by purchasing shares of the company's stock (p. 285)

Sole proprietorship a business that is owned and operated by one person (p. 284)

Speculative risk when there is a chance for gain or loss (p. 42)

Standards the rules used for the measure of quality (p. 18)

State tourism agencies public/private partnerships that promote tourism in a state (p. 37)

Storyboard outline with rough drawings of each scene in a television or other visual broadcast advertisement (p. 238)

Sustainable development strategies defined by the United Nations as "development that meets the needs of the current generation without compromising the needs of future generations" (p. 39)

T

Target market specific group of potential customers (p. 82)

Time utility the product or service is available when the customer wants it (p. 220)

Timeshare equity ownership or fractional ownership in a property (p. 134)

Touchpoint each point that a travel or tourism business makes contact with customers—over the Internet, by phone, or at hotel checkin—where an opportunity exists to increase sales for the business (p. 244)

Tour a guided or escorted travel product that bundles several elements, such as transportation, hotel room, sightseeing, admission to local attractions, and possibly meals (p. 143)

Tourism traveling for pleasure (p. 9)

Transportation cars, trains, airplanes, buses, ships, and any other mode of moving people or goods (p. 15)

Travel and tourism marketing a series of activities that creates an exchange that satisfies the individual customer as well as the travel and tourism business (p. 4)

Travel insurance insurance that provides coverage for a financial loss on an expensive trip (p. 262)

Travel journalist a creative writer who submits articles he or she has written on a particular travel destination that meet the needs and interests of a publication's customers (p. 57)

Travel protection plan insures a traveler against unforeseen problems that may hinder or cause travel plans to be canceled; also insures that a tour operator is in sound financial condition (p. 85)

Travel suppliers tour operators, cruise companies, airlines, hotels, and resorts that provide travel services (p. 56)

Travel trade any individual or company that creates and/or markets tours and/or independent packages, including tour operators, travel agents, individual travel planners, and online travel companies (p. 159)

Travel warning issued by the State Department when it is recommending that U.S. citizens do not travel to a specific country (p. 269)

Traveling leaving overnight the region in which one lives (p. 9)

U

Uncontrollable risk occurs when a business could not have prevented the loss (p. 42)

Union a legal organization of workers that collectively represents the workers to management (p. 62)

U.S. Department of Transportation umbrella organization for all of the administrative agencies that oversee transportation in the United States, such as the Federal Aviation Administration and the Federal Highway Administration (p. 16)

U.S. Green Building Council a coalition of building design and construction businesses; group has developed the LEED (Leadership in Energy and Environmental Design) Green Building Rating System^{tm}, a system focused on the construction of high-performance and environmentally responsible structures (p. 39)

V

Variable costs portions of a business's budget that include items such as shipping charges or the cost of fuel; costs that change with the volume of business and are less easily predicted (p. 209)

Visa an official authorization added to a passport, permitting entry into, and travel within, a particular country or region (p. 31)

Visa Waiver Program allows citizens of 27 countries to enter the United States for tourism or business stays of 90 days or less without obtaining a visa (p. 31)

W

World Tourism Organization agency of the United Nations with 144 member countries and 300 affiliate members; affiliate members represent private businesses and professional travel and tourism organizations (p. 16)

Y

Yield revenue per person (p. 214)

Yield management software tool used by businesses to track and analyze demand patterns, cancellations, overbookings, traffic flow, and prices (p. 214)

Index